The Conscience of India

Creighton Lacy

The Conscience of India

Moral Traditions in the Modern World

Holt, Rinehart and Winston

New York   Chicago

San Francisco

Designer: Ernst Reichl
85114–0115
Printed in the United States of America

For Fran,

who will understand

always!

Contents

The Conscience of India

"Who knows the individual hour in which
His habits were first sown, even as a seed,
Who that shall point, as with a wand, and say,
'This portion of the river of my mind
Came from yon fountain'?"

William Wordsworth
Prelude (Book II)

Introduction

Discovery

India observes her Independence as of August 15, 1947, although
sticky monsoon weather makes it more expedient to schedule mammoth celebrations on Republic Day, marking the formal adoption
of the Constitution on January 26, 1950. But each Independence
Day, after paying his respects at the sacred spot where Gandhi's
body was cremated, Prime Minister Nehru addressed a crowd of at
least a hundred thousand people from the ramparts of the Red
Fort.

On one such occasion, Pandit Nehru, as New Delhi papers put
it, "departed from past practice and struck a despondent note."
Appealing above all for progress in India's villages, he challenged
the mass of people before him—and the nation by radio—to "hard
work and privations." Those who condemn an avowedly socialistic
program would have been surprised to hear its leader declare: "It
is the people in the villages who will . . . make India prosperous
 . . . I am for the least governmental interference." And in a world
where ends seem often to justify any means, he warned that "it is

not enough to have big factories or increase agricultural production. What is more important is the manner in which we achieve this."

Yet in December 1961, India annexed the last remnants of European colonialism on her subcontinent by a flagrant invasion of Goa. Even those who defended her "right" to the territory and condemned Portuguese intransigence were shocked at this apparent betrayal of Gandhian principles. In America Herblock drew a cruel but apt cartoon entitled "Liberation," showing the Indian Prime Minister, his inseparable rosebud in one hand and in the other a bloody knife, with which he had just slain, not Goa or Portugal or the United Nations, but his own conscience. Less than a year later world sympathy turned toward India once more as Chinese Communist troops swept over the long-contested Himalayan border and then came to an unexplained and unreliable halt. But not before the invasion had produced strong international reaction (including military aid from both Russia and the United States despite India's persistent refusal to join any alliance) and—of equal significance—a belated disillusionment on the part of Jawaharlal Nehru.

More and more people have come to realize that what happens to India in the next few years—religiously as well as politically and economically—may be decisive for Asia and the rest of the world for many decades. Consequently there has been a steady stream of visitors to the second most populous country in the world: scholars to study, economists to build, statesmen to woo. In the single winter of 1959–1960 New Delhi received the United States' President Eisenhower, Soviet President Voroshilov, Soviet Premier Khrushchev, United Arab President Nasser and Communist Chinese Premier Chou En-lai. On his arrival at Palam Airport, Eisenhower, the first American president ever to set foot, while in office, on Asian soil, paid tribute to his distinguished host, Jawaharlal Nehru:

Your Prime Minister wrote a very great book about discovering India.[1] I was intrigued with the book, but I am here to do what I can in four short days to do a little bit of personal discovery about India. But some of the things I know. India won its freedom and its independence through peaceful means. This in itself . . . has challenged the ad-

miration of the entire world. But more than that, India, determined to
live in peace, has devoted her entire efforts, all her treasure, all her talent, all her brains, to raising the standards of her own people, to give
them a better chance for a better life. . . . The deepest purpose that I
have in coming here is this: to symbolize if I can . . . the fact that
the United States stands with India . . . in our common quest for
peace. And the Lord permitting, nations and peoples so inspired will
yet be successful to the complete freeing of man from the fears and
tensions that have plagued humanity. . . .

In the tumultuous welcome that followed, the President of the
United States dramatized by his presence and his personality not
only the universal longing for peace (a silk banner at the hub of
the capital bore the inscription: "Welcome, Prince of Peace!"), but
also the gradual meeting of East and West, and the new status of
"neutral" Asia.

It has become an aphorism that democratic India and com-
munistic China are engaged in a social and economic struggle
whose outcome will determine the course of history. (It can be convincingly argued that India's limited but admirable achievements to
date helped to provoke China into the border attacks of 1962.)
China has the advantage of homogeneity in race and religion, written language and cultural heritage, which makes national unity
vastly easier. Centuries of British rule in India have left a legacy of
education and democratic ideals at the top, but also a disturbing
network of fissures in the basic structure of society. Whether China
or India meets the "revolution of rising expectations" more rapidly
and more successfully may well depend on various elements of external support—slow though the West seems to be in realizing this
fact.

Many Americans, as well as Marxists, view this competition in
strictly economic terms. As India's problems are debated at countless dinner parties and conferences—by foreign service diplomats,
employees of the Agency for International Development, representatives of private foundations, Fulbright scholars and missionaries—it is often argued that culture is moulded by material factors, that raising India's economic standards will solve her social
problems, that ideas and ideals are irrelevant and derivative.

But Indians have been called a "God-intoxicated people." For a century or more, scholars of many lands have been glorifying the spirituality of the East as contrasted with Western materialism. Max Müller in Germany, Sir Edwin Arnold in England, Swami Vivekananda at the Parliament of Religions in Chicago in 1893, all have described Hindu culture as the expression of the oldest and richest religious heritage in world history. To be sure, there are many Indians—as well as Westerners—who assert with some validity that India's vaunted spirituality is a myth, that masses living on the verge of starvation cannot afford to be anything but materialists.

Nevertheless, India stands in the eyes of the world as a profoundly spiritual civilization, a land where the social structure has been part of the religious pattern, and vice versa. For centuries to come the debate will continue as to whether Mahatma Gandhi was a saint with a keen political insight or a shrewd politician with an aura of saintliness—or both. Without a doubt his greatest contribution to the world was to demonstrate that politics and religion meet at the focal point of ethics. "The essence of religion is morality," he said in the introduction to his autobiography.[2] At Gandhiji's death Albert Einstein paid this tribute: "In our time of utter moral decadence he was the only statesman to stand for a higher human relationship in the political sphere." [3]

But Gandhi is dead. In the years which followed his assassination by a fanatical Hindu nationalist, a new India emerged as an avowedly secular state. Jawaharlal Nehru, also a man of towering moral stature in world affairs, had publicly confessed: "Religion, as I saw it practiced, and accepted even by thinking minds, whether it was Hinduism or Islam or Buddhism or Christianity, did not attract me. It seemed to be closely associated with superstitious practices and dogmatic beliefs." [4] Where, then, are the spiritual traditions of India? On what foundations in Hindu society can modern democracy be built? What are the religious and philosophical and ethical sources of social change in Indian life? These are some of the questions which tantalize students of comparative religions, international relations and social ethics.

As a teacher of philosophy and theology in China, I had seen the transition from the National People's Party of Chiang Kai-shek to the People's Democratic Republic of Mao Tse-tung, and the blame is still being scattered indiscriminately. American political parties still ask: Why did the United States Government "lose" China? Christians who once supported in China the largest single mission field abroad inquire plaintively: Why did the Church fail there? Experts in Far Eastern history and politics still argue: Why did Western-style democracy fail to take root on Chinese soil? Sociologists and psychologists continue to wonder: Why did Confucian loyalties, the family system, village autonomy and individualism collapse under Communist regimentation? These questions are all misleadingly worded. Yet if they are dismissed as irrelevant to India today, they may be asked with tragic pertinence of India tomorrow.

No visitor to Southern Asia can fail to be impressed by the complexity of the Indian scene. An American industrial advisor declared bluntly: "India has more problems than any other country in the world." Some other nations may have higher rates of illiteracy and disease, fewer trained civil servants, greater population density, a more critical shortage of raw materials, less experience and less inclination for democracy. But what other land can equal India's combination of difficulties? Where else are the people of a single state so divided by language and religion and caste and class and regionalism? Where do so many human beings live on such arid soil with such debilitating climate? Where is the chasm more vast or the tension more acute between the intellectual leadership and the dead weight of village tradition? Where else are financial resources so inadequate to put to use the reservoir of "white-collar unemployed"? It will take more than economic determinism to meet these obstacles. It will take vision and purpose and unity.

In searching for India's springs of vitality, it quickly becomes obvious that many varied streams of thought have flowed together to form the great rivers of Indian culture and contemporary outlook. It would be satisfying for a Christian to point out the direct contributions of the missionary enterprise to social reform and social welfare in India. But non-Christians are understandably reluctant to admit even the more obvious currents of influence, and these can seldom be isolated. How can one separate the impact of Western literature and philosophy from their visible expression in education and legislation? Hindu culture prides itself on two immovable pillars: Its avowed tolerance of many ways of thought as leading to the same goal, and its inclusive claim that all truth (even, among some extremists, to flying machines and atomic power) can be found in the Vedas. Yet ironically these firm convictions lead to an extremely intolerant refusal to acknowledge the value or validity of differing views.

In spite of these difficulties, it is possible—nay, essential—to examine the sources of India's social thought, to inquire what elements are assets or liabilities in creating a democratic society, to discover what modifications and adaptations are being made in traditional patterns to enable India to take her rightful place in the modern world. Thoughtful Indians today are recognizing both sides of their dilemma. Some bemoan the fact that their people have been too contemplative, too passive, that in recent centuries they have meditated on Life and Truth and Spirituality to the neglect of constructive activity. They would point to the fact that Hinduism's most beloved scripture, the *Bhagavad-Gita,* is treated as a devotional classic although its conclusion is a clarion call for action; its appeal for Hindus of every rank and status has usually lain in the speculative mental and moral struggle, rather than in the final decision and practical consequences.

On the other hand, there are keen and vital leaders in academic and political life who are concerned that India is plunging ahead too rapidly—in technology, bureaucracy and industry—without giving sufficient consideration to national purpose and ethical principles. They see a moral and spiritual vacuum arising, as old traditions and outworn faith are discarded. Yet religion is often feared because it is regarded as divisive sectarianism. Are there old foundations—or new—for a society in revolution? For India is caught up in irresistible change. Asserting that the chief cause of socio-economic change is political change, the coming of railways and commerce and just taxation, two Western observers add:

How is the transformation to be explained? The new-born spirit of enterprise among the Indians themselves, the example of the rest of the world, the Zeitgeist—all these have been factors. . . . Social institutions, customs, manners, all the pageant of human life, are but the outward show of what is passing in the human mind. It is there we must look in order to see what is to come to-morrow and the day after. And in the Indian mind the signs are not those of conservatism and stagnation but of rapid and perhaps shattering change.[5]

People, then, are the focus of this journey of discovery. Whatever the relationship of the soul to the body politic, the conscience of India is moulded both by four millennia of history and by powerful forces of modern environment. In this particular study the historical background, the tremendous social progress of recent decades and the inspiring hope for the future took on life and meaning through scores of private conversations. It is hardly conceivable that in any other nation of the world could an unknown student-professor, without official sponsorship or personal introduction, secure appointments with the outstanding men and women simply by explaining his concerns in a letter. Yet in India, Government officials from the President and Prime Minister on down, Opposition spokesmen, college presidents and social workers, swamis and saints, graciously accorded this writer interviews averaging an hour in length. Some of these new friends are mentioned in subsequent pages; others prefer to remain anonymous. To all of them—the "man in the street" and the "personality behind the headlines"—I owe inexpressible gratitude for many insights into the heart and mind of India. Thanks are due also to the American Association of Theological Schools, which made it possible for my family to reach the other side of the globe, and to Duke University, which permitted a sabbatical leave for a year.

The discovery of India moved in many directions along many paths. Often these probing inquiries led to unexpected doorways for the discovery of America! I had gone half way around the world to study the moral and political motivations of India, while in my own country the peripatetic President finally followed up his earlier proposal to appoint a National Goals Commission to define America's aims.[6] (Commenting on the delay, *The Christian Century* remarked editorially: "Meanwhile we continue to define our national purposes by the actions we take. Characteristically we move toward goals without taking the trouble to subject them to critical examination." In the same issue a drama critic, reviewing the theatrical version of *The Andersonville Trial*, commented: "In all the talk about the moral fibre of the nation, which is very popular these days, very few persons seem to be asking what basic assumptions must underlie a moral stance." [7])

While this student sought to appraise certain moral practices in India, the conscience of America flared into heated debate over television scandals and payola. While India and Pakistan drew perceptibly—if temporarily—closer against a common threat from their northern borders, an American U-2 plane took off from Pakistani territory on an ill-fated mission. While I was turned away from a few Hindu temples and photographed a "Brahmin hotel and restaurant" (caste segregation in public accommodations is forbidden by the Indian Constitution), hundreds of white and colored students in the United States "sat-in" at lunch counters—inspired in part by the nonviolent campaigns of a Hindu ascetic named Mohandas Gandhi. While the Indian Ministry of Education released an official report on "Religious and Moral Instruction," concerned educators and churchmen in America wrestled over ways to retain Bible study and religious values in public schools, without incurring sectarian protest or legal restriction. And the very day that I visited the filthy Kali temple in Calcutta, where Hindu reverence for life is subordinated to daily animal sacrifice, *Time* magazine described a Tennessee church service in which a lamb was slaughtered on a cross, its blood dripping onto the altar beneath. (The "Christian" pastor claimed that "almost everybody . . . thought it was a wonderful experience.") [8]

More scholarly, definitive volumes than this have been written on the ethical teachings of Hinduism, on the significant contributions of nineteenth-century social reformers, on the programs and personalities of Independent India—although too few of these books are read widely in the West. Here is one effort to show how the great currents of moral and philosophical and political thought in India's past are being reflected and expressed in her society today. Among many interpretations of what constitute social ethics, the areas selected must be recognized as illustrative rather than comprehensive. In writing simply and sympathetically of India's social conscience, one need only affirm the convictions that no nation dare throw the first stone, that in this interdependent world what happens in India has vital relation to the United States (and vice versa), and that "beyond the contrasts of East and West in the sphere of institutions and doctrines, there lies a realm of values common to all humanity." [9]

Chapter 1

Ethics of Early Hinduism

"He who beareth no ill-will to any being, friendly and compassionate, without attachment and egoism, balanced in pleasure and pain, and forgiving . . . he who neither loveth nor hateth, nor grieveth nor desireth, renouncing good and evil, full of devotion, he is dear to Me." [1] Thus spoke Krishna, god in the guise of a charioteer. The *Bhagavad-Gita,* or "The Lord's Song," takes its place with "The Sermon on the Mount" and *The Communist Manifesto* among the most inspiring and influential writings in all history. Albert Schweitzer has called it "not merely the most read but also the most idealized book in world literature."

Around this beloved but controversial episode in the much longer epic, *Mahabharata,* centers the major problem of Hindu social ethics. Do the sample verses quoted above represent the sublime pinnacle of morality? Or do they describe an impersonal super-deity, who deprives his followers of the involvement essential to genuine ethical choice? Whence cometh compassion, forgiveness, and devotion, without love or desire or goodness? Can the

13

gods of detachment and divine approval lead past the blind alley of duty to the broad highway of social concern?

Before giving fuller analysis to the *Gita,* brief reference must be made to earlier classics and doctrines of Hinduism. Only such aspects of Hindu thought as bear directly on ethical theory and practice can be discussed here. The task is complicated by the fact that Hinduism encompasses a wide variety of beliefs and interpretations and possesses no official orthodoxy. In fact, Indian philosophy demands no "logical" consistency or precision. Furthermore, ancient texts have been handed down in such a variety of forms that completely contradictory conclusions may be drawn by equally competent scholars. Thus, while Hindu writers cite proof-texts to refute their critics, any objective appraisal must resort to generalizations of ethical theory and to observations of moral practice.

The Vedas

The Vedic period of Indian history stretches roughly from 2000 to 500 B.C. and includes the major invasions of Aryan peoples from the Middle East. In such a fluctuating society, high intellectual concepts were mingled with primitive rites and superstitions. The *Rig Veda,* the basic scriptural compilation from this era, contains little or no evidence of caste, child marriage, bars to widow remarriage, or other such antisocial practices. Women wore the sacred thread of Brahminism, participated in metaphysical discourse, and enjoyed a moral and intellectual status never achieved since then. Ethics appear to have been based on obedience to divine law, but whether this law came from Isvara, the Supreme God, or from an eternal, nonpersonal, natural order, cannot be clearly determined. In either case, *"Rta,* the law or order of the world—literally 'the cause of things'—provides the standard of morality. . . . Virtue is conformity to the cosmic law." [2] It remains for individual commentators to read into it varying degrees of love and fear, kindness and benevolence, order and duty. Certainly *Rta* supplied the basis for the central ethical concept of *dharma* in subsequent moral philosophy.

By the end of this formative period, however, the Brahmin or priestly class had erected a framework of religious sanctions. Caste groupings became more rigid, presumably to protect the vested interests of the dominant clergy, and "happiness" or salvation became dependent on appropriate rites and duties. The Vedic age still showed an affirmative view toward life, rather than the later ideal of renunciation. But Brahmin authority gave to the developing mysticism an element of pride that one might attain union with the Universal Soul, in contrast to Western mysticism's devotion and surrender to God. To this emphasis can be traced a lack of humility, compassion and ultimate ethical concern in Hindu mysticism. Gradually the ideal of sainthood became withdrawal rather than service, spiritual achievement not abasement. (And to this tradition of spiritual pride may be attributed the tinge of self-righteousness with which Indian philosophers and politicians claim moral superiority over the West.)

The Upanishads

The stress on union with the divine found expression in the *Upanishads,* a collection of metaphysical treatises dated from 700 to about 300 B.C. These defined ultimate reality as Brahman, the Supreme Soul. Man's highest spiritual aim was to blend his individual soul (or breath or *atman*) with the Universal, creating Brahman-Atman, which is impersonal, without attributes, supramoral. Because this spiritual goal possesses no moral characteristics, the process of salvation includes no moral challenge. "Brahmanic mysticism has nothing to do with ethics. It is through and through supra-ethical," says Schweitzer.[3] To be sure, the *Upanishads* contain various instructions and prohibitions, chiefly for the priestly caste: to speak the truth, respect gods and ancestors, honor parents and guests, control desires, avoid theft and drunkenness and specifically murder of a Brahmin or adultery with a Brahmin's wife. But "love and pity for one's fellows are still beyond the horizon of these ethics," as Schweitzer points out,[4] contradicting his own previous denial of the term, ethics. In fact the *Upanishads* explicitly disclaim any transcendent moral judgments beyond these caste duties. "The immortal man overcomes both the thoughts—'I did evil' and 'I did good.' Good and bad, done or not done, cause him no pain" (Brhad-Aranyaka Upanishad, IV, 4).

A second reason for the nullification of ethics in the *Upanishads* is the denial of the material world. If Brahman-Atman, the impersonal and supramoral Soul, represents the only reality, then obviously the physical universe and human existence must be *maya* (illusion), *lila* (play), a sport or mirage. In such a society one may have prescribed duties, like assigned dramatic roles, but any free, spontaneous, creative relationship to other beings becomes imaginary and meaningless. The attainment of Nirvana (a Buddhist as well as Hindu term for the extinction of desire and attachment) may be described as deep, dreamless sleep in which there is no consciousness to distinguish subject and object, a transcendence of all relativity and relationships. A devout Hindu or Buddhist would insist that this supreme union with Brahman is a positive experience of sheer being, even ecstasy. But clearly in the arena of human ethics, this concept of salvation offers neither guidance nor incentive. Even if moral standards still exist for those unhappy mortals who have not yet reached Nirvana, their spiritual goal cannot help but be an antinomian escape from such mundane restrictions.

A third reason for the "demoralization" of ethics can be found in the development during this same period of two doctrines crucial to all subsequent Hinduism: *karma* and *samsara*. The latter, transmigration or reincarnation of souls, appears in a number of primitive cultures in place of a doctrine of heaven or hell. All those who die (unless they achieve absorption into Nirvana) will, according to belief in *samsara,* reappear in another and yet another birth, either higher or lower in the orders of creation and the social scale. The law of *karma* (works or deeds) simply offers an explanation of transmigration:

Those who are of pleasant conduct here—the prospect is, indeed, that they will enter a pleasant womb, either the womb of a Brahmin, or the womb of a Kshatriya, or the womb of a Vaisya. But those who are of stinking conduct here—the prospect is, indeed, that they will enter either the womb of a dog, or the womb of a swine, or the womb of an outcast (Chandogya Upanishad, III, 14, 3).

Many Indians and some Westerners today, without justifying caste discriminations in any sense, uphold the doctrine of *karma* on various grounds. Metaphysically speaking, it provides a consistent theory of evil and suffering. No theistic system, including Christianity, has been able to reconcile the goodness and omnipotence of God with a world of pain and sin. Ethically speaking, the law of *karma* simply recognizes that man reaps what he sows, if not in this life, then in a life to come. The Hindu advocate of *karma* may be quite right that such a belief provides a powerful incentive for personal ethics. Who wants to be reborn a cockroach—or a mere woman? But the particular motivation, the specific type of moral responsibility engendered by fear of *karma,* depends entirely on the concept of what the automatic process demands. *If,* for example, one's duty extends only to one's family and caste, or only to rituals and formal laws, then *karma* offers no dynamic for social change or sacrificial love.

At best, therefore, these basic Hindu beliefs inspire a self-centered morality, whose sole criterion for ethical behavior is the merit being stored up by *karma*. Critics often protest that such a doctrine serves as an obvious drag on social ethics. If one's whole duty can be fulfilled within the bounds of prescribed behavior, if no divine imperative summons one to go the second mile, if God Himself has made no supreme sacrifice, why should one bother to do anything more than law or tradition require? If a neighbor's misfortune can be traced directly to his own misdeeds in a previous life, if neither society as a whole nor casual chance can be blamed, then one has no clear responsibility to improve the situation. In actual practice, many Hindu *pandits* will argue strenuously against any kind of social welfare on the precise grounds that (a) you will be tampering with the *karma* of both server and served, and (b) inequalities obviously exist and must be accepted in the nature of things.

The Code of Manu

"Of course Manu remains the basic authority for India's legal and moral philosophy today." Such an assertion by the chairman of the philosophy department at Delhi University surprised me. The *Code of Manu* is a law book as archaic and irrelevant as the Book of Leviticus. Yet Warren Hastings, the eighteenth-century administrator, chose it as the main text for translation and official use by the British East India Company. The period covered by Manu may range from the sixth century B.C. to the third A.D., though the present form probably crystallized shortly before or after the time of Christ. Obviously many progressive Indians recognize the social and ethical anachronisms contained in this anthology and are eager to discard them. Nevertheless, Manu (presumably a pseudonym for the compiler of much earlier social regulations) continues to hold the rational esteem as well as popular reverence of millions, despite the fact that his major role has been to petrify some of India's greatest social evils.

In Manu, and in the earlier *Rig Veda,* can be found the mythological rationalization for caste: that the Brahmins (or priests) sprang from the mouth of Brahman (thus wielding verbal authority), the Kshatriyas (or warriors) from his arm (for defense), the Vaisyas (craftsmen and farmers) from his thigh (for manual skills), and the Shudras from his feet (for menial tasks). Without a doubt this religious basis of caste has been discarded by enlightened Hindus, and the brutal exploitation of caste stands universally condemned. Nevertheless, many Indians, including Mahatma Gandhi and Rabindranath Tagore, have defended the caste system on other grounds. Caste reflects, for one thing, the inherent spiritual differences among men. Social and occupational groupings, it is argued, provide security and congeniality and division of labor within an integrated community. (For these socio-economic classes, now split into hundreds or thousands of subcastes, *jati* is a more accurate term.) Since the original word, *varna,* means color, and undoubtedly represented some segregation and prejudice between Dravidian settlers and Aryan invaders, caste has been hailed as an alternative to genocide. In a world torn between atomistic individualism and tyrannical collectivism, caste is regarded as a viable compromise, where the individual has a recognized place and status within the group. Some Christians have likened caste to the Platonic scale, the Thomist architectonic structure, and the Lutheran doctrine of calling. Whatever the source of such distinctions, the consequences have been all too clear. As Sir Sivaswamy Aiyer admits:

The social order of the Hindus was founded not upon the comparatively modern democratic principle of equality, but upon the conception of a social hierarchy based upon caste and sanctioned by religion . . . While the principle of equality was applicable within the limits of each class or caste, the principle of discrimination was adopted as between one caste and another . . . [and] reflected in the administration of law and justice.[5]

In Manu, also, can be found the codification of family ethics and a lower status for women. Prepuberty marriage, polygamy, divorce (or supersession under certain limitations), voluntary *sati* (widow cremation), and bans against widow remarriage—all found acceptance in the Hindu law book. No one reading these and similar requirements that a wife must worship and treat her husband as a god can accept the current Hindu contention that *sati, purdah* and other restrictions on women arose from fear during Muslim rule. In Manu appear such petty and—to all but professors —ludicrous admonitions as these:

[A student must abstain from] perfumes, women, use of shoes and umbrella, sensual desire, anger, covetousness, dancing, singing, gambling, idle disputes, backbiting and lying, looking at and touching women, hurting others . . . Let him not pronounce the mere name of his teacher [without an honorific title] behind his back even, and let him not mimic his gait, speech and deportment. By censuring [his teacher], though justly, he will become [in his next birth] an ass. (Manu II, 177—201)

Such admonitions may demonstrate profound insight into human nature—and the universality of student temptations over thousands of miles and of years. It suggests, however, that neither lawmakers nor philosophers of ancient India sought to construct any systematic ethical theory. Morality consisted in obedience to a divine law, expressed less in legal commandments than in social custom and religious sanction. But into the ritualistic order of Manu crept some Buddhist hint that vice arises from greed and desire,

some Greek awareness of ignorance or rational error, some Jainist
impulse to despise no one and repay abuse with blessing.

The Bhagavad-Gita

"The Song of the Celestial Lord" (as the *Gita* is often called)
ranks as one of the devotional classics of all time. Millions of Hindus turn to it for daily inspiration and guidance; many can recite
the entire text. Yet, like all sacred scriptures, it is subject to myriad
interpretations. Put in the most elementary terms, its central
theme is this: *Perform your duty with detachment.* One group of
pious devotees and scholars—perhaps the dominant school of
Hindu philosophy—has emphasized *detachment,* the freedom from
emotional involvement and concern for consequences. The other
group—increasingly influential in modern India—puts stress on
action, on courageously making decisions. The one perspective
leads to what Schweitzer calls "world-and-life negation"; the other
represents "world-and-life affirmation."

The *Mahabharata,* of which the *Gita* is an interpolation, dates
roughly from 400 B.C. to 400 A.D. Composed of numerous epi-
sodes among Kshatriya (warrior) clans, it also provides clues to an
ethical transition. Where early Hinduism based morality on laws
and ritual, "middle" Hinduism gives new weight to the personal
conscience. The Supreme Soul may be supramoral ("In God is no
evil"), but the hope of union with It suggests a spiritual worth in
man which, in turn, calls forth benevolence toward others. "Morality, which is eternal . . . consists of universal friendliness and is
fraught with beneficence to all creatures" (Santiparva 262:5).
"Neither with eye, nor with mind, nor with voice should one injure
another . . . He indeed is exalted in heaven who looks on all
other beings with an eye of affection, who comforts them in afflic-
tion, gives them [food], and speaks kindly to them, becoming one
[with them] in their grief and joy" (12:279, 297, 298). It is
difficult to reconcile such admonitions with true detachment. Yet
the *Mahabharata* also offers a Golden Rule closely akin to the
negative Silver Rule of Confucius: "Whatever action a man would

not like if done to himself by another, that he shall refrain from doing to others" (Santiparva 260:20).

It is in the *Bhagavad-Gita,* however, that the inner tension of
Hindu ethics pulls at the soul of man. Arjuna, a young warrior,
draws back in revulsion from battle, not simply at the sight of
physical pain and slaughter, but at the horror of fighting against
relatives and friends. This moral dilemma inspires some deathless
poetry and spiritual insights that have undergirded pacifists in
many lands and many centuries. Debate still goes on as to whether
Mahatma Gandhi, the Great Soul of modern India, based his nonviolent resistance on a partial or even inaccurate reading of the
Gita, or whether both critics and admirers who make such an assumption have more seriously misinterpreted the man or the poem.

The final message of the *Gita* seems unmistakably clear: "Perform thou right action [defined in a footnote as regulated, prescribed duty], for action is superior to inaction. . . . Therefore,
without attachment, constantly perform action which is duty, for
by performing action without attachment, man verily reacheth the
Supreme" (III, 8, 19). For Arjuna, as a warrior, the summons
was even more explicit: "Taking as equal pleasure and pain, gain
and loss, victory and defeat, gird thee for battle; thus thou shalt not
incur sin" (II, 38). In other words, a soldier's duty is to fight.
"Theirs not to reason why, theirs but to do and die" (Tennyson).
Schweitzer points out that the *Gita* represents the first sharp conflict between negation and affirmation of life. Accepting the Brahmanic view that the world is only a shadow-play, a magical illusion
which God acts out, Krishna nonetheless rejects Arjuna's natural
impulse to withdraw. Both action and escape may lead to salvation, he admits, but the former is the nobler choice. The paradox
of the *Gita* is not that it took so many introspective lines of reasoning to reach that conclusion. It is rather that so many readers
through succeeding ages have focused attention and value on the
moral struggle of Arjuna, in disregard—both rationally and practically—of the central conclusion.

One lesson of the *Gita,* then, is that each man should do his
own duty, fulfill his own *karma,* accept his lot in life. "Better one's
own duty, though destitute of merit; than the duty [*dharma*] of

another, well discharged" (III, 35; cf. XVIII, 47). Such a doctrine has two sides. It may be used to elicit faithfulness in assigned tasks. It is better to be a good slave than an immoral master, for example. Here a moral standard is implied, though it be no more than fulfillment of duty. A still more devastating interpretation, however, has also emerged in Hinduism: that it is better to be a bad priest than a good sweeper or farmer—or doctor or chemist. This doctrine of *karma* may not only stifle individual ambition, but social progress as well. "Even the man of knowledge," Krishna tells Arjuna, "behaves in conformity with his own nature; beings follow nature; what shall restraint avail?" (III, 33). What shall it profit a man to improve the community, if the members of it are conformed to an inevitable pattern by their inherent nature and status? Negatively speaking, what value are education and legislation and reform if human engineering cannot lead people out of ancient channels?

A second emphasis of the *Gita* is equality. If this basic element of Hindu ethics could be examined apart from the caste system, or even within the framework of a single caste or community, it would be seen to have many advantages. Krishna's insistence on detachment leads to impartiality, fairness, justice—at least within the group. "An action which is ordained, done by one undesirous of fruit, devoid of attachment, without love or hate, that is called pure" (XVIII, 23). This equalitarianism has something in common with the humanistic emphasis of the Enlightenment, which carried over into the Declaration of Independence. There is also good Biblical comparison, for "your Father who is in heaven . . . makes his sun rise on the evil and on the good, and sends rain on the just and on the unjust" (Matthew 5:45). But this is God's impartiality, and the equality of *dharma* (here meaning that each has his ordained duty) represents for many Hindus the excuse for noninvolvement, lack of concern. One of the Hindu arguments in defense of *karma* is that it puts ethical responsibility where it belongs, on the person himself, leaving him dependent neither on other people nor on the whim of God. Such a view admittedly, and without apology, leaves no room for vicarious suffering by the innocent, nor for atonement by an incarnate deity.

Krishna tells Arjuna, "The same am I to all beings; there is none hateful to Me, nor dear" (IX, 27). A superficial critic may point to the opening verses of this chapter, or to the preferential assurance that "I am supremely dear to the wise, and he is dear to Me" (VII, 17), as evidence of divine favoritism. Yet this same blend of unqualified love coupled with a qualified preference for men of faith can be found in Peter's dramatic discovery that "God shows no partiality, but in every nation any one who fears him and does what is right is acceptable to him" (Acts 10:35). Even the distinctions of caste are caught up in this universality of divine love. "The four castes were emanated by Me, by the different distribution of qualities and actions" (IV, 13).

A third major element of Hindu ethics developed in the *Bhagavad-Gita* is the concept of *dharma*. In ancient Vedic times it meant the whole body of truth, the cosmic law. But whereas Buddhism narrowed it to the particular set of teachings, the creed, the doctrines, Hinduism gradually expanded the idea until *dharma* came to mean many things—or the all-inclusive focus of ethics. *Dharma* is translated by Mrs. Besant in the *Gita* as "customs," "traditions," "duty," "righteousness." It may also refer to law, nature, justice, virtue, merit, morality. *Dharma* is the cosmic process, the Kantian moral law, the Quaker Inner Light, the Communist dialectic. It is the Decalogue, the Mosaic Covenant, and the "righteousness" of prophecy. For the Hindu it is what he does and why he does it.

There are those who criticize Hindu ethics, and the notion of *dharma,* as lacking specific content. But if the transition from the universal moral law to practical moral conduct is difficult for Hinduism, it is no less difficult for Christianity or any other religion. Krishna spells out the attributes of the righteous man near the end of the *Gita* as follows:

Fearlessness, cleanness of life, steadfastness in the Yoga of wisdom, alms-giving, self-restraint and sacrifice and study of the Scriptures, austerity and straightforwardness, harmlessness, truth, absence of wrath, renunciation, peacefulness, absence of crookedness, compassion to living beings, uncovetousness, mildness, absence of fickleness, vigour, forgiveness, fortitude, purity, absence of envy and pride—these are his who is born with the divine properties (XVI, 1–3).

Note that the final phrase tosses responsibility back to one's *karma,* denying the freedom essential to moral action or growth.

This suggests a further value of the *Gita,* perhaps the central reason for its abiding popularity. The impersonal atheism (or deism) of Brahma had been counteracted by a confused and confusing polytheism borrowed in part from primitive paganism, and the human yearning for a personal god had been satisfied with numerous incarnations: the multiarmed Shiva, the epic Prince Rama, but above all the "blue boy" of Hinduism, Krishna. Beloved most for his romantic escapades as a cowherd, he speaks in the *Gita* with all the authority of his god-form Vishnu.

Whenever there is decay of righteousness [*dharma*], O Bharata, and there is exaltation of unrighteousness, then I Myself come forth. For the protection of the good, for the destruction of evil-doers, for the sake of firmly establishing righteousness, I am born from age to age (IV, 7–8).

The significance of the *Gita* for Hindu ethics lies precisely here: that in this dialogue with Krishna Indians have found a god concerned with human problems, human temptations, human values. Chinese Buddhism co-opted (and even changed the sex of) Kwan-yin, the Goddess of Mercy (Kwannon in Japan), in order that worshippers might have the assurance of "One who hears and answers the cries of the world." Christians base their faith and particularly their moral concern, on the belief that "God so loved the world that He gave His only begotten Son." When this Christ tended to be drawn too remotely into the Godhead again, Roman Catholicism turned its adoration and sentiment to "the Mother of God." So Hindus have the assurance from Krishna that "he who seeth Me everywhere, and seeth everything in Me, of him will I never lose hold, and he shall never lose hold of Me" (VI, 30). The faith that Krishna offers and rewards is more tolerant, more universalistic than most. In fact, this constitutes one of Hinduism's chief claims to superiority—and its chief criticism of Christian dogmatism. The *Gita* reiterates such inclusive promises as these: "However men approach Me, even so do I welcome them, for the path men take from every side is Mine" (IV, 11). "Any devotee who seeketh to worship with faith any such aspect, I verily bestow the answering faith of that man" (VII, 21). Whatever the weaknesses of nonattachment, duty and eclecticism in formulating ethics, the freedom and open-mindedness of Hinduism present a strong appeal. And the personal theism of the *Gita* has enabled many sincere seekers to overlook the crude polytheism of Hindu mythology as a whole and the even cruder moral and ritualistic practices derived from it.

This devotion to Krishna, as poetically expressed in the *Gita,* became generally accepted as a third way of salvation in Hindu thought. The oldest (*Karma-Marga,* the Way of Works) consisted chiefly of rituals and sacrifices rather than ethical conduct. Gradually the simple but sufficient ceremonial demands were supplemented by the *Dharma-shastras,* law books including the *Code of Manu,* which regimented every detail of daily life, from a child's first haircut to the food for the household gods. The Way of Knowledge (*Jnana-Marga*) represented the effort of priests and scholars to achieve salvation by learning, by conquering the primary cause of misery and evil, which is ignorance. Methods included the search for Enlightenment on the Buddhist pattern, the repetition of the sacred syllable OM, and various forms of *yoga.* None of these held emotional appeal for the masses, who found true religious experience only in the Way of Devotion (*Bhakti-Marga*). Such worship may be—and is today—directed toward many deities, from the Black Goddess Kali to Nandi, the White Bull. But Krishna retains a unique position in the heart of India. Without rejecting Brahminism or the Vedas or caste, "Krishnaism" has injected into Hinduism an element of ethical monotheism, an emphasis on activity rather than withdrawal, an insistence on *bhakti* (devotion) as the highest attitude toward God. "It nowhere makes the demand, which is such a matter of course to Christianity, that love to God shall be actively realized in love to man." [6]

What, then, is the nature of moral character, as defined in the *Bhagavad-Gita?* Above all, it depends on a faithful performance of duty without regard to consequences. "Thy business is with action only, never with its fruits; so let not the fruit of action be thy motive, nor be thou to inaction attached" (II, 47). By the same token, no attention is to be given to conscious motivation. One follows, without question, the universal law of *dharma* and the particular law of *karma*. "The man consists of his faith [i.e. faith shows character]; that which his faith is, he is even that" (XVII, 3). This type of determinism explains not only the lack of missionary outreach in Hinduism, since a man's faith is bestowed on him at birth, but also the fierce resistance to religious conversion—or cultural change. It explains also why even the *Gita* has not inspired many Hindus to creative social and ethical reform. As Schweitzer says of Lord Krishna: "When he speaks of action, he never means more than the exercise of the activity dictated by caste, not subjective action proceeding from the impulses of the heart and self-chosen responsibilities." [7]

Later Developments

Succeeding centuries brought few decisive changes in Hindu ethical theory. Among various reformers and reinterpreters, three might be mentioned as possessing ethical significance. The *Artha-Shastras* of Kautilya may have been composed as early as the third century B.C. or as late as the third A.D. Its author has been called "the Machiavelli of India," and it is possible that the writings were known and used by the Machiavelli of Italy. Stressing the divine right of kings, Kautilya warned that "he who does not protect his people or upsets the social order wields his royal scepter in vain" (Artha-Shastras III, 1). As an ethical realist, he accepted widow-remarriage and prostitution. As a thoroughgoing rationalist, he acknowledged the priority of sacred law over evidence and history, but "whenever sacred law is in conflict with rational law, then reason shall be held authoritative," since the original text of sacred law "is not available" (III, 1).

If Kautilya was the Indian Machiavelli, Sankara was the Hindu Aquinas. Basing his exposition on the *Upanishads,* this eighth century scholastic developed a subtle analysis of *advaita* (nondualism), contending that apart from Brahman there is nothing but *maya* (illusion). Not only the sensible world, but all notions of personal deity or individual existence or rebirth, are but the product of ignorance. The only truth, according to Sankara, is to realize that there are no separate selves, no reality but Brahman. Such a doctrine nullifies not only concern for neighbor, but even one's individual *karma,* transmigration, caste, all human experience. What Sankara did not bother to tell us was how to live in a world of *maya.*

Three centuries later another scholar tried to salvage some basis for religion and ethics from the nihilism of *advaita.* Ramanuja asserted that the ultimate reality is a personal god, that individual souls and the physical world are "forms" of Vishnu, and that he manifests himself in creation and in his *avatars* (or incarnations). Such an approach restored the validity of *Bhakti-Marga* (devotion), replaced the cold intellectualism of Sankara with a kind of theism, and even introduced a heaven in which Vishnu receives back the scattered sparks of divinity called souls. Ethically speaking, however, this concept restored the mechanical justice of *karma* on one hand and the emotional ecstasy of *bhakti* on the other, rather than offering a new basis for moral responsibility. Ramanuja's doctrine did perform one further vital function: it reopened an avenue of communication with the approaching creeds of Islam and Christianity, an avenue which Sankara had quite obliterated.

Understanding of Ethics

This brief sketch of Hindu ethical philosophy points to certain significant weaknesses. It points, also, to some crucial perspectives that differ between East and West. Father Raymond Panikkar, a member of the Institute of Philosophy of the Higher Council of Scientific Research in Madrid, and former lecturer on Indian Philosophy at Benares Hindu University, focused attention on these differences. *If* we define ethics as involving intention, will, freedom, the relation of one individual to another, said Father Panikkar, we are imposing a Western concept on India. Admittedly, Hinduism has little or no ethics in this sense. But *if* ethics involves a set standard of behavior, based on duty, social custom, religious faith in *karma,* then Hinduism puts a high premium on moral conduct. "Hinduism has no concern for others—*as* others, as individuals deserving separate treatment," this Roman Catholic scholar explained, "but it does have concern for others as members of the group or as part of Universal Reality."

This basic problem of definition—and of moral demand—accounts for much disagreement between Hindu and Western scholars. It lies at the heart of the great debate between Albert Schweitzer and Sarvepalli Radhakrishnan as to whether Hinduism is "world-and-life negating." It is crucial to an understanding of the strengths and weaknesses of Hindu ethics—yesterday, today and tomorrow. From a polemical point of view, Hopkins is quite right: "It would really serve no useful purpose to prove that India's ethical systems of more than two thousand years were not erected on modern ideas of social service and philanthropic institutions." [8] But if we are concerned to examine the foundations of India's contemporary social and political ethics, then we are justified in asking to what extent the negation, the detachment, the stratification of Hinduism are compatible with modern democracy and social progress. Answers for the future must be found in the past as well as in the present.

Chapter II

Other Religions of India

Christianity is rediscovering what other religions in India have learned to their peril in centuries past: that Hinduism's vaunted tolerance poses a subtle threat to the survival of any distinctive, organized faith. On one hand, the inclusive, syncretistic acceptance of all beliefs or no belief seems to absorb and obliterate sharp doctrinal lines. On the other hand, the identification of Hinduism with an ancient and rigid social structure makes it difficult for alien creeds or systems to take root in India. Inevitable borrowings have occurred, the natural interaction of cultural factors through centuries of coexistence. But elements adopted from other sects and movements become an almost indistinguishable part of Hinduism, whereas Hindu forms and practices tend to make the receiving cult more Hindu and less unique. Nevertheless an effort should be made to appraise certain ethical influences which other religions have injected into Indian life.

Jainism

Jainism, the oldest indigenous offshoot from Hinduism, slightly antedates Buddhism. Nataputta Vardhamana, more commonly known as Mahavira (Great Man), lived—presumably—from 599 to 527 B.C. Little is known of his personal career or even his original teachings. Legends focus on extreme asceticism, his effort to free the soul from the oppressive evil of matter. This represented no new goal in world religions, but few others before or since have regarded renunciation of material existence as the *summum bonum* and built an entire system on that premise. Mahavira denied the reality of Brahman-Atman, the Supreme Soul, and thus discarded the Hindu conviction that each individual contains a portion of divinity. Instead, he placed on every human being the responsibility for his own salvation, which consisted in escape from matter. "There is no higher god than man himself. . . . This means that [for Jains] there is no saving power outside themselves, so there is no such thing as forgiveness or grace coming to them from another and higher being." [1]

If the goal is hazy, the path of austerity is unmistakable. Jainist interpretations of life and of moral demands are eminently simple. Asceticism as practiced by Mahavira included nakedness, silence and endurance of torture—from biting dogs and sadistic people. In disciplined meditation he, like Buddha, reached Nirvana (or Kevala, the elimination of desire) and thus became the Jina (Conqueror). To these rigors his followers added fasting and trances in their effort to follow him into a state of deliverance from matter. The Five Great Vows for monks were presumably drawn up by disciples rather than by Mahavira himself: no injury, no lying, no stealing, no sexual pleasure, no attachments. The master is reported to have declared that "the greatest temptation in the world are women" (sic).[2] But freedom from attachments—physical, psychological, emotional, even spiritual—represents the supreme conquest, for this aim comprehends the rest.

For the survival of the sect—not to mention the human race—modification of these requirements proved a practical necessity.

Laymen who could not or would not adopt such extreme asceticism might follow a less arduous twelve-point program. A good Jain should never knowingly take a sentient life, never lie, never steal, never be unchaste, never be greedy, avoid temptation, limit the use of "things," avoid evils, meditate, practice self-denial, give alms, spend certain periods as a monk. Thus Jain ethics are profoundly concerned with behavior, but with behavior to protect the spirit from contamination by matter. In terms of motivation, all of these moral demands were strictly egocentric. For example, the purpose in giving away excess wealth was to check the donor's temptation to greed, although alms were especially commended when given to ascetics. One must restrain the impulse to criticize ethical behavior solely because it stems from unworthy motives. Those who do right acts for wrong reasons are not necessarily immoral. But it can be fairly asked whether morals based on one's own salvation, with neither vertical nor horizontal reference, can ever be modified and expanded into genuine social ethics.

Over the centuries Jainism has absorbed certain Hindu characteristics and attitudes. Without actually approving caste, which Mahavira denounced, Jains have become in effect a caste within Hindu society. Today its members, numbering approximately a million and a quarter, are treated officially and legally as Hindus. Jain temples are—to risk a generalization—cleaner, neater, more ornate than Hindu temples, and have incorporated (except for the Sthanakavasi sect) idolatry from the surrounding culture. Jains have followed Mahavira in accepting the basic Hindu doctrines of *karma* and transmigration. Their major division has been between the Svetambaras ("white-clad") and the "stricter and more conservative Digambaras" ("sky-clad"), who believe with their founder in nudity as a religious duty. In short, Hinduism has permeated and assimilated Jainism until it remains little more than an austere Hindu sect, flourishing chiefly in the vicinity of Bombay.

One indispensable contribution Jainism *has* made to Indian thought and ethics: the emphasis on *ahimsa* or noninjury. Such an impulse, deep-rooted in the better nature of man, cannot claim a specific origin or date. The *Upanishads* mention the term only in passing. It seems clear that the importance of *ahimsa* as a fundamental tenet of Indian life, leading also to vegetarianism, came from the teachings of Mahavira and the example of his followers. To extreme Jains this moral law prohibits plowing (lest earthworms be cut up), walking in the rainy season (lest insects be trampled), scratching (lest vermin be clawed). It requires, at its highest, sweeping tiny creatures gently from one's path, straining water and even breath, careful inspection of food and beds. The killing of animals or the cooking of meat and eggs cannot be condoned, but Mahavira accepted left-over food providing the life had not been sacrificed *for him*. In like manner today there seems to be no opposition from Hindus or Jains to the spraying of DDT by government agents, so long as the "beneficiaries" themselves are not directly responsible for the injury to life.

In an effort to avoid taking life through outdoor activity, Jains gradually concentrated on professional and sedentary occupations: banking, commerce, law. In these they became eminently successful, with the ironical result that "their essentially world-renouncing religion has, in the devious course of events, secured their economic advantage among the struggling masses of India." [3] There seems little reason to doubt that Mahatma Gandhi, a native of Gujerat, where Jainism is strongest, owes to this small sect much of his profound dedication to *ahimsa*. Albert Schweitzer, whose famous creed of "Reverence for Life" draws deeply from Indian thought, has paid this tribute:

The laying down of the commandment not to kill and not to damage is one of the greatest events in the spiritual history of mankind. . . . In a period when in other respects ethics have not progressed very far, [Indian thought] reaches the tremendous discovery that ethics knows no bounds! So far as we know, this is for the first time clearly expressed by Jainism. [4]

But while he acknowledges the significant moral advance of this doctrine, Schweitzer points gently but unequivocally to its weakness. The practice arose, he believes, from a desire to remain undefiled, to seek perfection, "for his own sake, not from a fellow-feeling for other beings." Thus, *ahimsa* "keeps within the bounds of compassionate non-activity and completely disregards helpful sympathy," Schweitzer declares. Only much later, have Indian philosophers sought to interpolate a genuine personal concern for the object, or a positive attitude of kindness. Two final criticisms Schweitzer raises. First is the question whether an extreme and sweeping ethic does not defeat its own purpose. "Ethics without limits cannot indeed be complied with, but Indian thinking did not discuss this fact. It did not admit it at all." [5] (Does Schweitzer not see that this is equally the problem—and the glory—of Christian ethics?) Second, Jains and Hindus never seem to raise the question as to whether death may not be preferable to suffering (for a maimed or starving cow, for example). True *ahimsa,* Schweitzer would remind them, must be the servant of compassion rather than of legalism.

Whatever its inadequacies, in practice or in motivation, the concept of noninjury, expressed in nonviolence, still challenges mankind. It is a sad commentary that persecuted minorities in the West who attempt to use its power in the nineteen-sixties attribute the idea more often to Gandhi than to Jesus. Among many expressions of human brotherhood in all times and all places, the doctrine of *ahimsa* stands as Jainism's clearest contribution—to India's social conscience and to the world.

Buddhism

The ethic of compassion was born in India. Those who hasten to claim that honor for Palestine would do well to weigh the distinctions between ethic and religion, compassion and love. But those who underestimate the influence of Buddhism on India and the world should be aware of Asian perspectives on war and religious persecutions in Western Christendom. It is impossible here to present a complete or even adequate interpretation of Buddhism, but it is possible to suggest certain strengths and weaknesses of Buddhist moral teachings in India.

Siddhartha Gautama was born in 560 B.C. The fact that Mahavira, Buddha, Nanak, Gandhi and numerous other reformers have belonged to the second caste may be coincidence. More likely it reflects the fact that only the Kshatriya have both the incentive to challenge Brahmin domination and the education and cultural advantages requisite for independent thought. The story of Gautama's quest for salvation is a familiar one in the history of religions. Born into wealth and nobility, he was surrounded by material comforts, shielded from awareness of evil in the world. At length in early manhood he encountered four sobering sights (variously interpreted as divine apparitions or stark reality): a feeble old man, a loathesome disease, a corpse, and a serene but penniless ascetic. After ten years of marriage and the birth of his only son, Gautama left home, resolving to penetrate these mysteries of life.

Six years of intellectual exercises and extreme asceticism brought no answers. Eventually, after weeks of meditation under the famous Bo-tree, Gautama became the Buddha, the Enlightened One. The secrets he expounded were simple but profound. There are Four Noble Truths: all life is suffering; suffering is caused by desire; the way to end suffering is to eliminate desire; the way to end desire is the Eight-Fold Path. This path, variously translated, consists of right belief, right aspiration, right speech, right conduct, right livelihood, right endeavor, right mindfulness, right meditation.

These insights and these goals represented a new explanation of life, a new gospel of salvation, and a new law of moral behavior. Negatively speaking, Buddhism offered a challenge to Hinduism, an alternative to Brahminism which remained viable for over eight hundred years. First, Buddha rejected the efficacy of the Vedas as an authoritative view of man's place and his duty. Second, he denounced the rule of the Brahmin caste in social and religious affairs. Third, he criticized ritual observances as a means of salvation. Fourth, he condemned polygamy, child marriage, female infanticide, divorce, and so forth. Fifth, he disregarded the caste system by preaching the universal inclusiveness of the Noble Truths and the Eight-Fold Path.

It is not right to call men white who virtue lack;
For it is sin and not the skin that makes men black.

(Jataka 440)

Not by the cut of his hair, not by his clan or birth,
May a Brahmin claim the Brahmin's name, but only by moral worth.

(Chamma Pada 393)

Prime Minister Nehru paid this humanistic tribute to Indian Buddhism:

"Go into all lands," had said the Buddha to his disciples, "and preach this gospel. Tell them that the poor and the lowly, the rich and the high, are all one, and that all castes unite in this religion as do the rivers in the sea. . . . Not by birth, but by his conduct alone, does a man become a low-caste or a Brahman." . . . Whether this is a God or an Absolute or not, he does not say. He neither affirms nor denies. . . .[6]

To be sure, Buddhism in other lands became one of the most idolatrous of all religions. The Buddha himself, who denied any transcendent deity and taught a strictly humanistic ethic, came to be worshipped in numerous forms, perhaps from the influence of the Hindu pantheon and its doctrine of reincarnation. With amoeba-like ingestion Hinduism gradually turned Buddhism into a caste of its own and solidified Brahminism in rigid self-defense. By the time the White Huns (470–530) drove Buddhism almost completely out of India, it had already lost its dynamic, and by compromise and isolation had yielded to a renascent Hinduism. Yet as a modern Hindu writer noted, Gautama Buddha, "a rational thinker and confident reformer, a prince turned religious wanderer, and a philosopher turned moralist, . . . ushered in a millennium of moral earnestness." [7]

During that millennium one of the greatest rulers of Indian history left his mark and the imprint of Buddhism on the country. Asoka ascended the throne in 273 B.C. Twelve years earlier he had been so horrified by the slaughter involved in his own military exploits that he adopted the Buddhist "Middle Way." Though impartially sharing imperial patronage among Brahmins, Buddhists and Jains, Asoka devoted himself to policies of gentleness and compassion. He forbade the sacrifice of birds and animals, condemned immoral practices at religious festivals and encouraged higher family ethics. His public works have been described as "nothing less than the welfare state dedicated to righteousness. . . . In his capacity as the temporal head of India he preached a simple creed of commonly accepted morals and endeavored to bring humanity in the place of cruelty, ethical earnestness in the place of empty form." [8] For example, he founded hospitals, for animals as well as humans, twelve centuries before the first European hospitals. He built roads and dotted them with shade trees and rest houses. "He infused into the administrative machinery built up by his predecessors a regard for humanity almost unique among the governments of the ancient world, curbed its oppressiveness, and applied it to the advancement and civilization of this people." [9] He made of Buddhism the first genuinely missionary religion by sending embassies to Burma and Ceylon (which remain to this day predominantly Buddhist lands) and as far west as Egypt, Syria and Greece.

What was this creed that calls repeatedly for the word "humanity"? Philosophically, metaphysically, Buddhism shared with its Hindu environment a tacit acceptance of successive rebirths and ultimate release in Nirvana. Like Jainism, it sought escape from an essentially evil world. The original Buddhist has been called an egoistic hedonist because his concern centers in his own *karma,* his own ultimate salvation. But Buddhism has always been more pragmatic than speculative; perhaps that is why it eventually died out of India and took deeper root in China and Japan. What Sir Charles Eliot said of Asoka in his classic *Hinduism and Buddhism* might describe the ideal follower of Gautama in any age: "He stands isolated as perhaps the one man whose only passion was for a sane, kindly, and humane life, neither too curious of great mysteries nor preoccupied with his own soul, but simply the friend of man and beast." Nehru, too, recognized the social consequences of this individualistic approach in these words:

Buddha may not have thought of himself as the founder of a new religion; probably he looked upon himself as a reformer only. But his dynamic personality and his forceful messages, attacking many social and religious practices, inevitably led to conflict with the entrenched priesthood. He did not claim to be an uprooter of the existing social order or economic system; he accepted their basic premises and only attacked the evils that had grown under them. Nevertheless he functioned to some extent as a social revolutionary.[10]

Some scholars trace the manifold developments in later Buddhism to the various lands in which it has flourished, but it seems clear that some of these changes began in India itself. The most important doctrine from the ethical standpoint was the introduction of *bodhisattvas,* saints who have achieved enlightenment and the right to enter Nirvana, but who remain outside in order to help others find the way. On one hand, this concept has encouraged dependence on saviors, on salvation by grace. In a sense, such reliance on external aid undermines an ethic of responsibility. But as in the case of Christianity, when this charge is made, a new motivation for morality is advanced. This is the idea that sin grieves these deities or potential saviors. "To be good is to please them, to be sinful is to pain them; it is wrong to do wrong because it wrongs divinity. This is an entirely new conception to the Buddhist, though it is not so remote from the Vedic notion that sin makes divine beings angry." [11]

On the other hand, the example of *bodhisattvas* gives fresh meaning to the central term of Buddhism, compassion. From Buddha himself comes an example of gentleness, of kindly feeling. Edmund Perry expresses this attitude well when he writes. "In our compassion for the miserable creatures of existence we create in ourselves and in them a hitherto and otherwise nonexistent dignity." [12] In that sentence he reveals also the essential weakness of Buddhist compassion; namely, that the dignity of selfhood, of personality, of individual worth, is nonexistent until it is created by a sentimental pose. Because there is no god, the self has no objective reality, and therefore the supreme emotion—and ethic—of love has no meaning. Max Müller, the great German scholar of Oriental philosophy, once said of Buddhists: "While condemning love, they preached pity—a splendid substitute. . . . That pity means a great deal, it may mean all that is best in love." [13]

It may mean the highest emotional involvement of which human beings are capable—*if* they lack a divine point of reference. In that sense, pity violates the detachment from people or things which Buddhism recommends. For pity represents a subjective response to something finite and immediate, whereas the Buddhist ideal would seek escape from feeling, except in the most impersonal, dispassionate terms. Since the transient is rejected, the ultimate and eternal is sought. Yet it is precisely when the metaphysical detachment is laid aside, when the transient and human suffering calls forth sympathy and compassion, that Buddhist ethics transcend those of Hinduism and most other religions. Hopkins says of Buddhism's attempted reform: "The Brahman is not urged to love other people, especially low-caste people, only to be kind to them, to pity them, and to sympathize with them, which, indeed, may be enough." [14]

But it is *not* enough, and this failure to hold out a revolutionary challenge to Hinduism may have played a significant part in Buddhism's failure to capture the heart of India. Hopkins goes on to declare, some pages later, that "the crowning glory of Buddhism is not the doctrine of non-injury, which early Brahmanism also teaches, but the inculcation of that devotion to man which leads to self-sacrifice." [15] But this kind of sacrifice cannot be claimed by any one religion. It is too universal—yet too rare! In a world of suffering and a soteriology of escape, an ethic of compassion appears at best an irrational impulse of human nature. "Devotion to man" without devotion to God leads to inconsistent and undependable involvement.

At the same time it calls forth admiration and loyalty from enlightened humanists. In *The Discovery of India* Prime Minister Nehru explained his attitude toward an essentially nonreligious Buddhism:

It was the ethical and social and practical idealism of Buddha and his religion that influenced our people and left imperishable marks upon them, even as the ethical ideals of Christianity affected Europe though it may not pay much attention to its dogmas, and as Islam's human, social, and practical approach influenced many people who were not attracted by its religious forms and beliefs.[16]

Why a profound and influential interpretation of life vanished almost completely from the land of its birth, to take up new and altered forms in all the adjacent lands of Eastern Asia, remains one of the imponderable riddles of history. Perhaps this represents the supreme tribute to Hinduism's social cohesion. Perhaps Nehru is right that the doctrines proved unconvincing but the moral idealism permeated Indian life. Perhaps, on the other hand, it failed until it became in different cultures a more genuine religion. That Buddhism has become a part of India's heritage cannot be denied. With unconscious neglect of prior Hindu claims, a recent government publication asserts:

We have had social welfare programmes, social service organizations, social reformers and workers in the cause of social welfare in India from the earliest times. Right through the centuries, *commencing* with the reign of King Asoka or going back *even* to the days of Buddha, there have been rulers and many among the common people of India who trod the path of service to their fellow beings and adopted it as a life mission.[17]

Like the Jains, Buddhists are legally and constitutionally listed with Hindus. The elaborate modern Lakshmi Narayan (or Birla) Temple in New Delhi has an entire wing devoted to Buddhism. And the wheel of Asoka, which happens to be the Buddhist Cycle of Life, waves proudly in the center of free India's orange-white-and-green flag.

Zoroastrianism

"In many ways it is the most dignified community in India." [18] So writes Edmund Soper of the one hundred thousand Parsis, almost lost in a population of some four hundred million. These are really followers of Zoroaster (c. 660–583 B.C.), known generically as Parsis because of their ancestors' migration from Persia in the early eighth century. Like the Jains, the community is centered in Bombay, with a few members scattered "in small handfuls" to other urban centers. Like the Jains, too, Parsis are engaged predominantly in banking and industry, although outstanding leaders have played a constructive role in India politics.

The essence of Zoroastrianism is dualism, ethical and metaphysical. Zoroaster himself offered a radical doctrine for his day; namely, that there is one god, Ahura Mazda, but arrayed against him are potent forces of evil. Thus the world is seen as a gigantic arena or battlefield for the perpetual clash of Light versus Dark, Life versus Death, Truth versus Falsehood, Right versus Evil. Although Ahura Mazda is abetted and represented by numerous

Amesha Spentas (the Immortal Holy Ones who are both attributes and modes of deity), it is noteworthy that Love and Mercy find no place in this galaxy. It should also be pointed out that Hindus and Zoroastrians shared certain primitive concepts (such as fire worship and soma juice) and certain terms (cf. *devas, deus, divinity*) from their common Aryan heritage.

Despite the assertion of Mazda's supremacy, such radical dualism has had difficulty resisting polytheism in practice. Similarly, though Zoroaster affirmed a freedom of moral choice in each individual soul, the later *Avesta* (sacred scriptures) put great emphasis on ceremonial purity and even magical incantations to guarantee victory over evil. Essentially an abstract thinker, Zoroaster inevitably concerned himself with the rural social problems of his people, particularly the care of cattle. This led to a ready accommodation to Jainist *ahimsa,* Hindu reverence for the cow, and even purification with cow urine. Parsi houses of worship are often called Fire Temples, and a separate order of priests tends the sacred flame, but Parsis prefer to emphasize that the fire is a symbol of divinity rather than itself an object of worship. One other distinctive practice is the exposure of the dead to vultures on *dakhmas* (or Towers of Silence), rather than the contamination of fire or earth by cremation or burial.

Among the ethical contributions Parsis have made in India might be listed the dignified place of women, the mature age for marriage, the acceptance of religious equality, and enormous community benefactions. As one of them remarked, Parsis were not active in the early social reforms (of Ranade in Bombay, for example) because those movements were directed to Hindu needs. "We were already given freedom of divorce, education for women, and a ban on child marriage, etc." Over the centuries there have been no distinct movements to divide the ingrown group, and few outstanding leaders, yet all India would acknowledge the virtues which have developed within the community. Recent history, however, cannot pass over certain conspicuous Parsi names: Sir Pherozeshah Mehta, Sir Dinshaw Edulji Wacha. In the present Indian Parliament at least six Parsis serve ably, including M. R. Masani, Secretary of the new Swatantra Party. Distinguished Parsis control the great Tata steel and industrial complex, numerous banks and factories, and dominate the national airways.

Like many other religious groups, the Parsis today face a serious threat, not of apostasy but of indifference and ultimate dilution of faith. In 1937–1938, as terms of Indian independence were being discussed, ten thousand Parsis (one-tenth of the total community) sent to Clement Atlee a petition declining "British protection" and asking that they *not* be treated as a separate communal group, but accepted politically and socially as Indians first. A tiny community which for twelve hundred years has maintained its radical dualism against the prevailing spiritual monism of Hindu thought may continue to resist absorption into a single national culture. If it does so, the achievement will be due in large part to its ethical character. Says Edmund Soper: "This religion is on a high level because it gives the rightful place to morality in religion, such as has rarely been surpassed." [19]

Islam

It was a Parsi who told this Christian that some Hindus in India today would choose a Muslim neighbor "because once this man accepts you as a person, he will give his life for you." Yet the months following Partition in 1947 were marked by some of the most brutal, indiscriminate slaughter between two religious communities in all history. Today, despite the establishment of an adjacent Muslim state in Pakistan, forty million Mohammedans have chosen to remain in "secular" India, comprising one-tenth of the total population. The often bitter coexistence began in the eleventh century, when Mahmud the Turk invaded India, plundering and destroying sacred Hindu shrines at Mathura and Somnath and massacring thousands of inhabitants. This pillage was repeated sixteen times in his reign and extended throughout northern India by his successors. In the fourteenth century the Mongols (or Moguls, as they are called in India) swept over the mountains under the leadership of Genghis Khan and then withdrew. At the end of the century, however, his grandson Tamerlane directed a sack of Delhi so completely devastating that "for two whole months not a bird moved a wing in the city." Meanwhile the Turkish sultans penetrated for the first time to southern India, ravaging the countryside and setting up an assortment of princely states. Thus for eight hundred years, subject to recurrent uprisings and increasing European encroachments, Muslims wielded political power over most of Hindu India until Queen Victoria asserted her sovereignty in 1858.

During this period inevitable cultural interchanges occurred. Persian language, architecture and ceremony came to dominate the north, especially in court circles. Hindus among the upper classes secluded their women more strictly than before, though whether from cultural imitation of *purdah* or for moral protection remains a debated point. Conversion has taken place, first, by occasional force or conquest or coercion; second, by social necessity, when association with Muslims has caused loss of Hindu caste; third, by "missionary" persuasion; and fourth, by the influence of mystics and miracles, particularly in the fifteenth and sixteenth centuries.

But the creed of the Prophet did not attain that success in India which had been achieved in Egypt, Persia and Byzantia. The change in religion did not change their environment and atmosphere, which was permeated through and through with social isolation, superstitious ideas and caste restrictions.[20]

On the whole, more cultural "borrowings" have taken place from Hinduism into Islam. Village deities, nature and fertility cults, worship of saints, household shrines, the festivals of Shiva and Hanuman, the omission of circumcision, accepting a "bride price" for a daughter's marriage, caste observances of various kinds—all these can now be found in certain Muslim communities. Converts from Hinduism often continued to practice female infanticide or to commit suttee by burial (not cremation) with their husband's corpses.

While the political and military power of Islam, coupled with the authority of its dogmatic creed and practice, failed to conquer the deeply entrenched social and religious institutions of Hinduism, neither was the alien faith swallowed up. Frank Moraes, a brilliant journalist with highly Westernized perspectives, describes the net results in these terms:

The impact of the Islamic invaders on India was altogether different from that produced by the previous intruders. Hinduism was able to absorb and assimilate in its social fabric Greek and Saka, Kushan and Hun. But the Moslems it could not absorb. Nor was Islam able to up-root Hinduism and destroy its ideas and institutions. Hitherto Hindu society was divided horizontally; but with the intrusion of Islam into In·dia, society was split vertically, living in two parallel but separate worlds, divided one from the other by differences in outlook, ideas, religious and social philosophy, dress, manners and customs.[21]

The most conspicuous effort to break through this deadlock was made by the Emperor Akbar, who reigned from 1558 to 1605. Religiously curious although illiterate, Akbar took delight in the intellectual joustings of his Muslim *maulvis* (scholars) and the Jesuit priests who were welcomed at court. He compared the teachings of Hinduism, Jainism, Islam, Christianity and Zoroastrianism and dreamed of creating a Universal Faith (Din-i-Ilahi). When his advisors branded the newly compiled Sikh Granth as a dangerous book, Akbar had it read to him and declared that he found nothing subversive in it. He permitted conversion from one faith to another, abolished the Mathura pilgrim tax that had been imposed on Hindus by his predecessors, and even practiced vegetarianism. Although Muslims did not ordinarily marry their girls before puberty, the Hindu custom of child marriages had become so prevalent in both communities that Akbar imposed a law against it. He built a separate district in Delhi for prostitutes and called it, half-humorously, Shaitanpur (The Devil's Quarter). He also sought to end discrimination and caste, to make brotherhood and equality the practice rather than a social ideal. "It was for the first time that Akbar started the policy of India for Indians, service was opened to talent, absolute freedom of conscience was granted, toleration and brotherhood were the orders of the day." [22] For these and other expressions of liberal thought, Akbar was condemned by orthodox Muslims, and his son and grandson reverted to more rigid Islamic traditions. Nevertheless, as a modern Muslim admits, "during the reign of Akbar Muslims on the whole were better *men* though indifferent Musalmans." [23]

Partly because of their own social compromises, partly in de-fensiveness against Hindu nationalism, partly out of resentment toward the British usurpation of power, most Muslims in the nineteenth century withdrew from public life. As late as 1920 some *maulvis* taught that learning English would bar a devout Muslim from heaven. As a result, few took an active part in the Independence Movement, and many suffered educational, social, economic and political handicaps. A notable exception was Sir Syed Ahmed Khan (1817–1898), probably the outstanding Muslim in nineteenth century India. Born in Delhi from a long line of court officials, Syed Ahmed received little formal instruction himself but determined to raise the educational level of the Muslim community, including girls. Having entered British government service at 21, he supported the ruling power during the Mutiny of 1857 and on his first trip to Europe in 1869 paid tribute not only to the material goods and natural differences which he saw, but also to the "politeness, knowledge, good faith, cleanliness, skilled workmanship, accomplishments, and thoroughness, which are the results of education and civilization." [24]

On his return, he founded, on the model of Oxford and Cambridge, the Aligarh Anglo-Oriental College for Muslims, resolved to prove that Western education was not atheistic or heretical. He sought also to attack social evils through editing the *Mohammedan Social Reformer*. Like most Muslims, he remained aloof from the Indian National Congress, fearful that its policies would have an ultimately divisive effect, that representative government might prove unfair to minorities, and that Hindu nationalism could destroy the values of social progress under the British. Despite his communal outlook based on genuine religious loyalty, despite his unwitting contribution to the tragedy of Partition much later, Syed Ahmed Khan is still honored in India as the man who almost single-handedly lifted the Islamic community out of its medieval rut. "Other men have written books and founded colleges; but to arrest, as with a wall, the degeneration of a whole people—that is the work of a prophet." [25]

Even today Muslims differ widely in their attitude toward social change. Vice-Chancellor Mujeeb of Jamia Millia Islamia, New Delhi, insists that the Shariat (Islamic code) contains all that is necessary for moral reform if only it were observed more faithfully by Muslims. For example, he approves religious restrictions on polygamy and claims that it has never been practiced widely in India, yet resents any discrimination against polygamists or any attempt to prohibit polygamy by law. Islam has failed, he would maintain, to preserve the high standards of social equality, women's rights, just inheritance and the like that are commanded by the Koran. He himself would acquiesce in the political system adopted by the Hindu majority, but one of his faculty colleagues conceded that most Islamic states today are autocratic as well as theocratic and that "this is the question the West asks: whether democracy is compatible with Islam?"

Another prominent Muslim educator in the capital represents a very different approach. Milsa Mahmud Begg, Principal of Delhi College, openly and deliberately criticizes what he calls "the perverted religious sanctions" of modern Islam. By way of illustration, he cited two boys in filthy clothes who said they did not feel dirty because they were *pak*, ceremonially pure, uncontaminated in the prayer sense. Hindus, Begg added, would have found a religious sanction for washing themselves *and* their clothes. Or again, he explained:

The Hindu under a religious sanction saves money, because at the end of the year he has to worship Lakshmi, the goddess of wealth. The Muslim doesn't save because it would indicate lack of faith in God. This I call a perverted religious sanction, because otherwise we could teach them the plain economics of saving.[26]

Much of this irresponsibility Begg frankly blames on traditional priests, who proclaim a conservatism and a fatalism disastrous to social reform. The Koran, he points out, asserts that "God loves him who does his best and leaves the rest to the will of God," but reactionary *maulvis* have ignored the first clause and stressed inactivity based on utter trust. The *burq'a* (veil worn by Muslim women) was prescribed by priests, not by Mohammed or the Koran, Begg declared, and he refuses to admit to Delhi College any girl who remains technically in *purdah* (seclusion). "In India it will take a long time to change motives, urges, basic urges," he said. "But it is not too necessary to change them. A good religion will produce good social and economic conditions."

Like the other minority religions in India, Islam—increasingly cut off from Muslim states by dominant national loyalties—can escape corruption or absorption only by making a positive contribution to social and ethical progress.

Sikhism

The latest of India's religions—and the most purely indigenous since Buddha—is Sikhism. Nanak, the first *guru* (teacher) (1469–1538), owed many of his fresh insights to Kabir, a beloved Hindu poet-reformer. Kabir (1440–1518) eloquently condemned idolatry, ritualism, asceticism, scriptures and other religious externals if they bear no ethical fruit from spiritual root. A strict monotheist, he asserted that unqualified love of God (by which is apparently meant love *toward* God, not love *from* God) is sufficient to free man from the law of *karma* and rebirth and to assure absorption into the Absolute. Rejecting the unique authority of the Vedas and the barren forms of both Brahminism and Islam, Kabir introduced the idea of an inspired personal leader as the essential aid to spiritual insight and ethical goodness.

These principles Nanak incorporated in his own "enlightenment." Rather than adopt any one title for God, he referred to him as the True Name, who is one, sovereign, and omnipotent, predestining all his creatures, as the Muslims believed. From Hinduism he adopted the concept of *maya* (illusion) to describe the mystery of truth behind the veil of matter. But to each faith he insisted that religion consisted not in ashes smeared on the body, not in shaven head, not in wanderings to places of cremation, not in contemplation or bathing, but in purity of act and motive, faithfulness to wife and teacher, humility and harmony. "There is no Hindu and no Musalman," said Nanak when he emerged from his forest retreat. "Let no one be proud of his caste. . . . The world is all made out of one clay," declared the second *guru,* his successor. The first five Sikh leaders practiced a gentle pacifism, but under the cruel torture of Akbar's son, Jehangir, this policy changed at the beginning of the seventeenth century, and Sikhs became a militant sect who ruled their own kingdom from 1767 to 1849, served as policemen and watchmen in British colonies throughout Asia, and still make up the core of the Indian army. Fanatical Muslim persecution turned their religious syncretism into bitter hatred of Islam, so that Sikhs were fearfully involved in the bloodshed of 1947. Most chose Indian citizenship, but today they are still agitating under the bellicose Akali Dal for a separate Sikh state in the Punjab, with its own religion and its own language.

One prominent Sikh told a Western audience in Delhi that the visible signs of the faith (long hair and beard, a steel bracelet, a dagger, comb, and khaki shorts) are being preserved *because* the spiritual tenets are gradually being abandoned. However, an army officer remarked, on inquiry about his short-haired son, that many Sikhs were giving up the outward forms and slipping consciously or unconsciously into Hinduism. At the point of belief, of simple sincerity and moral integrity, it might be claimed that Sikhism and Christianity have more in common—or at least less in contrast— than either did with the prevailing religions of India. To those who emphasize faith in a single, personal God, this may be true.

Professor Teja Singh has defined "the essence of Sikhism as Nam and Sewa, or adoration of God through repeating his name, and service to mankind." [27] On the other hand, he goes on to admit that "the Sikhs, unlike the Buddhists, and Jains, have made little contribution to Indian culture." Their time has been shorter by many centuries, their periods of persecution more acute. It remains yet to be seen whether their ethical monotheism can resist the syncretism out of which their faith was born and in which it is destined to live. It remains yet to be seen whether the Sikhs can serve the social conscience of India as they have so conspicuously served its military arm.

Chapter III

Under the British Raj

When the British withdrew from India in 1947, they left a vast reservoir of goodwill. However reluctant the "dismemberment of Empire," however bitter the previous decades of struggle, the actual granting of Independence was handled between friends. The atmosphere of mutual respect and even appreciation was—and is— in marked contrast to the bitterness still festering in Indonesia, Indo-China, the Congo, and elsewhere.

Nevertheless, history can never be erased. Anglo-Indian relations during the past three hundred and fifty years will continue to be debated for at least that length of time to come. Enlightened scholars and even recent participants no longer paint the picture in stark contrast, blaming England for every Indian problem or glorifying the contributions of benevolent colonialism. A century ago many Westerners—often without first-hand observation—idealized Hindu philosophy and culture and village life. A century ago Indian social reformers welcomed avidly the blessings of Western science and education. Then, during the period of conflict and mutual disillusionment, each side grew blind to its own faults and the other's virtues. Now, with statesmen and writers in both countries free to acknowledge mistakes and misunderstandings, one can still detect a national bias in most accounts of recent Indian history. This will always be so, for one cannot measure human exploitation against railways, or genuine democracy against bureaucracy. When man chooses—or wanders accidentally—down one path of history, the other fork remains irrevocably closed to any knowledge of what might have been.

This chapter sketches some of the contributions, positive and negative, which the period of British rule in India brought to social and ethical values. First were the motivating principles and consequences of official British policy, under the East India Company and later under the Crown. Second, the abolition of suttee and other social evils by legislation. Third, the influences in Western education and literature which moulded India's modern political thought.

By the Elizabethan Charter of 1600 the East India Company was given authority to make and execute laws for the governing of itself and its servants and officers and for the advancement of trade, providing these rules and penalties were not contrary to English laws or customs. Under Charles II, the Charter of 1661 introduced English law into the Presidency towns of Calcutta, Bombay and Madras by giving the Governor and Councils jurisdiction over all persons belonging to the Company *or* living under them. Colonialism had begun. In December 1687, the East India Company was authorized to create such civil and military institutions "as may be the foundation of a large, well-grounded, sure English dominion in India for all time to come." [1]

One of the first moves by officials in Bombay to implement the Charter of Charles II was to adopt in 1662 a policy that proved fundamental for nearly three hundred years, a policy misleadingly labeled "toleration." Orders were issued that there should be "no compulsory conversion, no interference with native habits, and no cow-killing in Hindu quarters," in short, no pressure of any kind on non-Christian religions. By the end of the century, however, Parliament had recommended, in the Charter renewal of 1698, that Company representatives "should apply themselves to learn the languages of the countries, the better to enable them to instruct the Gentoos (Hindus), who should be the servants of the Company or their agents, in the Protestant religion." [2]

The eighteenth century brought drastic changes on both sides of the globe. British control in India expanded many-fold, partly by the "natural" extension and protection of commercial interests, partly by decisive victories of Robert Clive over the French, at Plassey in 1757 and at Pondicherry in 1761. Meanwhile the Evangelical Movement in England stirred a sense of moral responsibility for the burgeoning Empire. This was not yet a concern for the Christian conversion of the "Gentoos"; the Protestant missionary movement had still to burst into bloom under William Carey. For two centuries a pious solicitude for the welfare of the "natives" appeared too often to be rationalization for the basic policy of non-interference. Nevertheless a flame of idealism had been lit in Great Britain and India, a flame which neither Deistic indifference nor demonic avarice could wholly extinguish. As early as the famous trial of Warren Hastings in 1788, Edmund Burke had put the case for moral and social reform to the House of Lords in these terms:

Will your Lordships ever bear the corrupt practices of mankind made into the principles of government? It will be your pride and glory to teach man that they are to conform their practices to principles, and not to draw their principles from the corrupt practices of any man whatever.[3]

This was *not* the aim or purpose of the East India Company. Both missionaries and schoolteachers were banned from its territories. Even shipping agents who accepted such unlicensed passengers were liable for punishment, and one early missionary who attempted to defy this ruling actually died "before the mast" on his penal journey back home. When the brilliant young Wilberforce, whose name was to go down in history as the vanquisher of slavery in the British Empire, attempted to repeal these restrictions before the East India Company Charter was renewed in 1793, he received a resounding political defeat. Not only did the ban remain in force, but the Commons Resolution calling for "religious and moral improvement" in the social and economic conditions "of their Indian subjects" was ignored in the new Charter itself. Even officials who were practicing churchmen at home hesitated to apply their religion abroad. For example, Earl Cornwallis sought in various ways to raise the moral level of life in India during his brief term as Governor-General in 1805, yet he kept government offices and factories open on the Sabbath because he was "not yet persuaded that Sunday observance east of Suez was profitable or practicable." [4]

Indeed, "profitable or practicable" seemed to be the watchword of the Company. Its representatives admitted frankly that their concern was with markets not reforms, with profits not souls. As one spokesman put it, "The Hindus had as good a system of faith and morals as most people, and it would be madness to attempt their conversion." [5] Conversion, however, was not the only matter at issue. The deeper questions foreseen by Burke became increasingly acute: Were rulers from Western Christendom to tolerate not only "heathen superstitions," but antisocial and even immoral practices, or were they to impose alien ethical standards on an ancient and honorable civilization? In either case, was the motivation to be preservation of law and order for the sake of commercial profits, or was it to be the welfare of the governed? In the clash of politics and cultures, perhaps more than in any other sphere, it may be disastrous to do "the right thing from the wrong motive"—or vice versa.

The Company was not wholly to blame. England herself at the end of the eighteenth century had hardly set foot on the road to social reform. Many a so-called "rotten borough" was openly bought and sold; why should mere morality obstruct the profitable exploitation of India? If appointments to the E.I.C came often through influence rather than integrity, this happened ten times as often in Britain, according to Sir John Shore, an eminent Governor-General.[6] Mountstuart Elphinstone, one of the "great" Governors of Bombay (1819–1827) had plotters blown from guns because it was "painless to the criminal and terrible to the beholder." [7] Parliament legally abolished the slave trade in 1807, slavery itself in 1833. Not until the 'thirties, also, came the first annual state grant for education in England, thirteen years after government aid to education had commenced in India. The astounding fact seems to be that anywhere east of Suez ("where there ain't no Ten Commandments," as Kipling pointed out many decades later) reform movements followed as closely as they did the vacillating conscience of Mother England.

By any standards of measurement, progress can be traced in this period. Twenty years after Wilberforce suffered his first defeat, his opposition in Parliament girded for another battle of expediency versus morality. Tracts were circulated to glorify Hinduism, even referring to the "softening influence" of the Saugor dedications involving human sacrifice, or the "cheerful and well-ordered" system of infanticide at the sacred city of Benares.[8] Others with less hypocrisy asserted that paganism was preferable to unrest and dissent, profits of more concern than ethics. But William Carey was at work in India, and William Wilberforce in England. When the Charter was renewed in 1813, two concessions were made to the Evangelical conscience. Missionaries who had been refused a license to enter India might appeal that ban. One hundred thousand rupees were appropriated by the Company for education, science and literature, although significantly no mention whatever was made of religion.

The next twenty years saw even greater change, in attitudes and in legislation. There were those in England and in India who uncritically admired the philosophy and the piety and even the local polity of Hindu society. Others displayed a condescending tolerance based often on ulterior motives, like a tea merchant who urged that Indians should be left free to follow "their own religious prejudices and absurdities." More pragmatic realists argued that social harmony and political stability constituted the *summum bonum* of colonial administration, and that this required a policy of strict neutrality or noninterference. "Although the Directors' attitude was often based on honest if uncritical conviction, equally often their apparent interest in religious impartiality served as a useful cloak for their greater interest in dividends." [9]

On the other hand, supporters of social reform expanded the range of their arguments. Wilberforce was not the only man of influence in the British Parliament who believed with deep and simple evangelical fervor that every Indian—contemplative saint or ignorant idolator—needed the Christian Gospel. William Carey and the Serampore Mission had attracted a host of friends in England and America and had stimulated the formation of a dozen mission boards, Bible societies and other evangelistic groups. Equally important, despite his initial banishment from Calcutta to the Danish colony of Serampore, Carey had used his linguistic genius to earn a post as tutor and interpreter under the East India Company, and his personality and versatility to win the friendship and private support of many officials and traders.

Furthermore, both profiteers and politicians began to realize that a long-range development of Indian markets, resources and labor force would require widespread education and social change. Thus far, Christian schools were the only institutions providing such Western orientation, and missionaries stubbornly insisted on including moral and religious teachings. Responsible men in the government were beginning to echo the concerns of Sir Thomas Munro, Governor of Madras from 1820 to 1827:

There is one great question to which we should look in all our arrangements: What is to be their final result on the character of the people? Is it to be raised, or is it to be lowered? Are we to be satisfied with merely securing our power and protecting the inhabitants, leaving them to sink gradually in character lower than at present; or are we to endeavor to raise their character, and to render them worthy of filling higher situations in the management of their country, and of devising plans for its improvement?

Slowly and spasmodically, to be sure, the British hand in India grew firmer, if the heart still vacillated. Lord William Bentinck, the most outstanding Governor-General of those early days (1828-1835), quite frankly disliked bishops and the Established Church. He also detested child marriage, widow-burning, human sacrifice, and gross forms of polygamy, but he believed in principle that these practices had better be left to a gradually enlightened public opinion. For this reason he supported Indian social reformers in their efforts, defended free speech in British India, and encouraged a purely secular Western type of education. But when "the chips were down," when the lines of battle were drawn, Lord Bentinck used his authority in behalf of Christian ethics and British justice.

The most notorious issue, of course, was suttee (from *sati,* the original term for a faithful wife). The live cremation of widows on the funeral pyres of their husbands was never numerically serious, perhaps a thousand a year, over half of them in Bengal. Yet the practice struck the European mind as so barbarous, so inhumane, that its eradication took precedence over principles of neutrality and fears of rebellion. Over the centuries this particular demonstration of loyalty had become accepted as a certain road to salvation, not only for the widow but for her deceased husband. One text in the *shastras,* a set of interpretative writings sometimes called the Hindu Apocrypha, glorifies suttee and promises the woman a place with her earthly lord in paradise—if such a view can be reconciled with the doctrine of transmigration. In recent times this text has been variously analyzed: some maintaining that it is a corrupt passage, others that it permits but does not require immolation, still others that it exalts chastity and faithfulness in life rather than in death.

Behind these questionable religious sanctions lie social and ethical factors. Indian men have traditionally found it difficult to believe that any widow (as young as many of them were) could live alone and remain pure and chaste. No husband wanted to leave a pretty wife, often a child bride, to others. This possessive fear allegedly gained added validity in the periods of Turkish and Mogul rule. In addition, there loomed the very real problem of a "useless mouth" for the family to feed, in a society where single women had neither status nor vocation. Many scholars deny that suttee was common in Vedic times; Nehru asserted that early Sanskrit literature denounced the practice. Akbar the Great is reported to have said of suttee: "It is a strange commentary on the magnanimity of men that they should seek their deliverance through the self-sacrifice of their wives." [10] In any case, the moral and spiritual value of the act depended above all on its being voluntary.

The earliest European authorities in India were less hesitant than the later British to attempt outright suppression. The Portuguese, the Jesuits under St. Francis Xavier, the Danes, the Dutch, the French and some Englishmen sought to ban the practice in their respective areas. By the turn of the nineteenth century the presence of the Serampore missionaries in Bengal—and their embarrassingly frank reports to England—pricked the British conscience. When William Carey witnessed his first suttee in 1799,

what horrified him most was the use of bamboo poles to hold
the victim on the funeral pyre, providing clear proof that the sup-
posedly noble act of sacrifice was often far from voluntary. Later
investigations revealed that Brahmin priests exerted threats and
emotional pressures in many instances, that greedy families were
eager to be relieved of an unwanted female and to assure full control of the husband's estate.

Realizing that something should be done, yet fearful of the consequences, the Governor-General in Council, Lord Wellesley,
sought advice from an official court of Hindu pandits or scholars.
On June 5, 1805, they replied:

The practice of widows burning themselves with the bodies of their deceased husbands is founded on the religious notions of the Indoos, and
is expressly stated, with approbation, in their law. . . . The court have
reason to believe that the prejudices in favor of this custom are at present so strongly impressed on the minds of the inhabitants in most parts
of these provinces, that all caste (sic) of Hindoos would be extremely
tenacious of its continuance.[11]

Following Lord Wellesley's recall that same year, the British—
weighing morality against expediency—did nothing about suttee.
Finally, in 1813, prodded by Hindu leaders themselves, the government issued specific regulations for the ritual, most of them based
on shastric conditions listed by the *pandits*.

First, there should be no suttee without official permission; this
in itself set the stamp of approval on an act which had previously
been strongly condemned. Second, an Indian police officer must be
present to certify formally that the *sati* was not forced, drugged,
pregnant, or under sixteen years of age. The attendance by a representative of the government gave not only legal sanction, but an
aura of prestige to the sacrificial rite. The order further emphasized
that the government had no intention of infringing on the religious
tenets of the people, thus tacitly acknowledging the shastric authority. As a consequence, the number of recorded suttees in the
Presidency of Fort William (Calcutta) increased markedly during
the next five years, to the embarrassment of the Governor-General.

Meanwhile William Carey and his associates, shocked by a

number of such sacrifices in their immediate neighborhood, had delved deeply into Hindu classics and reached the positive conclusion that suttee was countenanced but by no means commanded in the *shastras*. Even missionary opinion, however, was divided on the matter of legal prohibition. Bishop Reginald Heber, for example, had expressed his conviction before his death in 1826 that the primary purpose of evangelism should not be jeopardized by outlawing any religious practice, even so barbarous a one as suttee. On the whole, however, Carey's careful scholarly investigations of sociological conditions and Hindu teachings were generally ignored until another powerful crusader entered the fray.

Raja Rammohun Roy was a remarkable man. If few Indians realize the extent of his political and social achievements, Westerners are even less familiar with this pioneer reformer. Although he must have witnessed many suttees, his opposition was crystallized in 1811, when he watched his own sister-in-law forced back onto his brother's funeral pyre, "a hysterical and unhappy sacrifice." [12] His formal campaign began with a petition in 1818, declaring that the use of force in throwing victims back on the fire, or even threats and emotional coercion, constituted "murders according to every *Shastra,* as well as the common sense of all nations." [13] He further charged that selfish economic motivation, the desire to avoid sharing a dead man's possessions with his widow, often encouraged complicity in the act.

His tract—and others that followed—probed still deeper into psychological analysis of this practice. It assumes, he argued, the intellectual inferiority of women and their complete dependence on husband and family. It accuses women of a lack of resolution, when relatives apply undue persuasion or forcibly "assist" the victim to adhere to her "voluntary" resolve. It brands women as untrustworthy, if they should be allowed to survive their husbands. It implies that women are more subject than men to sexual passions, an insinuation denied by the practice of polygamy for men and suttee for women. Furthermore, Roy upheld Carey's contention that the scriptures did *not* require such sacrifice as a religious duty; on the contrary, he declared, it urged as preferable a life of piety and chastity. So effective were his pamphlets, his personal persuasion, and his on-the-spot protests that a group of prominent Hindus in

Calcutta submitted a petition to the government in 1819, echoing Roy's arguments.

By this time, the Directors of the East India Company in London were distressed by appeals from Carey, Roy and the Governor-General. On one hand, they were warned by the Governor-General that "nothing but the apprehension of evils infinitely greater than those arising from the existence of the practice could induce us to tolerate it for a single day." [14] Lord Bentinck, appointed to the highest post in British India in 1828, faced the problem head on, and collated widely divergent views. He personally favored official support for Muslim and Hindu festivals, government collection of pilgrim taxes, and other acquiescence in popular religious custom. He did believe that suttee was "grossly immoral and revolting to humanity," but he needed evidence that it was not positively commanded by Hindu scripture and that immediate abolition would not incite violent revolt. The first assurance he accepted from Carey and Roy; the second no one could guarantee.

The Minute on Suttee (November 8, 1829) which prepared the way for legal action was a moving document because it revealed so clearly the inner wrestling of conscience. In it Bentinck paid tribute to "that enlightened native, Rammohun Roy, a warm advocate for the abolition of suttees, and of all other superstitions and corruptions, engrafted on the Hindu religion. . . ." He also reported that four out of five of the Hindu judges had recommended immediate prohibition, but he made no reference to William Carey, perhaps because he did not want to focus resentment against Christian missions. His passages of moral struggle deserve fuller quotation.

To consent to the consignment, year after year, of hundreds of innocent victims to a cruel and untimely end, when the power exists of preventing it, is a predicament which no conscience can contemplate without horror. . . . But . . . to put to hazard, by a contrary course, the very safety of the British Empire in India . . . may be considered as a still greater evil. . . .

The first and primary object of my heart is the benefit of the Hindoos. I know nothing so important to the improvement of their future condition, as the establishment of purer morality, whatever their belief, and a more just conception of the will of God. The first step to this better understanding will be disassociation of religious belief and practice from blood and murder. . . . When they shall have been convinced of the error of this first and most criminal of their customs, may it not be hoped, that others which stand in the way of their improvement may likewise pass away, and that thus emancipated from those chains and shackles upon their minds and actions, they may no longer continue, as they have done, the slaves of every foreign conqueror, but that they may assume their just places among the great families of mankind. I disown in these remarks or in this measure any view whatever to conversion to our faith.[15]

"Sunday, December 5th, 1829, was one of the most joyful days in Carey's life." [16] He was busy preparing a sermon when an urgent dispatch arrived from the Governor-General, a request to translate immediately into Bengali an official paper. Carey's muttered word of protest changed to cheers when he saw the document. It was the famous Resolution #17, issued by Lord Bentinck the day before. "No church for me to-day!" Carey shouted; "if I delay an hour to translate and publish this, many a widow's life may be sacrificed." It was a moment for which he had worked and prayed for thirty years.

The Regulation not only outlawed suttee unconditionally, but also branded any collaborators who might assist a widow in her suicide as accomplices in murder. The Preamble reaffirmed two basic positions involved in the long and not-yet-ended controversy. First, it declared that

. . . the practice of suttee, or of burning or burying alive the widows of Hindoos, is revolting to the feelings of human nature; it is nowhere enjoined by the religion of the Hindoos as an imperative duty; on the contrary, a life of purity and retirement on the part of the widow is more especially and preferably inculcated. . . .[17]

[Therefore] "The Governor-General in Council, without intending to depart from one of the first and most important principles of the system of the Government in India, that all classes of the people be secure in the observance of their religious usages so long as that system can be adhered to without violation of the paramount dictates of justice and humanity, has deemed it right to establish [these rules prohibiting the practice of suttee].[18]

Conservative Hindus remarshaled their arguments—and their condemnation of the traitor, Rammohun Roy. In England a British advocate argued for repeal of Bentinck's Resolution, on the ground that it gratified only a few Christians and that suicide was no worse than officially supported idolatry. To such fatuous arguments one might repeat the retort of Sir Charles Napier, when a Brahmin pleaded suttee as a national custom: "My nation also has a custom. When men burn women alive, we hang them. . . . Let us all act according to national custom." [19]

Who ended the shocking practice of suttee? A partnership across differences of race and creed and purpose. Then and recently certain educated Indians, jealous of Parliamentary tribute paid to Christian missionaries, claimed the credit for Rammohun Roy and Dwarkanath Tagore. Nehru said of Roy: "It was largely because of his agitation for the abolition of sati that the British government prohibited it." But the Prime Minister hastened to add: "This sati, or the immolation of women on the funeral pyre of their husbands, was never widespread." [20] To be sure, Roy's contribution was indispensable. Not only did he strengthen the hand of the Governor-General in India, particularly among progressive Hindus, but he labored almost singlehandedly to block the requested repeal in England.

Yet it is questionable how much Roy could or would have accomplished without the encouragement of the Christian missionaries. Nor should it be forgotten that Roy himself advised the Governor-General *against* a frontal legal assault on the practice, fearing that Resolution #17 was too abrupt. Without doubt William Carey and his Serampore colleagues carried the steadiest, most consistent amassing of facts and distributing of propaganda against suttee. In many respects they paved the way, both in India and in England. But neither Hindu reformers nor Christian missionaries had the authority to abolish suttee. Lord Bentinck, in a very real moral and political dilemma, showed courage and decisiveness— and a sensitivity to the still weak voice of India's social conscience.

It is said that Mrs. Pandit, sister of Prime Minister Nehru and long the distinguished Indian High Commissioner in London, once asked to know one good thing which British rule had brought to India. "If it hadn't been for the British," came Lady Asquith's biting reply, "you would have been burned to death on your husband's funeral pyre." [21] There is truth behind the devastating repartee. The legal abolition of suttee, therefore, represented the interdependent cooperation of Church and State and progressive people. Each of these elements, to overcome the weight of tradition and religious reaction, had to use intelligence and courage and vision. Each also had to conquer mutual suspicion and fear. In removing this one social evil Raja Rammohun Roy, Lord William Bentinck and the Reverend William Carey proved that India could move forward into other areas of social progress without losing her cherished Hindu soul.

The banning of suttee was not the only social reform initiated by Lord Bentinck. In cooperation with one of the despised bishops, he laid the foundation for later laws that protected Christian converts against being deprived of property and civil rights. He commanded that no Indian should be disqualified from public office by reason of religion, birth, descent or color. His agents took drastic measures against infanticide and thuggee (or *thagi*), the ritual strangling of victims in honor of Kali. Between 1826 and 1835 some 1500 "thugs" were convicted in the courts, in disregard of religious sanctions which still upheld their barbaric acts. As a British writer remarks satirically: "To the insidious assault of reason, the English had now begun to add legislative interference."

The year 1833 proved a landmark of social legislation in Britain, with significant repercussions in India. In that year William Wilberforce, who had fought for reform at home and abroad since his conversion nearly half a century before, passed from the scene. But in that year the first Factory Act put a check on the exploitation of child labor in England, reducing mill hours per day to nine for children and twelve for adolescents! In that year slavery was officially abolished from the British Empire. And in that year the renewed Charter of the East India Company eliminated the license requirement for missionaries entering Company territory. Finally, in that same year, Thomas Babington Macaulay, who two years later was to place his permanent seal on Indian education, introduced in the House of Commons a new bill for the Government of India, commending—

. . . that wise, that benevolent, that noble clause, which enacts that no native of our Indian Empire shall, by reason of his colour, his descent, or his religion, be incapable of holding office. At the risk of being called by that nickname which is regarded as the most opprobrious of all nicknames by men of selfish hearts and contracted minds—at the risk of being called a philosopher—I may say that, to the last day of my life, I shall be proud of having been one of those who assisted in the framing of the Bill which contains that clause.[22]

Even those who claim that India's social and ethical reforms stem from the great classics of Hinduism must acknowledge a debt to European scholars. Centuries had passed since any truly creative period of Indian literature or philosophy; only in very limited terms could this state be blamed on the stifling effect of foreign rule. On the contrary, European scholars were largely responsible for the translation of the Sanskrit classics and their reintroduction into Indian life.

Within India itself it soon became apparent that people were eager for education, that mission schools could not meet the demand, and that no embargo on knowledge could be imposed. Two fundamental questions immediately arose. First, should this be a classical education, instilling the historical and philosophical riches of Hindu civilization, or should this be a full-scale introduction of Western science and culture? Second, should schools in India be operated in English or in the traditional Sanskrit or in the regional vernacular tongue? The issues are being debated today in very similar terms to those used a century and a quarter ago.

With the adoption of his famous Minute on Education (February 1835) Macaulay settled the matter firmly on the side of a Western educational system in the English language. His acknowledged aim was "to form a class who may be interpreters between us and the millions whom we govern; a class of persons, Indian in blood and color, but English in taste, in opinions, in morals and in intellect." [23] He has been charged with ignorance and condescension toward Hindu culture. In large measure the narrow, examination-centered curriculum, which distresses practically all educators and many politicians in India today, can justifiably be laid at Macaulay's door. Government policy since Independence has aimed at

the adoption of Hindi as a truly national language, although protests from non-Hindi-speaking areas have forced a postponement of
the original 1965 deadline.

No thoughtful person can deny, however, that without Macaulay's decisive memorandum British policy would have continued to
drift, and without the establishment of a unified educational system, Indian progress—measured by any standards whatsoever—
would have been severely delayed. In the linguistic field alone, the
use of English brought a unity to the country which few other
factors could or can provide. It opened the doors of science and
literature and of liberal political philosophy, far more widely and
rapidly than any indigenous system could have done. Critics, including Prime Minister Nehru,[24] have complained that Western education developed a new upper caste, divorced from the masses and
looking for patronage and position to their alien rulers. It is significant, however, that India's upper-class intelligentsia have never
traditionally been concerned with the plight of the underprivileged,
and that those social reformers who *have* served the masses are precisely those men, like Nehru himself, who have received the influence of Western education. When all the debits have been heavily
underscored, the credit remains that "it was this system of education that was the vehicle of western culture and brought about a
veritable revolution in the thought-climate of India." [25]

Who, then, were the instigators of such radical ideas as independence and social change?

Ironically most of the Indian reformers found their chief and
sufficient stimulus among political and literary writers in Great
Britain itself. John Locke's two famous essays *Of Civil Government* became clarion calls to liberty and human rights in Asia as
in America. Edmund Burke's defense of the American colonies
seemed to many Indians to have equal validity for them—although
far into the twentieth century British administrators in India
seemed determined to ignore Burke's pointed warning ("On Con-
ciliation with America"): "I do not know the method of drawing
up an indictment against an whole people." Sir Surendranath Banerjea spoke for most Indian liberals when he said: "To none do I
owe a greater debt than Edmund Burke, whose political philosophy
has so largely moulded my own views about government and soci-

ety." To anyone familiar with "Reflections on the Revolution in France" this tribute sounds almost incomprehensible, for Burke rejected the right of self-determination and stressed the values of rank, wealth, aristocracy and education in government. Yet on the problems of India, Ireland and the American colonies "his sympathies were magnanimous, his judgment far-sighted, and for these reasons he will always be an abiding inspiration to liberal statesmen." [26]

Increasingly in the nineteenth century prominent men of government and letters in England found themselves involved in problems of the Indian subcontinent. The most notable example was John Stuart Mill, who followed his father into the East India Company at the age of seventeen, became head officer in 1856, and retired two years later when India came directly under the Crown. His essay "On Liberty" was taken as a prime example of Britain's political ethics, and through him spread the Utilitarian view that the sanction of government lies in goodwill rather than coercion. As chief administrator of the East India Company, Mill prepared a "powerful memorandum" against the Act for the Better Government of India, passed by Parliament in August 1858, to place India under the rule of Queen Victoria. It is difficult now to judge how much of his argument rested on liberal opposition to the expansion of Empire, how much on vested interests of the Company. The summit of idealism was expressed in a speech by Gladstone, asserting boldly that "our title to be in India depends on a first condition, namely, that our being there is profitable to the Indian people, and on a second condition, that we can make the Indians themselves both see and understand it to be profitable." [27]

Over and over, Indian leaders pay tribute to the wider vision and the deeper hope they derived from the great minds of England. Through their speeches and writings march the names of Richard Cobden, Herbert Spencer, Thomas Carlyle and John Ruskin. A contemporary Indian writer lists Burke, Lord Acton, George Bernard Shaw and Bertrand Russell among those who "inspired in us the love of freedom." [28] Many a moderate reformer, particularly Gopal Krishna Gokhale, found guidance in John Morley's essay "On Compromise," where he admonishes "the wise conservative to accept the small change, lest a worse thing befall him, and the wise innovator to seize the chance of a small improvement while incessantly working in the direction of great ones." Other aphorisms of Viscount Morley (1838–1923) found echo as central tenets of Gandhi's program: "It is not enough to do good; one must do it the right way" ("On Compromise"); "Those who would treat politics and morality apart will never understand the one or the other" (essay on Rousseau).

British poets, too, sang their social and political philosophies into the heart of India. Of Rammohun Roy, the pioneer, it has been said that "the Raja's contributions to the freedom of the press flowed from Milton's *Areopagitica,* the fountain-head of English liberalism." Shelley's "Song to the Men of England" might even more appropriately have been addressed to the peasants of India:

> The seed ye sow, another reaps;
> The wealth ye find, another keeps;
> The robes ye weave, another wears;
> The arms ye forge, another bears . . .

Speaking of Shelley and of the political sonnets of Wordsworth ("On the Extinction of the Venetian Republic," "Toussaint L'Ouverture," "On the Subjugation of Switzerland," "London, 1802,"), India's greatest modern poet, Rabindranath Tagore, wrote: "The English authors, whose books and poems we studied, were full of love for humanity, justice, and freedom." [29]

It is little wonder that educated Indians assumed—naively perhaps—that "the flood of British freedom, which to the open sea of the world's praise, from dark antiquity hath flowed, 'with pomp of waters, unwithstood,' " (Wordsworth) would in time nourish the thirsty land of India. Only gradually, after the Mutiny of 1857 (which many Indians prefer to call the First War of Independence), did hope and trust give way to disillusionment and impatience. Queen Victoria's Royal Proclamation of power (November 1858) reaffirmed what had come to be the dominant administrative policy:

. . . Firmly relying ourselves on the truth of Christianity . . . we disclaim alike the right and the desire to impose our convictions on any of our subjects . . . and we do strictly charge and enjoin all those who may be in authority under us that they abstain from all interference with the religious belief or worship of any of our subjects on pain of our highest displeasure . . .

"While its effect politically was to freeze and petrify the India of 1858, in the field of social and religious customs its consequence was a 'hands off' policy on the part of the British government." [30]

What, then, was Britain's contribution to India's social conscience? One answer comes from Alexander Campbell, an able reporter who fulfilled an inexplicable urge to go "muck-raking" in order to produce an up-to-date *Mother India*.[31] He takes pains to attribute the following quotation to an Indian:

The British when they came to India found thugs who committed horrible murders not for gain but for religious reasons; widows who were burned alive; Bengal children who were thrown into the sea as human sacrifices; and Rajput female children who were customarily strangled at birth. When the British left India, they had abolished most of those practices.[32]

But *The Heart of India* is only part of India. Truth is many-sided —especially in the Orient. While certain spokesmen are reluctant to acknowledge either personal or national indebtedness outside the Vedanta, others refer gratefully to the catalytic stimulus provided by Western thought. Sachin Sen, writing on the social philosophy of Tagore—and other intellectual leaders—expressed it thus:

The mobile power of the European mind struck against the immobile Indian mind. It brought about a renaissance in the mind of India. The universal aspect of knowledge, the distribution of justice irrespective of castes and classes, the acceptance of an active and inquiring mind— all these were revolutionary doctrines which British rule brought forth in seeking to cement the connection between India and the West.[33]

Nor is the government of Free India unwilling to recognize the impact of the West. From a somewhat different point of view, the official volume on *Social Welfare in India* includes this observation:

If the impact of Christian Missionaries was primarily on the religious and social institutions, the British educator was responsble for the introduction of a new pattern of thinking whose major characteristics were rationalism, democracy and liberalism. . . . [These] had an innate appeal to the Indian intellectuals. In the social as well as religious reform movements that followed, we notice the effects of both these impacts. The conventions and forms of the joint family and the inequities of the caste system could not be reconciled with the individualistic and equalitarian trends of liberal thought imbibed by the newly educated middle classes.[34]

Frank Moraes, distinguished editor and journalist, says of the early nineteenth century—or later: "The educated Indian saw and recognized that British power was based on some positive qualities— on stability and strength, on unity, industrial initiative, economic enterprise, a live social conscience and discipline." [35]

Undoubtedly the moral influence of British rule would have been far greater if liberal ideas had been practiced as well as they were taught, and if they had not been imposed with an air of condescending superiority. But few Indians today would deny that Western education released fresh springs of ethical and social concern, that British legislation channeled them through a vast, heterogeneous society. In spite of eddies and whirlpools and a very different cultural streambed, the currents that ultimately forced reform and independence in India were the same currents that produced freedom and democracy in Mother England—and in her rambunctious colonies across the Atlantic. For no people can develop a truly indigenous social conscience until they are politically and spiritually free.

Chapter IV

Early Christian Missions

In any survey of India history it is obvious that

> . . . the consequences brought about by deliberate governmental ac-
> tion are only a part of the consequences of the British connection, and
> that no less important have been the influence of missionaries, of the
> non-official British community resident in India . . . of the ideas, po-
> litical and philosophical, current in British society and propagated as a
> result in India, and of the economic forces which were generated by the
> political union of the two countries and which operated so powerfully to
> change the structure of Indian society.[1]

Resurgent Hinduism and proud nationalism are loathe to acknowledge any foreign indebtedness, even in historical perspective. Indian friends pointed out how inextricably complex are the sources
of India's social conscience. Even the obvious contributions of
Christianity are diffused and often indirect. Yet immeasurable
though they may be, they are also immeasurably important.

It is not surprising that early missions focused their attention on conspicuous immediate evils. Even in the West, Christian ethics before the Social Gospel movement—and all too often since —has leaned toward pietistic judgments. Suttee, thuggee, infanticide, and human sacrifice may have been comparatively rare in Indian society, but they blatantly shocked the European conscience which encountered them. Idolatry and superstition offended Christian missionaries, but they could hardly be uprooted as crimes by a government devoted to "religious" toleration. One can hardly expect that imperialism (however defined) or labor exploitation or oppressive taxation or personal profiteering would be labeled as sinful, even by devout eighteenth or nineteenth century Evangelicals. The wonder is that missionaries—and even some officials—from pre-Victorian England felt obligated to combat child marriage, mistreatment of women, unjust systems of land holding and so forth.

If Christians could have restricted their efforts to obvious social evils, they might have avoided the worst conflicts in their own day and left a legacy of less suspicion and hostility. Indian leaders would gradually have acquired a humanistic and humanitarian conscience on these matters from Western culture, if there had been no missionary movement as such.

But religious and social reform proved to be inseparable in India. So, too, were both creative and destructive consequences. In the first place, missionaries came primarily in those early days from the ruling imperialist power, and the swelling tide of Indian nationalism resented and repudiated both. In the second place, India represented—perhaps more than any other nation in the world— "a civilization that demands religious sanction for all its customs, regardless of their moral values." [2] In other words, any attempt, however gentle, to change existing *mores* became inevitably an attack on the Hindu religion. It is easy enough for modern India and renascent Hinduism to distinguish between social practices which are unessential or even inappropriate to the Vedas and traditional philosophy. Such a distinction could *not* be made—except by a few far-sighted reformers—when the entire culture cowered defensively under alien rule. Furthermore, as even modern missionaries are aware, certain practical aspects of presenting the Christian gospel prove to be unexpectedly offensive to members of other cultural groups. To teach that God came to earth as a carpenter's son is to imply a low-caste status which Rama, Krishna, Buddha, Nanak, and other religious figures scrupulously avoided. To a Hindu the killing of a fatted calf is not regarded as a supreme honor, but as a repulsive insult.

There was still another reason for hostility to Christian ethics. This objection aimed at the very heart of the missionary motivation. Friends and critics alike have sometimes argued that if Christian missionaries—

. . . had limited their activities to social work and avoided all attempts at evangelization, they would have won nothing but praise from the Indian people. Such a statement not only overlooks the opposition which almost invariably greeted social reform, but also ignores the obvious fact that the importance of the missionaries' social campaign, as well as its weaknesses, were a direct result of the fervent desire to promote Christianity. The main aspects of their social work were undertaken as aids to, and almost inevitable expressions of, their main task of evangelization.[3]

This general thesis cannot be avoided. Missionaries differed as to how imperative social change might be. They differed even more as to methods which should be used in a complex non-Christian culture. But most of them had only "subordinate schemes for social reform"—subordinate to the central aim of conversion. For many Christians such a frankly avowed purpose is part of the very definition of "missionary"—that is why the word is in such disrepute in many lands today. But the tragic consequences of a narrow emphasis on theology at the cost of social ethics can be seen in the story of Raja Rammohun Roy—or Mahatma Gandhi.

Rammohun Roy was the first—and perhaps the greatest—of India's modern social reformers. From encounters with missionaries and his reading of the Bible, he wanted to present the ethical teachings of Jesus as a challenge and help to Hindus in their moral inertia. Therefore in 1820 he published a little pamphlet of Gospel excerpts under the title, "The Precepts of Jesus, the Road (or Guide or Way) to Peace and Happiness." In the Introduction he explained why he had extracted these particular sayings from their context of miracles and of Trinitarian theology:

I feel persuaded that by separating from the other matters contained in the New Testament the moral precepts found in that book, these will be more likely to produce the desirable effect of improving the hearts and minds of men of different persuasions and degrees of understanding. For historical and some other passages are liable to the doubts and disputes of free-thinkers and anti-christians, especially miraculous relations, which are much less wonderful than the fabricated tales handed down to the natives of Asia, and consequently would be apt, at best, to carry little weight with them. On the contrary, moral doctrines, tending evidently to the maintenance of the peace and harmony of mankind at large, are beyond the reach of metaphysical perversion, and intelligible alike to the learned and to the unlearned. This simple code of religion and morality is so admirably calculated to elevate men's ideas to high and liberal notions of God . . . and is also so well fitted to regulate the conduct of the human race in the discharge of their various duties to God, to themselves, and to society, that I cannot but hope the best effects from its promulgation in the present form.[4]

Roy's hope was doomed to disappointment. At a time of bitter prejudice, accentuated by increasing attacks on suttee, orthodox Hindus condemned the implicit support for an alien religion. Even more violent indignation came from the Serampore Mission. Carey's colleague, Joshua Marshman, insisted that Christianity must be accepted *in toto,* that Roy obviously did not understand either the Bible or the Good News it conveys. The presentation of precepts apart from doctrines, Marshman argued,

. . . perverts the grand design of the gospel, and frustrates the grace of God in the salvation of men. . . . These moral precepts were then presented to the Natives of India as being of themselves sufficient to secure happiness and peace to mankind, while the great Doctrines of salvation were omitted as comparatively unimportant. . . . What is it but to consign them over to eternal death? . . . Jesus must be regarded as God equal with the Father, expiating the sins of men, and saving them by his mighty power—or the whole of the Gospels, no less than the rest of the Sacred Scriptures, *must be* rejected as a cunningly devised fable, involving a tissue of arrogance and deception unparalleled in the history of mankind.[5]

Subsequent theological developments have not altered this basic stand of Christian orthodoxy. What may be questioned, however, is the lack of wisdom and grace in dealing with a potential ally and friend. When Carey and Marshman, in their paper, *The Friend of India,* accused Roy of "tampering with God's word," they refused to allow him to reply in their Bengali magazine, and finally denied him even the paid use of their press for his own publications.

Roy for his part maintained an extremely irenic attitude. Admitting that he was unfamiliar with English (he had studied it and numerous other languages for twenty years), he voluntarily abstained from further controversy for two years, during which time he learned Hebrew and Greek (and Syriac?) and read far more deeply into Christianity. At the end of this time, he wrote three *Appeals to the Christian Public* to defend a unitarian concept of the Godhead. Meanwhile onto the scene came another figure, to the acute embarrassment of the Serampore Mission. One of their own members, William Adam, announced his conversion to Roy's unitarian position, whereupon his ex-colleagues dubbed him "the second fallen Adam." Nevertheless, Adam boldly defended the Indian reformer, denying that Roy had ever depreciated the rest of the Scriptures in selecting his "Precepts," and reminding the missionaries that they, too, frequently distributed portions or commentaries on selected passages. Roy had merely expressed his conviction that these moral teachings were "more likely" to benefit his countrymen than some other parts. Furthermore, Adam argued that Roy had not repudiated Christian miracles; he had not likened their *truth* to "fabricated" Hindu miracles, but had merely suggested that they might *seem* less convincing because of their similarity. Finally, Roy's conclusion that "the regulation of the heart and life is the great end of all religion . . . showed that his heart was right in the sight of God and that his chief object was to lead mankind to true piety and virtue." Since the missionaries had achieved only "limited and imperfect . . . direct success," they ought to welcome the interest and support of a man like Rammohun Roy, Adam insisted. As it is,

They know neither their own spirit, nor the spirit of the Master whom they profess to serve, and . . . judging not by their professions, but by their conduct in this particular case, they might, without any breach of charity, be supposed to have come to this country not to spread Christianity, but to retard its progress.[6]

Theological intolerance and inflexibility were not the only self-imposed handicaps to Christian influence. The Church in India, as elsewhere, had accommodated itself to the prevailing social pattern in many respects. Among Syrian Jacobites, an ancient and ingrown minority, marriages were permitted between boys ten to twelve years of age and girls six or seven. Rituals of birth and marriage and death relied as heavily on animistic fears as on either Hinduism or Christianity. "At the beginning of the nineteenth century the Christian church in India, in its ancient forms of orthodoxy, had lost much of its inner power of reformation and revival. Like Hinduism and Islam, it had suffered for many centuries from a slow decline which had reached its lowest point as the eighteenth century drew to an end." [7] Among Roman Catholics, Robert de Nobili (1576–1636), the famous Italian Jesuit who followed Francis Xavier, frankly regarded caste as a social rather than a religious matter and even defended its functional values. For himself he adopted the sacred Brahminical cord (woven of three strands for the Christian Trinity), practiced vegetarianism and upheld his status as a Brahmin by avoiding contacts with other Europeans, most of whom were Portuguese. As an Indian Christian has explained, "What de Nobili wanted to teach was not socialism or practical democracy but Christianity. . . . He was a spiritual teacher, and the abolition of caste was the concern of the social reformer." [8]

Perhaps the greatest tragedy of the Church—then and now, in India or in the West—has been that Christians have been so ready to draw this dichotomy between the Gospel and its social imperatives, and to label the latter as "socialism" or "democracy" instead of Christianity. The Gospel is not a "system"—ethical, political or economic—but it cannot be effectively or faithfully taught by a "spiritual teacher" who is unconcerned with the social welfare of his hearers.

Yet many Protestants a century or two later still felt it necessary to respect the distinctions between pariahs and upper castes, even after their conversion to Christianity. The German Pietist,

Bartholomew Ziegenbalg, who arrived in Tranquebar in 1706 under Danish auspices (and soon received Anglican financial help), gave precedence to high caste Christians at Communion. Even the revered Reginald Heber, author of such great missionary hymns as "From Greenland's Icy Mountains," "Brightest and Best," and "The Son of God Goes Forth to War," found it impossible to have joint Communion in his churches. Only here and there local conditions or individual courage enabled Christians to take a vigorous moral stand against caste discriminations and other evils.

In social reform, as in every other area of missionary service, one name stands out for all time to come. William Carey always found time in the midst of multiple translations, botanical experiments and evangelistic preaching to combat social evils of every description. During his first decade in India (1793–1803), Carey undertook at government request an investigation into the Hindu ceremony of "dedicating" children to the Holy Mother Ganges by throwing them into the river at Saugor, sometimes to fulfil a vow by sacrificing the first-born. A son of Carey's colleague, Joshua Marshman, wrote of this study: "It had hitherto been the policy of the government of India to avoid most scrupulously all interference with the religious prejudices of the natives; and to permit the most sanguinary rites, whenever it was alleged by orthodox Hindus that they were sanctioned by the shasters" (or *shastras,* scriptural commentaries).[9] Carey concluded that the Saugor dedications were *not* enjoined in Hindu scriptures and could therefore be banned without fear of revolt, "whatever religious motives may be pretended." As a result, Lord Wellesley, the Governor-General, issued an order in 1801 forbidding this practice, and stationed fifty *sepoys* (soldiers) on the river bank to prevent it. A similar order prohibited the exposure of ill and aged persons to the ravages of white ants.

Fear that this kind of social disruption had helped to set off the Vellore Mutiny of 1806 made British officials extremely suspicious of missionary "firebrands," and proposals for further reform were received with "compromise and evasion." Nevertheless William Carey continued to collect his data and to present his views—to the government in India, to the public and Parliament in England.

As a child Carey had been distressed by the thought of human slavery, and the writings of Jean Jacques Rousseau confirmed him in his opposition. Once, shocked by an advertisement for the sale of a Negro, he wrote to a relative:

I hope no Christian keeps a slave. If this should be the practice (for custom often blinds the eye of even good men) in the Southern parts of the United States, it will not be difficult to answer the enquiry . . . why the churches are in so languishing a state; but I hope that . . . it is the practice of those only who are enemies of God.[10]

Early in his missionary career Carey concerned himself with the re-form of Indian marriage practices, including polygamy and the mistreatment of widows. In his circle of converts he allowed re-marriage (presumably after unilateral divorce) for those whose wives would not join them in accepting Christianity. This practice was presumably based on the "Pauline Privilege" (I Cor. 7:15), still accepted by some churches as the sole ground for dissolving a marriage. With more courage than many of his colleagues, Carey insisted "that the retention of caste was not something of minor im-portance" and sought to establish "a new Christian national sys-tem, without caste differences." One of his early Brahmin converts married a Christian Shudra girl and ate the wedding supper with the foreign missionaries, though the two most tenacious taboos of caste are intermarriage and interdining.

Nor did this bold Baptist hesitate to criticize his countrymen, at home and abroad, for their reliance on military force, for their cor-ruption, and for the political controversies which so often under-mined the moral purpose of British rule in India. For better or worse, in the activity of William Carey, "thousands of Indians, both Hindus and Muslims, felt for the first time the impact of en-thusiastic evangelism inseparably bound up with a programme of social and educational reform." [11]

Carey's impact on Indian society came also in ways which were regarded as unorthodox or even un-Christian among certain church groups. As a self-taught horticulturist, he exchanged plants with botanists in England and experimented with products which were to alter substantially the Indian economy: coffee, cotton, tobacco, sugar cane, cereals and fruit. By translating such Hindu classics as the *Ramayana* into English—thus making them available for many

Indians who could not read Sanskrit or local vernaculars—Carey helped not only to interpret Hindu philosophy and culture to the West, but also to revive among Hindus themselves the values and ethics of India's past.

Fortunately there were some government officers under the East India Company and under the Crown who took a more sympathetic stand toward Christian missions than did official policy in England. The complacency of eighteenth century Deism had fitted readily into the political policy of "tolerance," but a gradual change in attitude can be traced. Warren Hastings, whatever his faults, was a man who "thought of Indians as human beings . . . and treated them always with courtesy." He also sought to convince the Directors of the Company that the people of India were not savages, but had laws and customs which ought to be respected. A natural corollary of this position was his insistence that those who lived among the Hindus should "leave their religious creed to the Being who has so long endured it and who will in his own time reform it." [12]

A few years later came Sir John Shore, Governor-General from 1793 to 1798, who was in later life to become president of the British and Foreign Bible Society. A man of "mild evangelical religion," he posed the question, to himself and indirectly to the British Government and Christian people: "Has not Providence imposed upon you the care of millions?" Increasingly after 1800 churchmen looked upon the Indians as the "White man's burden," the Christian's responsibility, and on British rule as the will of God. Governor-General John Lawrence affirmed his policy and his faith in these words: "We must endeavour solely to ascertain what is our Christian duty and follow that to the uttermost, undeterred by any consideration. . . . Christian things done in a Christian way will never alienate the heathen." [13]

Not all colonial administrators showed such motivation or such insight. On the contrary, through much of this same period ran two practices which puzzled and amazed the Hindus as well as the Christian missionaries. The first was deliberate discrimination against Indian converts. The noble promises of religious equality and civil neutrality, made by Bentinck and Macaulay and others, seemed in practice to protect Hindu and Muslim but not Christian

rights. Christian converts were often disqualified from offices open
to other Indians, and up to the Sepoy Mutiny of 1857 British officials refused to enlist Indian Christians in the army. In matters of
employment the excuse might well be given that high-caste Hindus,
why by education and prestige received most of the positions given
to Indians, objected as strongly to working with Christians as with
low-caste Hindus. This reasoning does not justify in any sense
certain judicial cases where Hindu, rather than British or "Christian," law was enforced against converts. Bishop Heber recalled one
Indian Christian who was punished for refusing to help pull the
mammoth Jagannath chariot in the heathen festival. The only
explanation for this kind of discrimination seems to have been a
psychotic fear that any encouragement whatsoever toward Christianity among the "natives" would incite violent rebellion against
proselytizing—and against the government. Such policies, however,
even in the eyes of educated Hindus, amounted to a betrayal of
British justice as well as a denial, by the rulers, of their own moral
and religious faith.

This impression received further impetus from a second be-
wildering policy: the many instances of official support for Hinduism. A son of Joshua Marshman reported that a deputation went
in 1802 to the Kali Ghat in Calcutta (one of the most depraved and
depressing Hindu shrines in all India) to make a thank-offering of
five thousand rupees in the name of the East India Company for recent British successes in India.[14] Among official practices which
missionaries felt compelled to condemn were the following: dedicating government records to Ganesh, the elephant-headed god;
employing Brahmin weather ceremonies; awarding judgment on
idolatry questions in British courts; ordering official gun salutes to
pagan gods (as late as 1851).[15]

Certain "religious responsibilities" the British felt they had accepted in the process of extending their authority over various tribal
or princely domains. In some cases commitments to protect and
support Hindu and/or Muslim festivals and shrines had been a
condition of "surrender" to British rule, often merely transferring
obligations which local princes had inherited for centuries. These
usually included state endowments for the "support of mosques,
temples, and other pious and beneficent purposes." At one time

some 7,600 shrines in the Madras area alone were under the jurisdiction of the government. Far more than financial support, however, direct participation in superstitious and idolatrous ceremonies
shocked the Christian conscience in India and in England. Worse
still, the motivation could be clearly seen in profitable revenue, not
simply in preserving law and order. After deducting expenses, the
East India Company netted £95,206 in seventeen years at Jagannath, £159,429 in sixteen years at Allahabad, £445,942 in sixteen years at Gaya.[16] Under this dual heading of profits and peace
fell such practices as issuing certificates to pilgrims at popular
shrines, collecting entrance fees in temples, licensing *devadasis*
(dancing girls who were frequently temple prostitutes), conscript-
ing pullers for the Jagannath carts (pullers who not infrequently
died by accident or sacrifice under the giant wheels). Some of the
more flagrant pilgrim taxes were abolished in 1840, but subsidies
for festivals and temples continued long thereafter. "The Government in India remained unconvinced of having in any way acted
contrary to the dictates of humanity which they genuinely sought
to observe, and continued to interfere in the conduct of the great
Indian festivals with a steady blend of humane and profit-making
motives." [17]

No wonder this official sanction of idolatry and "paganism"
drew condemnation from those who sought to introduce Christian
ethics into Hindu society. Evangelicals in England bitterly assailed
the East India Company as a "dry nurse to Vishnu" and the
"churchwarden of Juggernaut." [18] George Smith in his *Life of William Carey* denounced what he called "a deliberate encouragement
of the worst forms of Hindooism by the East India Company and
its servants." [19] Missionaries on the spot gathered their factual data
and their eye-witness accounts to convince the British public that
the government was sponsoring gross superstition and social evil,
not merely practicing religious tolerance. They refused to accept
—or allow Christians back home to accept—the description of such
degrading practices as "quaint, fascinating or even childish." [20]

Arthur Mayhew, in his survey of *Christianity and the Government of India,* lists a fourfold program of reform followed by
missions between 1813 and 1857.[21] First, to secure not merely
toleration but protection and justice for Indian converts to Chris-

tianity. Second, to stimulate civil authorities to raise both moral and
social standards in India. Third, to encourage an all-too-timid government to profess and practice more openly the faith of the government and people in England. Fourth, to demonstrate that it was
possible to tolerate other religions without slighting or repudiating
Christianity, as official practice seemed to do. These aims appeared
mild and hardly objectionable. They were not formally adopted or
deliberately advanced. Yet their spirit and purpose achieved a
gradual change in administrative policy, even prior to the Mutiny.

Most of the conspicuous support of pagan idolatry came to an
end when the Crown took over the government of India in 1858.
Indeed, it may be argued that this one mistake in policy—the official sponsorship of heathen festivals and superstitions—cost the
East India Company popular support in England when it fought
for its "right to rule" after the Mutiny. As early as 1862 a civil
suit was actually filed against the "shamelessness, rascality and de-
ceit" of certain Vishnu temple priests. Despite a threat of excom-
munication for any Vaishnavite followers who might testify against
them, the priests were adjudged guilty, and the plea of religious
sanction was dismissed by the assertion that what is morally wrong
cannot be theologically right. In a radical departure from previous
policy in India, the court declared: "Practices which sap the very
foundations of morality, if established in the name and under
the sanction of religion, ought to be publicly exposed and denounced." [22]

In 1864, the great Methodist missionary pioneer, Bishop James
M. Thoburn, delivered an address to the first session of the Indian
Mission Annual Conference in Lucknow.[23] Deploring the fact that
the Church and church people had in earlier days accepted idolatry
and tolerated "a great moral pest house" in India, Bishop Thoburn
suggested seven reasons: (1) the selfish ends of the government
and churches; (2) the depreciation of their own religion by some
Christians; (3) the British policy of strict religious neutrality; (4)
the blunt assertion by Macaulay, in drafting the Education Act of
1835, that "we abstain from giving any encouragement to those engaged in the work of converting the natives to Christianity"; (5)
the deliberate withholding of government aid from many mission
schools (financial aid was granted to all educational institutions,

officially and universally, in 1854); (6) the common neglect of religion (and morality) by the British themselves; (7) the practices of the East India Company during its tenure.

Among the Company policies which Bishop Thoburn condemned were the following: (a) for fifty years it excluded any place of Christian worship in India (presumably there were no Roman Catholic or Syrian churches in the tiny British enclaves of the early period, although the Bishop might have considered only Protestant churches); (b) for two hundred years it sought to exclude missionaries; (c) it debarred Christians from "offices of respectability" yet repaired mosques and temples; (d) it "drew distinction between morality and religion," and displayed "worse" than polygamy in its own moral behavior. He might have added that until 1854 no government school in India could have a Bible in its library, and no teacher was permitted to explain religious references or to answer questions about religion in or out of school.[24] In extreme cases literary mention of Solomon was changed to "a wise man," and the word "Christian" to "soldier" in certain poems by Jane Taylor. Yet Hindu and Muslim literature, full of their respective religious traditions, were included in the curricula. "It was not the Christian aims of Government but the apparent lack of any religious aim that frightened many observers of its educational efforts." [25]

No sketch of Christian influence in India would be complete without mention of mission schools. The importance of education for the uplift of India was recognized by missionaries long before the government gave its attention to the problem. No matter how true it may be that the primary purpose of Christian institutions was evangelism, there can be no denial that they released a flood of Western science and literature and philosophy into Indian society. In the long run, the difference between government and mission policy was one of emphasis and method. Many officials firmly believed that India would be evangelized naturally and inevitably through Western education. For example, despite his opposition to evangelism, Macaulay anticipated that under a system of British schools no idolator would be left in Bengal within forty years. Missionaries, on the other hand, believed that India would be Westernized through Christian education and conversion.

"Many agents of the Government, and practically all the agents of Christian missions, held that the gift of Western civilization, divorced from all knowledge of its religious foundations, was educationally unsound and morally dangerous." [26] This striking statement should have wider acceptance and implementation—then and now.

Through missionary teachers and institutions, Christianity has touched the lives and thought and ethics of countless Indian leaders who have never forsaken the social and religious roots of Hinduism. Raja Rammohun Roy, though rebuffed by the Serampore missionaries, became an intimate friend of Alexander Duff, the great Scottish educator, and helped him to open his first school in Calcutta. Like his revered friend, Carey, Duff refused to condemn everything in Hinduism. He acknowledged its moral and spiritual values, but did not believe that they were adequate to raise the nation out of its slough of ignorance and superstition. Therefore he made no secret of his confidence that science would gradually undermine Hinduism and point the way for all Indians toward Christianity. Incidentally, in a day when economic problems still lay outside the scope of most Christian ethics, Duff helped to remove injustices in the system of land tenure in Bengal.

From the days when fathers scoffed at Duff and others for proposing a school for girls ("You might as well try to educate my cow!") Christian missions have pioneered in education and social equality for women. Isabella Thoburn College in Lucknow and Madras Christian College for Women have become two of the outstanding schools in the entire country. K. C. Sen brought the Brahmo Samaj, the first significant social reform movement, even closer to Christianity than had Rammohun Roy, its founder. Swami Vivekananda studied in a mission school and reputedly conceived the idea of the Ramakrishna Mission while telling the story of Jesus one Christmas Eve.[27] Gopal Krishna Gokhale was influenced "to some extent" [28] by the Cowley Fathers in Poona in the founding of the Servants of India Society. Mahatma Gandhi's admiration for—and frequent use of—the Sermon on the Mount are well known. President Radhakrishnan studied in mission schools, including Madras Christian College, before going abroad to Oxford, although most of his biographical sketches and "who's who" descriptions pointedly omit this fact.

Such contacts are obviously immeasurable, even by the person concerned. Still more difficult to evaluate are the subtle, indirect influences on millions of humble Indians and on society at large. Detailed mission histories may be able to say, in certain instances: this village abandoned polygamy and prostitution because the Christian Gospel was preached; or that community opened its walls to all castes because a missionary showed the universal love of God; or this primitive tribe gave up head-hunting—or infanticide—or thuggee when they became acquainted with Christ.

If it is possible for biased Christians to make extravagant, often unwarranted claims in this respect, it is equally possible for bigoted anti-Christians to reject the most obvious connections, to point to Muslim condemnation of caste or to Hindu concern for the stranger, and say dogmatically: Here, *not* in Christianity, lie the roots of India's social conscience. Yet most impartial observers—if there be any—would agree with Farquhar when he suggests that "the old religions are the soil from which the modern movements spring; while it will be found that the seed has, in the main, been sown by missions." [29]

Chapter V

Nineteenth-Century Reform

In their effort to understand the heart and mind of modern India many Westerners have overlooked a vital period of transition. They have analyzed the ancient Vedic scriptures and the impact of Muslim and European rule on Hindu society. They have probed the ineffable character of Mahatma Gandhi as mystical saint and practical politician. They have scrutinized the statesmanship of Jawaharlal Nehru. But all too often they have remained ignorant of the intellectual currents and cross-currents, the social reform movements and the religious tensions that marked the nineteenth century awakening of India.

Wherever the responsibility may lie, at the beginning of this period Indian civilization had reached a low level of degradation and corruption. Polytheism and idolatry had usurped the thrones of monotheism and philosophy. Relying on distorted interpretations of the Vedas, Brahmin priests had debased the simple religion of the people. Social evils had made of a noble nation a prime example of "heathenism" at its worst.

Raja Rammohun Roy

But "a great personality arises in revolutionary times," and that man for India was Raja Rammohun Roy (1772–1833). Called "the Father of the Indian Renaissance," "the Herald of a New Age in India," "the great pioneer of modern Indian thought," Roy deserves an even larger podium. In the words of a distinguished member of a distinguished family, Saurendra Nath Tagore, Roy's contribution was "not a particular creed but a *Weltanschauung* . . . not only for Bengal or for India, but for the whole world." [1] In depth of religious and intellectual insight, in breadth of social vision, in height of moral courage, Roy ranks among the great reformers of any age or culture.

Born into a devout Brahmin family, which had abandoned the priestly profession, the young princeling was married three times by the age of ten, his first "wife" having died in infancy, his other two never congenial partners in his monumental career. Early contacts with liberal Islam inculcated in the boy a revolt against idolatry, bibliolatry and narrow sectarianism. At the age of 16 he wrote a booklet, in Persian with an Arabic introduction, in which he condemned idolatry and urged a comparative study of religions. This caused a break with his family, made final years later by his protest against his sister-in-law's suttee. For an uncertain period he wandered to Nepal and back, studied in the sacred city of Benares, then worked for a decade under the East India Company. Among his writings during this period were "A Gift to Theists" and "Discussions on Various Religions."

In 1814 Roy settled in Calcutta, where he encountered Christian missions—with mixed results. His partnership in the abolition of suttee has already been described. Through his friendship with Alexander Duff he

. . . played a great part in drawing the Christian missions into the field of Indian education. . . . All true education, the reformer emphatically declared, [to Duff], ought to be religious, since the object was not merely to give information, but to develop and regulate all the powers of the mind, the emotions, and the workings of the conscience.[2]

Yet Roy's profound and genuine interest in the Christian message met bitterly hostile rebuff from those missionaries, at Serampore and elsewhere, who condemned uncompromisingly his liberal "unitarian" interpretations. When he first moved to Calcutta, Roy organized the Atmiya Sabha (or Society of Friends). "In this society not only religious principles, but the absurdities and puerilities of the various Hindu social and other customs, connected with polytheism or idolatry, used to be discussed and condemned." [3]

In the last years of his life, Rammohun Roy journeyed to England on a threefold mission: to plead for more adequate stipends for the deposed emperor of Delhi; to block the efforts of conservative Hindus to repeal the Bentinck reforms; and to be in London during the debate on the renewal of the East India Company Charter. On this historic visit Roy sat in the diplomatic section for the Coronation of William IV and was presented to the King. The East India Company gave him a public dinner, at which he consumed rice and water while guests around him dined on turtle, venison and champagne. Jeremy Bentham (1748–1832), "the venerable but still fiery prophet of the rational love of mankind," with whom Roy had corresponded earlier, paid the unprecedented tribute of a late evening call at Roy's hotel and hailed him as "an admired and beloved fellow-worker in the service of humanity." [4] The Indian social reformer also met Robert Owen, "the father of British socialism," who attempted in vain to convert Rammohun to his views.[5]

Rammohun Roy had concerned himself over the years with international affairs. Back in 1821 he had given a banquet to celebrate the liberation of certain Latin American countries from Spain. He had sent a gift to famine relief in Ireland because of his sympathy for the Irish revolt against the British—and a century later Eamon de Valera expressed the nation's gratitude and pledged reciprocal support to India. On his way to England, Roy had left his own ship in Capetown, despite ill health, and boarded a French vessel in port simply to pay homage to a country which had fought for liberty, equality, and fraternity.[6] In 1831 Roy's first request for a visa to visit France was refused, and the Raja promptly composed a letter to the famous Foreign Minister Talleyrand, appealing for the abolition of the passport system, since both religion and science testify to the unity of mankind. In this letter he also urged the establishment of a "Congress" to which—

All matters of difference, whether political or commercial, affecting the Natives of any two civilized counties with constitutional governments (might be submitted and) settled amicably and justly to the satisfaction of both and profound peace and friendly feelings between them from generation to generation.[7]

(It should be added that Roy received his visa and even an audience with Louis Philippe.) But in his premature plea for a supranational organization, for a genuine world outlook, Roy was advocating "not the present fashionable internationalism in which nationalism dominates . . . not the most extraordinary internationalism being doled out to India from the West . . . not the diplomatic juggling (of) charity . . . diplomacy . . . and atom bombs . . . but real universal humanism."[8]

Was Raja Rammohun Roy a Christian? The debate still rages. On the affirmative side, the Synod of Ulster greeted his arrival in 1831 with "our admiration of his splendid talents and attainments, our high satisfaction in his accession to the cause of Christianity, our deep sense of his invaluable exertions for the diffusion of the Gospel."[9] According to Farquhar, Roy believed that "the highest form of education is . . . a thoroughly sound intellectual and scientific training, built on the moral and religious principles of Christ. To him the teaching of the Bible was the most essential element in the education he gave."[10] On the negative side, Prime Minister Nehru answered as follows:

Influenced in his early days by Islam, and later, to some extent, by Christianity, he stuck nevertheless to the foundations of his own faith. But he tried to reform that faith and rid it of its abuses and the evil practices that had become associated with it.[11]

To the over-all question Roy himself made occasional references. When he offered Alexander Duff the use of a Brahmo Samaj (Society of Believers in Brahma, or God) building and persuaded his friends to send their sons to Duff's school, he himself came on the first day to explain the missionary's purpose and to help remove anti-Christian prejudices against Bible teaching. "I have studied the whole Bible," he told Duff's new students, "and you know I am not a Christian." [12] More specifically, "he said himself, just before he set out for Europe, that on his death each sect, the Christian, the Hindu, and the Mohammedan, would claim him as their own, but that he belonged to none of them." [13]

In short, Roy's belief was a kind of "universal theism," in which he stressed the unity of God (with Islam, against Hindu polytheism or Christian Trinitarianism), the infinite love and goodness and power of the Supreme Being, and the immortality of the soul. He could not accept idols even as mere symbols; he could not accept rituals even though they might help the spiritually weak; he could not accept suttee even as a time-honored custom. In all religions at their best he found assurance of a personal God and a universal brotherhood. There are Indians today who ignore Roy's essential theism in their efforts to minimize the influence of Christianity. But his own statement reveals far far more accurately the basis of his respect for Christianity:

The consequence of my long and uninterrupted researches into religious truths has been that I have found the doctrines of Christ more conducive to moral principles, and better adapted for the use of rational beings, than any other which have come to my knowledge.[14]

Disappointed at the narrow dogmatism of traditional Christianity, rebuffed by those who originally brought the Gospel to nineteenth century India, Rammohun Roy sought to preserve the best elements of religious and social reform through the establishment of the Brahmo Samaj in 1828.

What Rammohun thought was needed most for the good of the individual and society, both here and hereafter, was the belief in, and service of, an infinite and perfect God, love to whom and peace and goodwill towards man, were to be the most potent factors for raising them in the scale of spiritual advancement, as well as of morals or conduct.[15]

The Brahmo Samaj had been suggested by William Adam, and some of Roy's disciples had urged an alternative to attending Unitarian services. The first meetings held on Saturday nights included Brahmin recitations of the Vedas, texts from the *Upanishads* explained in Bengali, and sermons and hymns. The theistic emphasis drew the common designation, Brahma Sabha (One-God Society), but orthodox Hindus condemned the new group most vehemently for its radical social stance. In their concern for the unity and equality of all men, the "Brahmos" attacked child marriage, suttee, polytheism, caste and sectarian prejudice of all kinds.

The Trust Deed of the Brahmo Samaj Worship Hall established in Calcutta in 1830 indicates something of the spirit and purpose of the founders. "The Hall is to be used . . . for the worship and adoration of the eternal, unsearchable, and immutable Being who is the Author and Preserver of the Universe . . ." but *not* under any particular (that is, sectarian) name or likeness or liturgy. On the other hand, no object of worship by any man or group was to be disparaged within the hall, and all sermons, prayers or hymns must encourage "contemplation of the Author and Preserver of the Universe" and promote "charity, morality, piety, benevolence, virtue, and the strengthening of the bonds of union between men of all religious persuasions and creeds." [16]

The Brahmo Samaj had barely gotten under way when Rammohun Roy departed for England, never to return. But the foundations had been well laid, and among those soon to take an active role in the Society were successive members of an illustrious family, the Tagores. The elder, Dwarkanath, broke Hindu caste by travelling to Europe, where he impressed Max Müller as a not learned, but intelligent man of the world. It may well have been his frank rebuke to the German scholar that gave stimulus to Müller's later investigation and admiration for Indian thought. "You are all alike," Dwarkanath Tagore said; "if anything seems strange to you and does not please you at once, you turn away. . . . You say our religion is no religion, our poetry is no poetry, our philosophy no philosophy." [17]

His son, Debendranath (1817–1905), grew up in a liberal, unconventional home, and joined the Brahmo Samaj in 1842. The Brahmo Covenant or Confession, which Debendranath composed in 1843, included these affirmations:

God is a personal being with sublime moral attributes. God has never been incarnated. God hears and answers prayer. . . . Temples and fixed forms of worship are unnecessary. Men of all castes and races may worship God acceptably. . . . Repentance and cessation from sin is the only way to forgiveness and salvation. Nature and Intuition are the sources of knowledge of God. No book is authoritative.[18]

Five years later Debendranath drafted a Book of Common Prayer for the Brahmo Samaj, drawn from the *Upanishads,* the *Code of Manu,* the *Mahabharata,* and other sources. As can be assumed from his language and sources, Tagore did not share Roy's reverence for Christ, and he seldom if ever quoted from the Bible. Yet references to repentance, forgiveness, and salvation sound strange within a Hindu context. Albert Schweitzer sums up Debendranath's creed in a simple sentence: "It was for him a matter of course that love for God must be proved by love to mankind." [19]

Keshab Chandra Sen

The chief successor to Raja Rammohun Roy was not Tagore, but Keshab Chandra Sen (1838–1894). Years later, in a lecture in England, Sen described his conversion thus:

English education unsettled my mind and left a void; I had given up idolatry, but had received no positive system of faith to replace it. And how could one live on earth without a system of positive religion? At last it pleased Providence to reveal Himself to me. I had not a single friend to speak to me of religion or God and immortality. I was passing from idolatry to utter worldliness. . . . When I felt that I wanted a church, I found that the existing sects and churches would not answer my purpose. A small publication of the Calcutta Brahmo Samaj fell into my hands, and as I read the chapter on "What Is Brahmoism?" I found that it corresponded exactly with the inner conviction of my heart, the voice of God in the soul.[20]

What were some of these compelling doctrines? Reliance on nature and intuition rather than revelation or authoritarian books as a basis of faith; fundamental truth at the heart of all religions; a progressive spiritual as well as physical development; One Supreme God with personality and intelligence and moral attributes, but *not* incarnation; repentance as the only way to atonement and salvation; faith in providential care, in prayer, in public worship (though communion with God is possible at any time anywhere, for "love toward Him, and performing the works He loves, constitutes His worship"). In the field of social welfare, Sen organized extensive famine relief for northwest India and a fund for epidemic victims in Bengal in 1861.

Despite their initial mutual respect, Debendranath and Keshab soon came to a parting of the ways. Sen became increasingly radical in his renunciation of Brahmin customs, not only abandoning caste, idolatry and the sacred thread for himself, but advocating intercaste marriages and widow-remarriage. Certain critics have implied that Keshab led the Samaj too close to Christianity, by changing the worship day to Sunday, addressing God as Father of all *men* rather than all living beings, and citing Jesus as the *Asian* Christ. Yet the brutality and racial prejudice which followed the Mutiny of 1857 led Sen to assert:

I have always disclaimed the Christian name, and will not identify myself with the Christian Church, for I set my face completely against the popular doctrine of Christianity. . . . Christianity has failed to produce any wholesome moral influence on my countrymen, yet their Muscular Christianity has led many a native to identify the religion of Jesus with the power and privilege of inflicting blows and kicks with impunity. And thus Jesus has been dishonored in India.[21]

The dispute with Tagore, however, stemmed not from religious differences but from attitudes toward social change. Debendranath composed a Brahmo ritual for births, weddings, funerals, and so on, and his own daughter was married by this form, as faithfully Hindu as possible without idolatrous elements. But he considered widow remarriage and intercaste weddings as highly dubious practices, and in fear of popular opposition he excluded members of the Samaj who discarded their Brahminical threads. Keshab believed that "social service and social reform were the bounden duty of every serious theist." Tagore feared that such excessive emphasis would weaken "spiritual religion." [22] "At bottom, the religious reformers were by force of circumstances socially minded, and the social reformers were by force of the same circumstances religious minded." [23]

In 1865 Keshab Chandra Sen broke from the Samaj and organized in the following year, the Brahmo Samaj of India, leaving Tagore in charge of the Adi (Original) Brahmo Samaj. But Sen's own activities and preoccupations split in two divergent directions. On one hand, he intensified his social protests, opposed untouchability, took his wife to public services (in defiance of *purdah*). He also appealed to Mrs. Josephine Butler, founder of the Association for Moral and Social Hygiene in England, against the "regular system of procuring Indian or Japanese women for British troops stationed in India" and the consequent rise of venereal disease among British soldiers to over 50 per cent. In a "singular achievement for those days" Mrs. Butler succeeded in getting Government policy changed, procuration ended, houses of prostitution closed and the women repatriated. On the other hand, K. C. Sen came under the influence of the mystic, Ramakrishna, and moved increasingly toward asceticism, renunciation and yoga.

In 1872 the Government of India had passed the Civil Marriage Act III, largely under pressure from Sen's Indian Social Reform Association. This set standards for civil marriage for those who would publicly declare that they "did not profess the Hindu, Mohammedan, Christian, Parsee, Buddhist, Sikh, or Jain religion." For such nonreligious persons (Christians, Muslims, and Hindus had their separate laws) the new Act forbade polygamy, allowed intercaste marriage and widow remarriage, and set the legal age at 14 for girls (though the medical commission had recommended 16) and 18 for boys. Unwilling to disown so fully their religious affiliations, unhappy over the low age limit and insisting that marriage should be regarded as a religious sacrament rather than a civil contract, even the Adi Brahmo Samaj opposed the measure. Few outside of Keshab's Brahmo Samaj of India made use of the new provisions. But six years later Sen announced the betrothal of his own daughter, under 14 years of age, to the prince of Kuch Bihar. His friends protested at the age, at the idolatrous Hindu ceremony, and at the probability that the prince would not remain monogamous. Sen assured them that a Brahmo service would be used, but the prince's will prevailed, and the wedding followed Hindu ritual. Nine days later some of his followers, disillusioned by their leader's "betrayal" and by his increasingly autocratic claims of divine revelation, broke away to form the Sadharan Brahmo Samaj under Pandit Sivanath Sastri, and Sen drifted still further into mystical faith in a New Dispensation.

This Church of the New Dispensation deserves special mention in any survey of religious currents in Indian thought, because it represents such a typical effort to blend diverse elements into a world faith. Although Keshab, convinced of his own messianic role, maintained that the New Dispensation stood logically above other religions, he conceded that all were true and made use of their respective scriptures as well as the Hindu trident, the Muslim crescent, and the Christian cross. In an apparent effort to mollify Hindu opponents, he abandoned his early opposition to idolatry and polytheism, accepted Durga Puja (one of the most popular sectarian forms of Hindu worship), employed the waving of lights and religious dance, and referred to God as the Divine Mother. On the other hand, he observed Baptism and Communion, acknowledged the supremacy of Christian ethics and the character of Christ, and spoke of the Trinity and of Christ as one with the Father, yet fulfilling Hinduism. The inconsistencies appeared as insignificant to Keshab as they seem obvious to readers today. To Christians he pleaded the New Dispensation in these emotional terms:

Woe unto me if ever I harboured in my mind the remotest desire to found a new sect, and thus add to the already accumulated evils of sectarianism! Woe unto us, if I ever conceived the project of setting up a movement against the Church of Christ! Perish these lips if they utter a word of rebellion against Jesus. . . . A new sect! God forbid. We preach not a new sect, but the death of sectarianism and the universal reconciliation of all churches. But the very idea of an electic church, it will be contended, is anti-Christian. To mix up Christ with the hundred and one creeds of the world is to destroy and deny Christ. To mix Christ with what? With error, with impurity? No. Mix Christ with all that is Christian in other creeds. Surely that is not un-Christian, far less anti-Christian. . . . The Church of the New Dispensation works faithfully upon the lines laid down by Christ, and only seeks to amalgamate the Western Christ and the Eastern Christ. . . . It is not the mixture of purity with impurity, of truth with falsehood, of light with darkness, but the fusion of all types of purity, truth and light in all systems of faith into one integral whole.[24]

Yet on his deathbed Sen is reported to have cried out: "Mother of Buddha, Mother of the Sakyan, grant me Nirvana!" [25]

Rabindranath Tagore

Meanwhile leadership in the Adi Brahmo Samaj moved into the hands of a third-generation Tagore, the poet-painter-philosopher, Rabindranath (1861–1941). The youngest of Debendranath's seven sons, this distinguished writer devoted the first half of his life to social reform and agitation against British rule, then retired to his literature and art and education, disgusted with the motives and methods of his political comrades. Profoundly influenced by his father and by the memory of Rammohun Roy, Rabindranath drank deeply of the *Upanishads,* the teachings of Buddha and liberal western thought. He wrote "ferociously" (a favorite word) on social issues, especially against child marriage. He criticized the Congress and the nationalist movement for pushing social reform into the background, for he felt strongly that political freedom for India would be meaningless until social injustice was wiped out. With scathing insight he pointed out how much easier and more popular it was to burn British cloth than to abolish untouchability (though he himself had composed songs for the *swadeshi*—native products —movement).

Tagore's was a world vision. Unlike many Indians today, he acknowledged frankly that India's real problem was not political but social—namely, the race problem. Yet he did not hesitate to tell Americans on his lecture tour in this country in 1916: "Until you have solved the question in America, you have no right to question India. . . . The call has come to every individual in the present age to prepare himself and his surroundings for this dawn of a new era when man shall discover his soul in the spiritual unity of all human beings." [26] Rabindranath always tempered his criticism with gentleness and appreciation. "I cannot but think that it is the special mission of America," he declared, "to fulfill this hope of God and man. You are the country of expectation, desiring something else than what is. . . . America is destined to justify Western civilization to the East." [27] She has not adequately done so yet, and time is running out.

Speaking more directly to the caste problem in his own country, Tagore confessed:

What (India) failed to realize was that in human beings differences are not like the physical barriers of mountains, fixed forever—they are fluid with life's flow, they are changing their courses and their shapes and volume. . . . In trying to avoid collisions she set up boundaries of immovable walls, thus giving to her numerous races the negative benefits of peace and order, but not the positive opportunity of expansion and movement. . . . Therefore Life departed from her social system, and in its place she is worshipping with all ceremony the magnificent cage of countless compartments that she has manufactured.[28]

In his penetrating analysis of Tagore, Albert Schweitzer refutes the claim that Tagore's buoyant, optimistic, affirmative outlook on life is derived from original Hindu thought. In identifying God with the Creator *and* His creation, Tagore "wanders to and fro between monism and dualism as if there were no gulf between them," and sees no difficulty in explaining the universe in terms of beauty, harmony, goodness and joy.[29]

In an appeal for the Tagore Centenary Fund, Prime Minister Nehru paid this tribute:

When all sensitive minds search for a solution and try to find some anchorage in the great principles and underlying truths which humanity has nourished and which have distinguished it from brute creation . . . in our country two mighty men of spirit and vision pointed out the path to us—Gandhi and Tagore.[30]

These two mighty men exchanged mutual admiration—in fact, Tagore is credited with first according Gandhi the title of Mahatma (Great Soul)—yet they were very different. Tagore rejected the Gandhian noncooperation movement as being negative, the independence movement as sacrificing social reform to political agitation, socialism as too mechanical to achieve social justice. In comparison with Gandhi, the ascetic, the frugal, the practical, Tagore was prodigal, affirmative, in love with life, eager for music and "hyacinths to feed the soul." In the words of Louis Fischer, Gandhi's biographer:

Sentimentally inseparable, soulmates to the end, they waged verbal battles, for they were different. Gandhi faced the past and out of it made future history; religion, caste, Hindu mythology were deeply ingrained in him. Tagore accepted the present, with its machines, its Western culture, and, despite it, made Eastern poetry.[31]

Mahadev Govind Ranade

Beside a teeming street of Bombay, stands a life-size statue bearing an inscription about a "scholar, judge, citizen, patriot, and social reformer—Mahadev Govind Ranade (1842–1901)." Research into India's social ethics reveals one of the keenest minds and dedicated hearts of the nineteenth century in any land. He was reared in an orthodox Hindu family, strictly bound by religious sanctions, and married at the age of twelve to a girl of nine. Already manifesting a brilliant intellectual capacity, Ranade became in 1859 one of the twenty-one students who passed the first matriculation examination at Bombay University. His biographer notes the experience in these terms:

The falling of the seed of Western education upon a mind nurtured in the Hindu tradition, and at the same time so able and so assimilative as Ranade's was, could not fail to be a momentous event. Ranade's English education was, without a doubt, the most formative influence upon his life and career.[32]

Within two years he was English editor of the *Indu Prakash* and a teacher in Elphinstone Institution (later College), his subjects ranging from English composition and poetry, through logic, history and geography, to arithmetic and economics. In the last-named field he assigned Senior and Malthus for his students and did not hesitate to criticize John Stuart Mill, "the high priest of economic orthodoxy" and presumed expert on India, for his irrelevance to Indian affairs. From its founding in 1870 until 1893 Ranade was the "life and soul" of the Sarvajanik Sabha, a society in Poona for interpreting public opinion to the government. This organization proposed responsible self-government, the inclusion of Indians in the British Parliament, and an electorate of taxpayers. At the great Delhi Durbar of 1877, when Queen Victoria formerly took the title of Empress of India, it was Ranade who urged the establishment of an Indian Council of Representatives and a Chamber of Princes. Like many an early reformer, who fearlessly criticized British and Indian evils and mistakes, he believed that God's providence had placed the British in India to uplift the country, and that Western education, machinery, capital—and ethics—were necessary for the rehabilitation of the nation.

From the start of his career, Ranade had been a respectful follower of Rammohun Roy in the field of social reform. He concerned himself directly and personally with the depressed classes, illiteracy, child-marriage, caste and idolatry. In an effort to win over the conservative Hindu opposition, he produced scholarly analyses of "Vedic Authorities for Widow Remarriage" (1870) and "Shastric Texts on the Subject of Infant Marriage" (1888). While many sincere reformers feared the consequences of government action against popular sentiment, Ranade boldly advocated laws which would raise the age of marriage from ten to twelve for girls and sixteen to eighteen for boys, treat sexual intercourse with girls under fourteen as rape, and forbid men over forty-five from marrying virgins. In a lecture on Women's Rights he declared:

We should feel shame that people all over the world, having advanced farther than we, are despising us—but leaving that aside, if the valour of our manhood is to be exercised against the womenfolk of our homes, that is the lowest depth of baseness.[33]

Yet when his wife died, and his principles might have led him to marry a widow, he yielded to filial obedience and accepted an adolescent bride his father had chosen. With true grace, however, he accepted the responsibilities of this painful decision, taught his young wife to read and write (using the New Testament as her English textbook), and shared his ethical convictions with her until she became a genuine partner in his career.

In other areas as well, Ranade showed himself great enough

to endure the accusation of compromise for the sake of pragmatic progress. He had lent active support to a home for widows run by an able Christian woman. But when some of the inmates were attracted to Christianity by the personal character of the director, Ranade withdrew his backing, not because he himself feared the new religion, but because he did not want the total cause of social reform jeopardized by charges of proselytizing. Condemned by his foes for attending a tea with foreign missionaries (though he himself did not eat or drink there), Ranade and his companions were excommunicated for breaking Hindu caste. After bitter debate he finally accepted the ritual penance required, partly for the sake of his colleagues (who could endure ostracism less casually than he), and partly because he did not wish to harm the reform movement by prolonging controversy over a trivial personal issue.

Even as the Brahmo Samaj in Calcutta fell on less effective days, another movement arose on the opposite side of the subcontinent. The Prarthana Samaj (Prayer Society) was founded in Poona in 1870 to defend the ancient purity of the Vedas, including widow remarriage, against the "corruptions" of idolatry, caste and child marriage. Eschewing the growing violence of his nationalistic critics, Ranade employed the instruments of tradition, conscience and legislation. In the first he demonstrated sympathetic respect for the sensitivity and suspicion of orthodox Hindus. In the second he asserted that all moral reform must be guided by the voice of God. In the third he regarded laws as "constraint imposed by the wise upon the ignorant in their common interest," to be used only when tradition and conscience have been tried in vain.

His own personal motivation for moral reform seems ever to have reflected a wise balance between religion and social realism.

Ranade's inner religious life was a very real thing, and lay at the very core of his personality. His deepest ideas easily expressed themselves in a religious form, and his heart was constantly aglow with the warm emotion of religious thoughts. . . . He constantly felt as if God were speaking at one end of a long tube, at the other end of which he was listening. . . . Ranade was a theologian—as was inevitable for a man possessing his richness of inner religious life and his keenness of intellect. He was a convinced Theist.[34]

Without denying the many unsolved problems of religion, without undergoing any significant change in his lifelong beliefs, Ranade consistently rejected the alternatives of materialism, pantheism, egoism, agnosticism or secularism, whether they came from Hinduism or from Western philosophers such as Sidgwick, Mill and Spencer. Condemned by liberals for preaching in idolatrous temples and by orthodox Hindus for using Biblical texts, Ranade repeatedly denounced

. . . the dreary alternative of agnosticism, which the young students are taught to accept as the final word of science on the grave mysteries of life and thought. . . . Hindu students especially need the strengthening influence which faith in God, and in Conscience as His voice in the human heart, alone can give. The national mind cannot rest in agnosticism. The experiment was tried once on a large scale by the greatest moral teacher of this or any other age. The failure of Buddhism is a warning that such teaching can have no hold on the national thought.[35]

When some of his colleagues urged that the Prarthana Samaj should change its name to the Brahmo Samaj, Ranade retorted that a society based on faith in prayer as the chief duty of man and the means of attaining God ought frankly to call itself a Prayer Society. When urged to abandon religious aspects of the reform movement because of their divisive effect, he replied: "This is the land of religion. Be it for good or evil, we cannot do without religion. Religious thoughts are in our blood. If we try to flee from it, it will pursue us." [36]

Yet Ranade never hesitated to probe the weakness of traditional religious belief. He preferred to emphasize *dharma* (duty) above *karma* (fate), and insisted that man's *karma* can be controlled by human will which is genuinely subservient to a Higher Will. The historic concept that life is vanity, illusion, dream, *maya*, Ranade labelled as "atheism in its worst form." To the Indian National Social Conference, which he helped to organize as a separate outgrowth of the Indian National Congress, Ranade warned against those ideas which had been "hastening our decline during the past three thousand years":

. . . submission to outward force or power more than to the voice of inward conscience . . . fictitious differences between men and women due to heredity or birth, passive acquiescence in evil or wrong-doing, and a general indifference to secular well-being almost bordering upon fatalism. These have been the root ideas of our ancient social system.[37]

Ranade was thus one of the first to realize that Hinduism must be drastically reinterpreted if it is to undergird a democratic welfare state. Nor did he hesitate to paint unflattering pictures of India in contrast to the colonial rulers. It was here that Mahadev Govind Ranade saw the deepest need and the highest hope for a renaissance in India's social conscience.

The important thing about any body of knowledge is that it should tell us what we are, what our duty is, what we are to do in this world, what our rights are, and such like matters. . . . Now that knowledge has been more or less discovered by the European learning, whereas even in the flourishing times of our Indian learning there is no trace of it.[38]

To this search, to this enlightenment, to this body of ethical knowledge and practice, Mahadev Govind Ranade devoted his life.

Gopal Krishna Gokhale

If Ranade had been influenced by Rammohun Roy, he in his turn guided the life of another great social reformer, Gopal Krishna Gokhale (1866–1915). Indeed, Gokhale—whom Mahatma Gandhi acknowledged as his "political *guru*" (or teacher) —regarded Ranade as *his guru* and held him in such "almost religious reverence" that he would not be seated in the master's presence. Ranade, for his part, recognized the potentialities of the younger man and helped to cultivate them, so that another Indian statesman, Sir Valentine Chirol, could refer to Gokhale as "perhaps the finest character that India has produced, blending accurate knowledge of Western history and Western thought with a profound understanding of the Indian mentality and of the ancient civilization that has moulded it." [39]

Although his ancestors, like Ranade's, were scrupulously orthodox Brahmins, Gokhale knew poverty and village life more intimately than most of the reformers. At Rajaram College in Kolhapur, Deccan College in Poona and Elphinstone College in Bombay, he displayed incredible memory, which included whole speeches by Burke and Bright and the entire content of *Paradise Lost*. As a student, he first met Ranade by unknowingly turning him away from a school function. Years later he became secretary of the Sarvajanik Sabha in Poona and thus had occasion to see his *guru*'s "utter, absolute unselfishness" in action. At the early age of 23, Gokhale was invited to give a minor speech before the Indian National Congress and soon became one of the leading figures in that movement, often in crucial controversy with the "father of Indian Nationalism," Lokamanya Tilak.

In the political realm, Gokhale led vigorous assaults against the salt tax, the extravagant military expenditures of the British, and the virtual exclusion of Indians from public service. In social reform, however, he hesitated to step forward because of what he regarded as his own sin against society. On the death of his father, his uncle had arranged a marriage with a girl who had an incurable disease and could never be a real wife. For that reason he finally yielded to relatives' persuasion to take a second wife. Nevertheless he did feel compelled to speak out against the inhumane treatment of depressed classes, especially when this shame coincided with indignant public protests about the plight of Indians in Africa. When excommunicated with Ranade for attending the mission tea in Poona, Gokhale ignored the agitation—and the penalties.

Of his many outstanding contributions to India's social progress, the most important was Gokhale's founding of the Servants of India Society in 1905. Admittedly based on the Jesuit Order, its avowed purpose was "to train men, prepared to devote their lives to the cause of the country *in a religious spirit* . . . [and] to promote, by all constitutional means, the national interests of the Indian people." [40] From applicants he demanded vows of service and sacrifice: that their best loyalties would be given first to the country, that they would seek no individual advantage, lead a pure personal life, and accept for themselves and their families only such subsistence as the Society could provide. Initiates spent five years of full-time service to the cause, partly in Poona, partly at home, partly in practical work. Often in his stress on the unity of India, Gokhale sent Hindus to live and serve among Muslims, or high-caste men to low-caste situations. "Above all, a Reconciler," he sought to combine the self-sacrifice of the East with the social service of the West, and to emphasize the inseparability of political and social problems. No wonder William Paton, ecumenical states-man and former missionary in India, called the organization "something between a monastic order and a Fabian Society."

Yet Gokhale did not shirk political responsibility. He served first on the Bombay Legislative Council and then (1902–1915) succeeded Sir Pherozeshah Mehta, the distinguished Parsi states-man, on the Imperial Legislative Council. Offered a post as the first Indian on the Secretary of State's Council, he preferred to remain in an Opposition role and even declined knighthood. In Parliament he urged compulsory education for boys and voluntary educational provisions for girls (only 12 per cent of Indian children were then receiving schooling), attacked the exploitation and immorality of indentured labor, and demanded greater voice for Indians in gov-ernmental and financial decisions. Sir Guy Fleetwood Wilson, Brit-ish Finance Minister from 1908 to 1913, once said of his Parlia-mentary opposition: "The one man I frankly feared was Gokhale, the Gladstone of India." He went on to describe how he avoided Gokhale, fearing some treacherous Oriental deception, only to have Gokhale send him in advance a copy of an intended speech in the House of Commons. "I do not believe that such a generous at-titude has ever been assumed by the Leader of the Opposition in any other country in the world," Sir Guy concluded.[41]

Gokhale's ethical springs are less obvious than those of Roy or Ranade. On one hand, he was branded an agnostic; on the other, "a rationalist but a believer." Friends who claimed that he had adopted the aims and aspirations of Vivekananda, or had reached a faith in God as Love, found no public confirmation. Subsequent writers have declared that the Servants of India Society "was prob-ably the first major organization in the field of social work which did not have a religious basis. It was a non-religious organization dedicated to the service of India." [42] Yet Gokhale "resented strongly in conversation the suggestion that it was a purely secular body," [43] and his entire life was devoted to serving his country "in a true

missionary spirit . . . in a religious spirit," which he demanded
from each of his recruits.

Conclusion

It is an imposing line of social reform through the nineteenth
century: Roy and K. C. Sen and the Tagores in Calcutta, Ranade
and Gokhale in Bombay, their disciples and supporters across the
land. They began within a profoundly religious context, proud of
their heritage and conscious of their obligation to deal gently with
the spiritual roots of India while pruning the rotten branches and
blighted fruit.

But even in the nineteenth century, for two decades an entirely different
tradition was being established by a new band of social reformers in the
four corners of the country. This was a non-religious, liberal tradition.
. . . They did not seek justification for their views in the *Shastras;*
they were agitated over the same questions . . . but their standpoint
was different. They were all individually—with some exceptions—men
of faith and belief, but the critical tradition they established was primarily an intellectual one . . . oriented to philosophic generalizations
rather than to analyses based on facts.[44]

There was also a third group arising in this period, men who
linked Hinduism with patriotism, who subordinated social reform
to the independence movement. The following chapter examines
the extent to which religious conservatism went hand-in-hand with
violent nationalism, increasingly overshadowing the moderate and
liberal currents of social and ethical change.

Chapter VI

Nineteenth-Century Revivalism

India's nineteenth-century leaders sought in a great variety of ways to utilize, to modify, or to replace religious sanctions for social change. Unlike some of their twentieth-century successors, none presumed to discard moral and spiritual foundations entirely, or to substitute thoroughgoing secularism for traditional faith. Yet two distinct streams of social thought can be discerned. The preceding chapter sketched one group of reformers, characterized—among other things—by their acceptance of Western influence and their willingness to use modern methods, such as British education and legislation. The second movement may be called very loosely "reaction." Its leaders too were concerned with reform of social evils, although some believed strongly that political freedom deserved priority. But they based their appeal to the masses on Hindu tradition, on religious nationalism, on a glorification and purification of the past, generally condemning everything not indigenous to India.

Dayananda Saraswati (1824—1883)

Mula Shankar (later to be known as Swami Dayananda) was born a Brahmin on the Kathiawar peninsula, the future home of Mahatma Gandhi. Since his father was an ardent devotee of Shiva, the boy donned the sacred thread of Brahminism at eight, had memorized the entire Vedas by fourteen. Led toward a religious life by his sister's death, he was repelled from it during an all-night vigil at a Shiva shrine. Watching the rats nibbling at the plaster image turned the youth permanently from idolatry and many other Hindu superstitions. At the age of twenty-two he ran away to escape an arranged marriage, and spent the next twenty-five years (the traditional period of family responsibility) studying with a succession of *swamis* and teachers. After brief contact with K. C. Sen of the Brahmo Samaj, he fell "easy prey to Madame Blavatsky's spiritual fascinations" in theosophy. Vyas shrewdly remarks that neither understood the other, but when they both did, an immediate breach ensued.[1] In 1875 Dayananda visited Ranade in Poona. Although each was impressed and eager for the support of a different but complementary character and temperament, they split over such doctrinal issues as the infallibility and divine inspiration of the Vedas. Among many Saraswati legends, his death is ascribed to poison, either by Brahmins who feared his social reforms or by dancing girls resentful of his moral censure.

Dayananda's lasting contribution proved to be the organization in 1875 of the Arya Samaj. One Indian editor describes it as "largely motivated by the desire to counteract the Christian missionaries."[2] Nehru stressed its opposition to Islam and Christianity, especially the former.[3] Clearly the new movement was intended also as a reactionary protest against the Brahmo Samaj in Bengal and the Prarthana Samaj in Bombay. These Dayananda condemned for abandoning Hindu traditions and adopting Western ideas. By going "back to the Vedas" he claimed all truth and knowledge could be found in germinal form, including steam power, railroads and the Copernican view of the universe. His Vedic literalism represented the antithesis of the liberal-rational Brahmo Samaj, yet it attracted solid, educated, middle-class civil servants by the thousands.

Despite his emphatic denial of any debt to the West, Daya-nanda displayed a social conscience which had not heretofore been found in non-Western-educated reformers. Although he accepted the four *varnas* as described in the Vedas, he condemned the multi-tude of subcastes and the evils of untouchability. He opposed child marriage and approved widow remarriage (provided the original union had not been consummated); he also endorsed levirate marriage (or concubinage of one's brother's widow) if necessary to provide an heir. He led his followers in vigorous opposition to idolatry, polytheism, sacrifice, temple prostitution and other de-grading forms of religion. On the other hand, he is said to have upheld Manu's punishment for adultery (the man to be burned alive on a red-hot bedstead, the woman to be devoured alive by dogs).[4] He professed the doctrines of metempsychosis (transmigration), *karma* and cow worship. He believed that the Lord of Creation re-wards all men on a basis of absolute justice, in exact proportion to their deeds. Such a strict view of *karma* ("forgiveness is for ever impossible") helps to refute Radhakrishnan's claim for mercy in traditional Hinduism.

In short, the Arya Samaj rests firmly on the revealed authority of the Vedas. Its Official Creed includes some noble guideposts:

All actions ought to be done conformably to virtue, i.e., after a thorough consideration of right and wrong. The primary object of the Samaj is to do good to the world by improving the physical, spiritual, and social conditions of mankind. All ought to be treated with love, justice, and due regard to their merits. . . . No one ought to be contented with his own good alone, but everyone ought to regard his prosperity as in-cluded in that of others.[5]

Today the organization has retained greater strength, in influence and numbers, than other nineteenth-century societies. As a re-spected agency in independent India it continues to operate private schools, with low fees but not government subsidy, and to offer both technical and moral instruction.

On one hand, Indian nationalists hail the stimulus which the Arya Samaj provided for Vivekananda, Tilak and other militant patriots. On the other hand, there are critics who believe that the early influence of Dayananda deserves condemnation. Farquhar expresses the opinion that "his unhealthy teaching has produced very unhealthy political fruit." [6] What can be questioned objectively is whether Dayananda's revival of narrow communalism ("India for the Hindus!") did not stiffen Muslim fear and resistance, thus contributing to the later demand for Partition. If this is the sense in which the Arya Samaj reawakened the past and prepared India for the future, then the tragic consequence of reactionary religion, as contrasted with rational reform, cannot be denied.

Annie Besant (1847—1933)

Reference was made above, in the life of Dayananda Saraswati, to the "spiritual fascinations" of Madame Helene Petrovna Blavatsky. A Russian with some occult power and perhaps a greater amount of graft and fraud, she teamed up with Colonel H. S. Olcott to form the Theosophical Society in New York in 1875. Four years later they transferred their operations to India, where they hoped to find Hindu *karma,* transmigration, and *maya* more receptive to spiritualism. Dayananda's contact with them began by correspondence in 1878 and ended, after personal encounter, by 1881. A greater-than-these was to bring fame to the Theosophical Society, one who was to play a unique and dramatic role in India's political and religious life.

Annie Besant married a minister at the age of twenty; six years later she left him and Christianity. For the next twenty years she participated in almost every conceivable social movement in England. With the Webbs and George Bernard Shaw she helped found the Fabian Society in 1884 and the early British Labour Party. She espoused atheism, socialism, woman suffrage, penal reform, trade unionism, birth control and antivivisectionism. She fought against sweatshop wages, capital punishment, colonialism, war and royalty as an institution. Then, looking for new worlds to conquer, she sailed for India in 1893. She found them there.

With what a modern Indian writer has called her "close study, magnetic personality and persuasive eloquence," [7] she won a large following of the intelligentsia caught in the turmoil of social and spiritual change. Readily granting the superiority of Hindu mysticism over Western materialism, Mrs. Besant also recognized the imperfections of Indian society and the need for discriminating reforms. In the *Code of Manu* she found warrant for adapting old principles to changing conditions and insisted that "customs should be kept flexible, instead of being inflexible as they are in the India of today." [8] As in England she had asserted the equal dignity of women, so in India she crusaded for the right of widows to remarry, for the abolition of child marriage, for the establishment of schools for girls. With Colonel Olcutt she founded the Central Hindu College, which later became the famous Benares Hindu University. In that college she refused to admit married students, a protest against child marriage.

Like many a European, Annie Besant arrived in India with an idealized concept of Hinduism. At the start she defended the social and vocational values of the four *varnas*. "This marvellous endurance [of India over Persia, Egypt, Greece and Rome], while primarily due to her profound spirituality, is partly due also to the stability given to her by her caste system, a social stability of home, answering to the inner stability of spirit." [9] Later she saw that the virtues of caste were overshadowed by its vices, declaring in 1908: "I am bound to say that I do not believe the caste system can continue in India in the changing life of the nation and with the heavy responsibilities which more and more still fall upon her sons." [10]

During this period the Theosophical Society established world headquarters in a suburb of Madras. Annie Besant became its president in 1907. Even more important, however, she took an increasingly active role in the Indian National Congress, which she chaired in 1917, working valiantly for Hindu-Muslim unity. Two years earlier she had helped to found the Home Rule League, and in 1918, her own countrymen arrested her for activities in behalf of Indian self-government. Strangely enough, she did not support the *swadeshi* boycott (to buy only Indian goods), partly because of her own latent patriotism, partly because she favored status for India within the Empire rather than complete independence, and partly because she preferred constitutional methods to mass action.

K. M. Munshi, one of India's great elder statesmen, has written: "Mrs. Besant was one of the makers of modern India; the greatest foreigner and the only European who threw in her lot completely and unreservedly with India. Her work cannot be divided into watertight compartments, such as social service or educational, religious, or political uplift." [11] Hers was a versatile mind, a cosmopolitan spirit. Louis Fischer claims that she regarded herself as a reincarnation of Hypatia of Alexandria and of Giordono Bruno, the Italian philosopher, and longed to be also the "bride of Christ." [12] Yet with all this eclecticism, she believed solely in Hinduism for India:

Without Hinduism, India has no future. Hinduism is the soil in which India's roots are struck, and torn out of that, she will inevitably wither. . . . India lived before other religions came; India could live after their passing. But let Hinduism go, Hinduism that was India's cradle, and in that passing would be India's grave.[13]

During her lifetime, however, political rather than religious activities had taken precedence. After 1933 the Theosophical Society moved completely out of political involvement, to concentrate again on the occult investigations and the world faith which Madame Blavatsky and Colonel Olcutt first intended.

Bal Gangadhar Tilak (1856—1920)

Like his chief opponents, Ranade and Gokhale, Bal Gangadhar Tilak was a Chitpawan Brahmin—perhaps the most typical of all. When the British undermined the glory and the leadership of the Maratha Empire at the end of the eighteenth century, the ruling caste (so the saying goes) converted its sacred thread into a bowstring, henceforth to be used in proud defiance against its conquerors. Tilak reveled in this heritage. His revolutionary activities earned him many terms in prison—and the title, "Father of Indian Nationalism."

Tilak was never opposed to social reform. In fact, he often criticized the so-called reformers for failing to practice what they preached. While Ranade, for example, married a child bride to please his father, Tilak kept his daughters single until the age of sixteen. He had accompanied Ranade to the ill-fated mission tea party, and like the judge, accepted *prayaschitta* (penance) in order not to offend the orthodox priests and peasants. He believed in widow remarriage, crossed the seas to England (against Manu's rules), and condemned caste discrimination in vehement language: "If God were to tolerate untouchability, I would not recognize him as God at all. . . . I do not deny that it was the Brahmin rule that introduced the practice of untouchability. This is a cancer in the body of Hindu society and we must eradicate it at all costs." [14]

But Tilak opposed unequivocally the means used by the liberal reformers to bring about social change. Ranade and Gokhale, in his estimation, proved themselves entirely too Western in attitudes and methods. For example, they worked for legislation in England and in India to rectify ancient wrongs, whereas Tilak insisted that no alien government had the right to interfere with the customs of the people, however worthy the cause. For this reason he opposed the Age of Consent Bill of 1891, giving rise to the unjust charge that he upheld every practice of orthodox Hinduism, including child marriage. An Indian biographer, perhaps equally biased in the other direction, explains the position of the *Lokamanya* (Leader of the People, a title bestowed by popular usage) as motivated by concern for the masses and their support. In order not to offend their religious feelings, it is claimed, Tilak resisted the rational reforms which rode roughshod over hallowed customs and practices.

His paramount concern, subordinating all others, was Indian independence. "Swaraj is my birthright, and I will have it!" became not merely Tilak's slogan, but the rallying cry for an entire nation. The man whom Gandhi called "The Maker of Modern India" gave himself with single-minded devotion to the one task of winning freedom. Convinced that social reform could and would come only from the midst of a free people, he attacked bitterly those who argued with equal sincerity that only a just and moral people are fit to be free. The liberals, in effect, trusted the British to grant self-government when Indians proved themselves worthy and capable. Tilak determined to break this hypnotism, which he blamed on the universally accepted myth of Britain's moral superiority.

He did this by reviving traditional Hinduism, not so much as a philosophy, but as an emotional center of loyalty and unity. "I regard India as my Motherland and my Goddess, the people in India my kith and kin, and loyal and steadfast work for their political and social emancipation my highest religion and duty." [15] He restored spiritual and national vitality to—and through—the great festivals of Ganapati and Shivaji. In unabashed criticism of both Sankara and Ramanuja, for implying that the liberated soul has no responsibility in the world, Tilak stressed the activist interpretation of salvation found in the *Bhagavad-Gita*. As with other mystic-politicians like Gandhi, it is difficult to judge which facet of character, which personal motivation, predominates. Most Indians would say they cannot and should not be separated. One recent writer has remarked: "Perhaps Tilak Maharaj (Great Ruler) was also the first man in our history who identified God with the masses and recognized Him in the form of Janata-Atma (Soul of the People)." [16]

In the last analysis, Tilak won his niche in the Indian hall of fame as a "freedom fighter." He had urged civil disobedience years before Gandhi experimented in Africa with *satyagraha* (truth force). At Tilak's death the Mahatma mourned: "My strongest bulwark is gone." Tilak, however, had regarded nonviolence as a strategy, not a moral principle, and even encouraged the use of force as the struggle for independence intensified. Speaking of his student days in Harrow and Cambridge, Prime Minister Nehru recalled, "Almost without exception we were Tilakites or Extremists." Where Gokhale and Ranade advocated moderation in politics and progressive action in social reform, Tilak "preached revolutionary tactics in politics and evolutionary moderation in social reform." Because he thus opposed the liberals and even the Indian National Social Conference, Ambedkar and other apostles of reform have called him "one of those social tories and political radicals with whom India abounds." Like Dayananda and most of these political reactionaries, he contributed directly to communal jealousy and strife by stressing the Hindu roots of India, to the alarm and resentment of Muslim neighbors. The most direct clash between Tilak and Ranade and Gokhale occurred in the Indian National Congress and the Indian National Social Conference, as described in the next chapter. But the evaluation of a distinguished scion of a distinguished liberal family, long-time editor of the *Indian Social Reformer,* cannot be ignored: "The agitation fanned by Tilak was to prove destructive of all steady sustained effort at reform." [17]

Aurobindo Ghose (1872—1950)

Just as social reformers sprang up simultaneously or successively in eastern and western India, so political and religious "revivalists" appeared first in Bombay and then in Bengal. Aurobindo Ghose left his Calcutta home at the age of seven to study in London and Cambridge, where he made a brilliant academic record.

During his fourteen years abroad he joined the secret Lotus and Dagger Society dedicated to Indian freedom, but he did not assume active leadership of anti-British terrorists until riled, like Tagore, by the partition of Bengal in 1905. Meanwhile he taught English at Baroda College and served as private secretary to the Gaekwad (prince) of Baroda, after proving (in K. M. Munshi's pithy phrase) "a self-invited failure in the Indian Civil Service." [18] At the Congress session of 1907, Aurobindo broke sharply with the moderates and proved himself even more radical than Tilak, thus paving his own road to Alipur jail for sedition. "Nationalism," he asserted, "is a religion that comes from God. Nationalism cannot die." [19]

In prison Aurobindo experienced a mystical vision which led him to renounce politics for a life of meditation. Some years earlier he had taken up *yoga,* the physical, mental and spiritual discipline characteristic of Hinduism. On his release he retired to the French settlement of Pondicherry, to inaugurate "the life divine" for himself and a handful of disciples. Although his outward choice was obvious—and faithfully maintained—the inner tension between activism and quietism remained. Occasionally Aurobindo would issue a political pronouncement from his ashram: supporting the Allies in World War II (in contrast to many of his nationalist colleagues), condemning the invasion of South Korea in 1950 just before his death.

In social and ethical matters his mind seemed equally divided. Aurobindo followed Dayananda in claiming that all science, technology and modern truth could be found in the Vedas through the "higher consciousness of the spirit." Like Vivekananda, he regarded Hinduism as sufficient for all mankind, in contrast to Tagore's plea for a world synthesis. With Ramakrishna he sought salvation in *bhakti* (devotion) instead of the more active *karma yoga* of Dayananda and Gandhi. Yet he stressed the ethical affirmation inherent in Hindu mysticism and represented, according to Romain Rolland, "the completest synthesis that has been realized to this day by the geniuses of Asia and the geniuses of Europe." [20] In his call for local and regional autonomy, with the village as the basic unit of society, Aurobindo anticipated Gandhi, Vinoba and J. P. Narayan. In fact, *The Spirit and Form of Indian Polity,* published shortly before his death, hints that national unity may be a difficult if not impossible goal for such a pluralistic culture. At least, he insisted, spiritual and cultural integration will be all the more essential to compensate for the lack of political and geographical unity.

Despite the seclusion of his last forty years, Aurobindo left a permanent mark on Indian life and thought. "The past must be sacred to us," he once said, "but the future still more sacred." In his struggle for national independence and in his subsequent devotion to contemplative retreat, he personified the schizophrenia of modern India. Radhakrishnan, himself a superlative scholar, paid this tribute: "Aurobindo was the greatest intellectual of our age and a major force for the life of the spirit. India will not forget his services to politics and philosophy and the world will remember with gratitude his invaluable work in the realms of philosophy and religion." [21]

Today the Aurobindo *ashram* at Pondicherry is presided over by "The Mother," a French woman presumably incarnating spiritual truth. It boasts far-from-ascetic comforts and elaborate facilities for a regimen which emphasizes meditation and sports. Guests have reported a tendency to "worship" both Aurobindo and "The Mother" (now in her eighties), and amidst wealth and luxury there is a distressing lack of concern for others, either in charity or in sharing the message of "the life divine." Indra Sen, a prominent member of the *ashram,* has written, in a mood of mingled confession and pride:

Leaders of thought and life in India have during the last century uniformly represented a life-and-world affirming outlook in place of the older life-and-world denying one. But while in action, we have adopted the affirming attitude, in inner feeling the denying attitude persists with considerable force. This makes us divided within ourselves and weakens our acceptance of science, technology, and the spirit of social progress of modern life. This calls for a proper philosophy to aid the necessary inner reintegration.[22]

The admission of India's earlier life-and-world negation, and the dating of the affirmative outlook in the British century, confirms one underlying thesis of this book; namely, that Hindu escapism has been only partially modified by Western thought and modern pressures. Whether Aurobindo's philosophy can supply "the necessary inner reintegration" for Indian society looks very doubtful at present. If it ever does so, it will be through the intellectual involvement of men like Radhakrishnan, not through the ingrown self-gratification of the *ashram* at Pondicherry.

Ramakrishna Paramahamsa (1834—1886)

For the conclusion of this chapter on religious revival and political reaction two figures have been held out of chronological context. Ramakrishna Paramahamsa and Swami Vivekananda are spiritual father and son, soul and voice. The Swami's appearance at the Parliament of Religions in Chicago in 1893 made him almost the only nineteenth-century Indian known in America. Today the Ramakrishna Mission, which he founded in honor of his saintly *guru,* draws praise from all quarters as the most active and influential socio-religious movement in modern India. But the relationship is tenuous and sometimes paradoxical.

Gadadhar Chatterji came from a poor Bengal family, had little if any formal education and remained virtually illiterate. In a story reminiscent of Jesus in the temple, it is claimed that the young boy settled a profound theological issue being debated by priests at a funeral. If (as tradition claims) he leaped from the trees like Hanuman, the monkey god, this may have indicated religious ecstasy or boyish energy. Because of his childhood trances, he was apprenticed with his brother to a Kali temple. Over the years he learned various scriptures and received visions of Kali and Shiva, Rama and Sita, Krishna and Buddha, Jesus and Mohammed (each list varies somewhat). From these he concluded that all religions are equally valid, that all roads lead to the same Truth, that man's spiritual duty is not to create a syncretistic world faith, but to show piety and devotion in one's own cultural experience.

Married at twenty-five to a bride of six, he later deserted her to become a *sannyasi* (seeker after truth). On this pilgrimage he abandoned caste distinctions, but conquered inner prejudice only by serving as sweeper and scavenger, cleaning up after outcastes and Muslims. According to tradition, he sat in a trance for six months, having to be forced awake to eat. Furthermore, he wore women's clothes in women's quarters to imitate the goddess, Radha, in order that he might achieve the love of her divine mate, Krishna. In his study of Sankara he accepted the orthodox dogmas that God is impersonal, that the human spirit is part of the undivided Supreme Soul, and that the world is unreal. Yet with no sense of inconsistency, he followed Ramanuja's account of the personal attributes of Brahma and the individuality of human souls. "God is in all men, but all men are not in God," he explained; "that is the reason why they suffer." [23]

The mystic took to himself the popular name of two deities, Rama Krishna. The title, Paramahamsa (which may mean Great Goose or Mighty Eagle), is applied by a reverent public to rare and saintly sages. Nehru described him as "a simple man, no scholar but a man of faith and not interested in social reform as such . . . fitting into India's many-colored pattern and accepted and revered by many of her people as a man with a touch of the divine fire about him." [24] Wherein lies his contribution—if any—to the social service of the Ramakrishna Mission? Although he stressed devotion (*bhakti–marga*), he recognized the merits of good works and prayed out of his own renunciations: "Oh, Mother (Kali), let me remain in contact with mankind; let me not become a hard ascetic." [25] Some critics have accused Ramakrishna of antinomianism, of ignoring ethical dangers in the confident reliance on salvation by knowledge. Indian and European "Pharisees" have complained that he did not "show sufficient moral abhorrence of prostitutes" or that he did not "honour the principle of teetotalism according to Western notions." [26] Neither did Jesus!

In the framework of this study, however, it is perfectly true that Ramakrishna was "the least socially minded of all the religious figures dominating the nineteenth-century scene, and he performed no social service himself." [27] Nevertheless, he contributed to what may be labeled "reaction" in two ways. First, "he practised and defended everything Hindu," demonstrating to the masses of India that the nation and the faith could be revitalized without Western accretions, thus helping to nullify not only Christian missions, but the influence of the liberal *samajes*. Second, as "a man who had pronounced his judgment against Western culture and the Western way of life," [28] he stiffened the religious nationalism of rebels like Tilak and Aurobindo. Whatever one may think of his trances, his superstitions, and his inconsistent theologies, few can doubt that Ramakrishna was "a God-intoxicated man." But as the patron saint of contemporary social service, his authority bears further examination. For that we must turn to his colorful and enigmatic disciple, Vivekananda.

Vivekananda (1862?—1902)

Narendra Nath Datta attended the Scottish Church College in Calcutta, where he responded eagerly to the fresh ideas of Herbert Spencer, among others. Attracted to leaders of the Brahmo Samaj by their criticism of idolatry and caste, he found an even more inspiring faith in Ramakrishna, whom he met about 1880. It is said that young Datta asked these religious *gurus* one question: Have you seen God? Debendranath Tagore, with all the rationalism and honesty of his Western training, said No! Ramakrishna, from the richness of his mystic visions, answered Yes! The story may be apocryphal, but it illustrates a dilemma which confronts religious liberals and conservatives in every land. Those who see God and His purposes in human beings and in social welfare instead of ecstatic trances find it more difficult to convince inquirers of their depth of faith.

Taking the name of Vivekananda, the young pupil attached himself to Ramakrishna and succeeded him as leader of the order in 1886. An avid reader, he absorbed the philosophies of Descartes, Hume, Hegel, Comte, Darwin and Mill. For his devotions he carried the *Imitatio Christi* and the *Bhagavad-Gita*. During the next few years he traveled over India, broadening the scope of the Rama-krishna movement (it was not formally organized until 1897 or legally incorporated until 1909) and deepening his own apprecia-tion of India's heritage. After giving away one sizable "travel fund" to the poor, Vivekananda decided that he should attend the Parlia-ment of Religions to be held in Chicago in 1893. Despite inade-quate resources and confusion about dates and geography, he reached the assembly and became its most sensational attraction. Here, for the first time, a brilliant linguist and philosopher inter-preted the beauty and spirituality of Hinduism to Western au-diences. They were captivated. The *New York Herald* promptly exclaimed: "After hearing him we feel how foolish it is to send mis-sionaries to this learned nation." [29] On this and a second trip to Eu-rope and America, Vivekananda became the lion of the lecture cir-cuit.

Believing with Ramakrishna that all religions are true for their own cultures, the Swami expressed bitter disappointment at finding that Christians in the West did not practice the teachings of Christ. Yet he frankly admired the social freedom and democracy of Amer-ica, above all the concern for human welfare which he noted. If these could be combined with Hindu spirituality, he insisted, a gen-uine kingdom of God on earth could be established. Even Nehru quoted Vivekananda's enthusiastic summons to his countrymen: "Make a European society with India's religion. . . . Become an occidental of occidentals in your spirit of equality, freedom, work and energy, and at the same time a Hindu to the very backbone in religious culture and instincts." [30]

In many respects it is difficult to classify the Swami's ethics or his theology. He recommended intercaste marriage and sought to re-move discriminations against unmarried women, widows and out-castes. However, he argued that since marriage is primarily for re-production, society may justly exercise certain controls. Despite its once-useful function, he spoke of caste as "filling the atmosphere of India with its stench." [31] Admitting that India lacked adequate mutual concern, he insisted that reform must come from within the soul of Hinduism itself. Unlike Gandhi, Vivekananda would have nothing to do with the "nonsense of politics." In fact, he warned his disciples: "India is immortal if she persists in her search for God. But if she goes in for politics and social conflict, she will die." [32] There are those who tremble in fear that this prophecy may yet come true, especially in view of the Swami's other miraculous insights. As early as 1896 he told Sister Christine, one of the British women who joined his retinue: "The next upheaval that is to usher in another era will come from Russia or from China. I cannot see clearly which, but it will be either the one or the other." [33]

An even more profound version of this augury lies in his theory of caste cycles, possibly derived from Auguste Comte. In *Modern India* he voices the conviction that the four castes, in each society, successively govern the world. The first, or priestly rule, reflected artistic and intellectual supremacy, perhaps the Middle Ages or Renaissance. Then came the absolute monarchy or oligarchy, the focus of political power which leads to tyranny. Next, in the late Victorian era, he saw the triumph of the mercantile class, based on accumulated capital wealth. This same pattern Vivekananda super-imposes on Indian society under the British, deploring the domination of foreign teachers, alien armies and avaricious traders. With uncanny wisdom Vivekananda did not elaborate the role of the fourth caste, except to say that under colonialism "only the Sudra-ness—the beast-of-burden-ness—is now left with the Indians themselves." [34]

But was he looking into the future? Did he anticipate the Revolutions of 1917 and 1949, the shadows that darken the world in mid-twentieth-century? Observing that the Shudras (workers) of other countries were awaking a little, but still lacked education and mutual trust, he realized that "that unity by which ten men collect the strength of a million is yet far away from the Shudra." Did he know how near? Was this young Indian mystic or psychic enough to foresee the rise of the worker-peasant class on the dim horizon—and to fit it into the timeless wisdom of Hinduism?

Vivekananda delves deeper into the "nonsense of politics" than he admits when he endeavors to explain the potential power of the Shudra class. His thesis is that ancient Hinduism gave freedom for caste mobility, that superior talent could move into higher social strata, whereas in recent times (blamed on the British) the lines have become more rigid. This picture may possess dubious historical accuracy; Farquhar remarks that "Vivekananda has no historical conscience whatsoever" in claiming India's influence on Greek, Roman, and Chinese civilizations. His point here, however, is that the "freezing" of caste lines, so that character and ability remain within the lower classes instead of aspiring to higher status, will give the Shudras education, wealth, leadership, which have hitherto been drained off. When even outcastes become cabinet members or state prime ministers, Vivekananda's forecast earns new respect. But whether this trend leads to "government by the Shudras" or to a truly casteless national unity remains to be seen. The outcome may well depend on the moral and spiritual factors examined in this book.

To philosophical or metaphysical insight the Swami contributed very little. As a Kshatriya rather than a Brahmin by birth, he was, after all, a popular vocal "fighter" for Hinduism rather than a saint or scholar. In full accord with Ramakrishna, he stressed that God is impersonal, unknowable, nonmoral, manifested in all things. Although he had once admired the Brahmos' attack on idolatry, his fervid nationalism led him later to defend images, on the ground that nothing Hindu should be discarded, but only purified and redirected. Despite the gracious charm which enthralled western audiences, Vivekananda could become nastily critical of Europe and America when he spoke to his Indian countrymen. "European nations and Western civilization are gross, material, selfish and sensual," he said. "Hindu civilization, since it springs from the oldest and noblest of religions, is good, beautiful and spiritual in every part. . . . All the criticism of European scholars is erroneous, and everything that missionaries say on the subject is wickedly slanderous." [35]

Yet the very next paragraph speaks of the necessity for Hindus to work among "the miserable and down-trodden people of India." For Vivekananda, unlike his master Ramakrishna, proclaimed a religion of service. Over and over, he railed against the narrow prejudices and practices of India society, what he scornfully termed, "Don't touchism!" Over and over, he asked, "Is there any fellow-feeling or sense of *Dharma* left in the country?" Over and over, he told his disciples, "Your duty is to serve the poor and the distressed, without distinction of caste and creed. . . . If you want to find God, serve man." [36]

No wonder, then, that Albert Schweitzer vacillated in his judgment between admiration and disgust. "For us people of the West the great spiritual and ethical personality of Vivekananda is rendered difficult to understand by what appears to us his boundless self-consciousness and by the hard, unjust and contradictory judgments in which he allowed himself to indulge." [37] Yet this fascinating, dramatic character became the pivot of a remarkable spiritual genealogy. Before him, apparently luring him from a Western orientation and political activity, sat Ramakrishna Paramahamsa, mystical, illiterate, purely indigenous. After him came a great social welfare organization known as the Ramakrishna Mission, stretching its network of institutions and lecture halls across India, and exercising continued vitality and popular appeal today.

Towering as the unlikely link between the simple mystic and the active program stands Narendra Nath Datta, Swami Vivekananda. He himself was neither a spiritual saint nor a social reformer— though he might have fancied himself as both. Rather he was orator and organizer, religious traditionalist and cultural modernist. Strangely enough, it was Ramakrishna, the ascetic recluse, who warned his promising pupil against purely egoistic piety and urged him to serve the poor. And Schweitzer the critic could pay this equally sincere tribute: "What is great in Ramakrishna and Vivekananda is that both experience and enjoy the state of ecstasy and yet are superior to it and draw their final criterion for the judgment of spiritual matters from ethical thought." [38]

Chapter VII

The Indian National Congress

A wealth of history and social change lay between the formation of the Indian National Congress and the achievement of national Independence. The three score men and ten who gathered at Poona in 1885 did not even have that goal in mind, much less imagine its fulfillment. Nor could they have foreseen

. . . the subsequent stormy history of this party, and its evolution into one of those giant organizations which, like the National Socialists, the Communist party, the Chinese Kuomintang, and the Italian Fascists, rule the fate and disturb the tranquility of so large a part of the modern world.[1]

Most of the seventy delegates were Hindu lawyers, educators and journalists; only two Muslims were included. Summoned at the suggestion of a retired British Civil Servant, with the encouragement and approval of the Viceroy, they used the English language to praise their English rulers for the privilege of such free speech and assembly. Many of them had studied in England; their "tone

119

was loyal and moderate"; they conducted themselves like well-bred Indian gentlemen. Sixty years later millions of their fellow-countrymen had shared that *pukka* (proper, quality) British training and had moved into a modern and Westernized world. Yet in that same period the Indian National Congress itself became a militant movement for political independence, led by a wizened little man who had exchanged his top hat and barrister's boots for a loin cloth.

Ever since Raja Rammohun Roy, in somewhat reluctant partnership with Lord Bentinck, had challenged his people to social reform, certain segments of Indian aristocracy had organized for particular types of welfare. In 1837 the Zamindary Association (later, and literally, the Landholders' Association) was formed. The Bengal British India Society was organized in 1843 "to secure the welfare, extend the just rights, and advance the interests of all classes of our fellow subjects." (Note the deferential acknowledgment of colonial status.)

Indian leaders, with Debendranath Tagore as secretary, established the British Indian Association in 1851 "to secure improvements in the local administration of the country and in the system of government laid down by Parliament," including a relaxing of the revenue system, improvements in judicial procedures, a more inclusive educational program, the employment of Indians in administrative offices.

Educated Indians followed with admiration the efforts of Garibaldi and Mazzini to unify Italy, for they recognized kindred problems of welding autonomous and highly diversified states into a single nation. Yet their aim, at this period, never went further than representative, constitutional government under British rule.

In the late eighteen-seventies a British Civil Servant named Allan Octavian Hume suggested that the Indian élite should be gathered into a disciplined body dedicated to "unselfishness, moral courage, self-control, and an active spirit of benevolence." This moral idealism found later expression in Gokhale's Servants of India Society. But it rested also on political realism, for Hume sensed the growing restlessness among educated Indians and sought to channel it into constructive service. Since the "National Revolt" of 1857 and the Royal Proclamation of 1858, which replaced the East India Company with the British Crown, conditions in the overseas empire had not improved, and relations between Indians and Englishmen had deteriorated. With blended—not divided—loyalty, Hume knew that British rule had brought peace and stability to the subcontinent, but he also realized that much more needed to be done for the welfare of the masses, that bureaucracy had lost touch with the Indian people at all levels.

Although dubious about public opinion in England on behalf of India, the Viceroy, Lord Dufferin, welcomed the idea of an organization which would serve as a "safety valve" for Indian discontent and provide a medium of transmission for Indian protests and demands. In fact, he advised Hume that the chairman of the new body should be an Indian, rather than a British governor. It was a measure of continuing good will, rather than colonial pressure, which led to the subsequent election of several Britishers as Congress chairmen.

Thus a group of Indian intellectuals came together at Poona for the last week of 1885. Years later Gopal Krishna Gokhale said in London that "no Indian could have started the Indian National Congress." How many English politicians since have had occasion to rue the day that anyone took that step! Yet some such powerful movement could not have been delayed much longer. At their first meeting these Indian gentlemen passed resolutions asking for an investigation of Indian administration, the abolition of the Indian Council in London, the submission of government budgets to legislative councils, and the establishment of standing committees in the House of Commons to receive petitions from Indian legislative councils. In later years they concerned themselves with education, with reduction of military expenditures, with wider employment of Indians in government, with the oppressive tax on cotton, and with the plight of Indians in British Africa.

At the outset British officials, tolerant and paternalistic, viewed the Congress as an amiable outlet for native frustrations, or as a political game for children. As Indian demands became more vigorous and more cogent, however, British attitudes shifted from scorn to suspicion to outright hostility. Sometime in the eighteen-nineties Sir E. Watkins declared in the *Pall Mall Gazette:* "I am strongly of opinion (sic) that Russian gold is being circulated . . .

among these native agitators." [2] Yet for the first twenty years the Congress made every effort to use orderly, democratic processes. Most of its leaders had been educated in England and retained a simple, idealistic faith in British liberalism, justice and fair play. When they were charged with seeking political power for illiterate mobs, Surendranath Banerjea replied in his Presidential Address of 1895: "I was not aware that any responsible Congressmen had ever asked for representative institutions for one woman or for the masses of our people," [3] but only for a qualified, educated electorate.

By the turn of the century the situation began to change. A critical famine in 1896 and a serious plague in 1897 produced two indirect but vital consequences. On one hand, they revealed the desperate suffering of rural India in a way that many Indian intellectuals had never realized it before. On the other hand, they destroyed in many of these educated leaders the last vestiges of trust in Britain's good intentions, sweet reasonableness and humanitarian concerns. The deep-seated racial prejudice displayed in the forced amendment of the Ilbert Bill in 1893 still rankled in many hearts. Now Indians were quick to blame British officials at the very least for indifference and mismanagement in the midst of crisis, at worst for deliberately exploiting the famine to tighten political discipline. Thus what might have led to a heightened social conscience, on the part of British and Indians alike, served instead to drive a wider breach between the two, and to strengthen those nationalistic extremists who saw their only hope—and therefore their single aim— in political independence.

A cleavage along similar lines had been growing within the Indian ranks ever since the inauguration of the Congress. Under the urging of Justice Ranade a parallel organization had arisen, known as the Indian National Social Conference. Enlisting Muslims and Christians as well as Hindus, the group focused attention on local work and on education for reform. Some members took vows of temperance, or against dowries and child marriage. A strong theist himself, Ranade rejected the appeal of the several Samajes on the ground that social change did not require such drastic religious upheaval and, conversely, that religious revolution did not necessarily produce social progress. In short, Ranade—"the guiding hand and the inspiring mind" of the Social Conference—was a moderate, who believed in gradual, constitutional methods. But the days of the moderates were numbered.

Strangely enough, the increasingly radical wing was sired and inspired by Dadabhai Naoroji, a Parsi merchant who during many of his years in England had served in the House of Commons and had profoundly influenced men like John Bright and William Gladstone. As chairman of the second session of Congress in Calcutta in 1886, Dadabhai confronted the question of purpose head-on:

It has been asserted that this Congress ought to take up questions of social reform (Cheers and cries of "Yes, Yes"). . . . But . . . we are met together as a political body to represent to our rulers our political aspirations, not to discuss social reforms. . . . How can this gathering of *all* classes (and religions) discuss the social reforms needed in each individual class? . . . Only the members of that class can effectively deal with the reforms therein needed.[4]

In his presidential address of 1892, W. C. Bonnerjee rejected the view that India must prove by social and moral reform her worthiness for political freedom. Citing as examples of political demands an amendment to a law on forests, or the separation of judicial and executive functions held by the same officer, he inquired bitterly: "Are we not fit for them because our widows remain unmarried and our girls are given in marriage earlier than in other countries, because our wives and daughters do not drive about with us visiting our friends? . . . I fail to see any connection between the two." [5]

The first serious break came in 1895. Because ardent reformers continued to criticize the Congress for not actively supporting the Social Conference in its crusades, Surendranath Banerjea declared in his presidential address:

We cannot afford to have a schism in our camp. . . . Here we have all agreed to bury our social and religious differences and recognize the one common fact that being subjects of the same Sovereign and living under the same Government and the same political institutions, we have common rights and common grievances. . . . Ours is a political and not a social movement.[6]

He and Naoroji and others took the position that social reforms were needed but that Congress was not the proper instrument for such efforts. On one side stood Ranade and Gokhale, urging that social and political reforms must go hand-in-hand and that only by improving their own society could Indians justifiably expect more democratic treatment from the British. On the other side were W. C. Bonnerjee and Lokamanya Tilak, the latter so belligerently opposed to any connection between the Congress and reformers that he threatened to burn down the *pandal* (tent) if the Indian National Social Conference were permitted to use it. Tilak's militant bluster won out, and though the tension between social and political goals continued to smoulder for another decade, the two organizations were effectively divorced. As a result, the outcastes or untouchables—deprived of any encouragement for their cause from Congress—burned the I.N.C. in effigy and (according to their militant leader, Ambedkar) adopted an attitude of suspicion and bitterness which not even Gandhi could fully overcome.[7]

Ranade and his followers were not to be cowed. While deploring such signs of "denationalisation" as adopting English dress or food, he continued to raise a critical voice against blind adherence to the past. At the 1897 session of the Social Conference he asked:

What shall we revive? Shall we revive the old habits of our people when the most sacred of our castes indulged in all the abominations, as we now understand them, of animal food and intoxicating drink? . . . Shall we revive . . . the eight forms of marriage, which included capture, and recognized mixed and illegitimate intercourse? Shall we revive the custom of many husbands to one wife or many wives to one husband? [8]

To the claim of Tilak and certain other radicals that no British interference should be tolerated and no legislative procedures used, Ranade insisted: "Wherever there is undeserved misery endured in a large number of cases, there is ground for State interference, always supposing that the State interference will lead to the redress of the wrong better than any individual effort can accomplish." [9]

Thus, with or without the backing of Congress, the Indian National Social Conference continued to pass resolutions on a wide variety of social issues: resolutions which were aimed at conservative

Hindu society, resolutions directed to the Government of British India and even to "the Mother of Parliaments." Among these concerns can be listed the following: adjustment of birth, marriage and death fees according to ability to pay (1888); raising the marriageable age of children (1888, 1897, 1899, 1914); protection or remarriage of child widows (1888, 1897, 1899); approval of intermarriage, at least between subcastes which recognize interdining (1888, 1915); greater educational facilities for girls (1893), for outcastes (1895), for physical training of boys (1899, 1900), for moral and religious instruction (1897); the establishment of local movements against temple dancing and prostitution (1893); for temperance (1893), for orphanages (1900); opposition to penance for sea voyages abroad (1888), to dowry demands (1891), to the *zenana* or *purdah* system of female seclusion (1902), to polygamy (1891, 1913); the "fusion of sub-castes" (1902), "relaxation of caste restrictions and rigidity" (1908), and "abolition of castes" (1915).[10]

Here in capsule form can be seen three decades of social change. It is impossible, looking backward and without intimate participation in Hindu society, to suggest which of these required religious reforms, which should be dealt with by legislation. The same problem still besets India today. Yet for a critical period in the early twentieth century the Indian National Congress had excluded itself from any direct influence on social welfare. Ambedkar undoubtedly overstated his case when he charged that the 1895 rebellion settled for the next twenty-five years the unwillingness of Congress to discuss reform. But even in refutation, Chakravarti Rajagopalachari admitted a twenty-two year gap when he wrote: "This policy of abstention in regard to socio-religious questions was modified in 1917. The Indian National Congress of that year adopted a definite resolution urging upon the people of India the necessity, justice, and righteousness of removing all disabilities imposed by custom upon the Scheduled Castes." [11] Part of the explanation for this renewed social concern lay in external events: the new tides in Asia, world-wide discussion of imperialism, loss of belief in white superiority.

By and large, however, the Congress did abdicate social responsibility to the Indian National Social Conference. What held these two remarkable organizations in loose relationship, despite their differing views, was the quality of moderate leadership. On Ranade's death in 1901 the mantle of social reform fell on Gopal Krishna Gokhale. For fourteen years he guided the Social Conference in attacks on indentured labor and on the intolerable financial burdens which taxes and usury placed upon the peasants. He appealed constantly, to Hindu and British officials alike, for a vastly expanded educational program, compulsory for boys six to ten and voluntary for girls, to be supported by joint State and local payments. Having been active in the Congress since his maiden speech at the age of twenty-three, Gokhale was chosen as its president in 1905, the same year in which he founded the Servants of India Society. To the predominant political focus of the session, he managed to add proposals for economic and educational reform. In his Presidential Address he told the delegates:

The real moral interest of a struggle such as we are engaged in lies not so much in the particular readjustment of present institutions which we may succeed in securing, as in the strength that the conflict brings us to be a permanent part of ourselves.[12]

No appeals for moderation or moral restraint could influence the extremists from this point on. At the session of 1906 Dadabhai Naoroji, serving his second term as President and now literally the "Grand Old Man" of Indian politics, called for *swaraj* (self-government). In the hands of Lokamanya Tilak this goal became the single obsession of the National Congress and the battle-cry for all India during the next four decades. Tilak clashed heatedly at this meeting with Gokhale, and an actual break was postponed only through mediation by the venerable Dadabhai. The following year, however, a riot broke out between moderates and extremists, during which, incidentally, Gokhale protected Tilak from physical violence. Quoting the Magna Carta, Milton, Gibbon, Spencer and Darwin, the middle-class advocates of restraint and gradualism met separately to appeal for constitutional reforms.

In 1908 British authorities arrested Tilak for sedition and sentenced him to "transportation"—meaning imprisonment abroad, in this case in Burma. His absence for the next six years, the tighter controls on all political activity which were imposed from the outbreak of World War I, and the gracious, irenic personality of Gokhale helped to hold the Congress together in tension, rather than divided in dispute. Yet Gokhale antagonized the radicals by offering, if absolutely necessary, to accept an increase in the hated salt tax (against which Gandhi was later to lead his famous March to the Sea) in order to finance broader education. He alienated them still further by writing from London: "Whatever the shortcomings of the bureaucracy, and however intolerable at times the insolence of individual Englishmen, they alone stand to-day in the country for order; and without continued order no real progress is possible for our people." [13]

As England—and a reluctant, protesting, noncooperative India—plunged into the First World War, a new star arose on the horizon of social and political reform. Mohandas K. Gandhi had spent most of his early manhood in London and South Africa, where Gokhale had visited him. For a number of years Indian nationalists had watched with admiration the nonviolent campaign against injustice and discrimination, as it was being waged by expatriate Indian minorities in Africa. Grateful tributes to Gandhi at the Congress session of 1913 first applied to him the term *Mahatma* (Great Soul). With fraternal frankness (he was only three years older) Gokhale had referred to Gandhi's *Indian Home Rule* pamphlet as "crude and hastily conceived," and extracted a promise that Gandhi would abstain from politics for at least a year after his return in 1915. At one point in his career Gandhi had sought to join Gokhale's Servants of India Society. But he insisted that it should practice greater asceticism and accept absolute poverty; this the Society was unwilling to do—for a young and unknown Gandhi.

When Gokhale died in 1915, just forty-nine years old, Indian moderates looked for guidance to Gandhi. He, however, not only determined to keep his pledge to refamiliarize himself with the Indian scene, but wisely preferred to avoid head-on conflict with the popular extremism of Tilak. By "sitting out" the radical-moderate split of the Indian National Congress in 1918, Gandhi managed to inherit the leadership of both factions at Tilak's death in 1920. From that time until his own assassination in 1948, the Mahatma wielded decisive power in the Congress and among all ranks of Indian people, occasionally in official position but more often by sheer force of personality.

That Gandhi began as a moderate social reformer, in the tradition of Ranade and Gokhale rather than Tilak, seems clear from the record. During those first few years back in India, before he became involved directly in politics, he attacked various social injustices which came to his attention: the exploitation of peasants by indigo planters in Bihar, unjust taxation in Gujerat. When he began to edit the influential magazine, *Young India,* he wrote: "Should not we the Hindus wash our bloodstained hands before we ask the English to wash theirs? This is a proper question reasonably put. . . . Swaraj is as unattainable without the removal of the sins of untouchability as it is without Hindu-Muslim unity." [14] Yet from the outset—or rather, from far back in the mistreatment he and his countrymen received from Englishmen in Africa—Gandhi's direction had been clear. It was no mere publicity move that enabled him to raise 13,500,000 rupees for a Tilak Swaraj Fund, as a memorial to "the Father of Indian Nationalism." His own increasing responsibility, as well as the agitation of the people and the blunders of the British rulers, pushed him continually toward the goal of full independence.

In the process Mahatma Gandhi changed a somewhat exclusive organization for the demanding of national rights into a mass movement for the active achievement of social, political and spiritual freedom. The Congress had been made up almost entirely of intellectuals, convening once a year to pass resolutions, but operating without funds and without machinery. Gandhi took the issues and the challenges to the people, transcending caste and class, and drew from them by his personal magnetism not only adulation and obedience, but millions of membership fees at four annas (slightly more than a nickel) per year. Whereas the militant forces of Tilak had been gaining ascendancy in Congress, with a single eye on independence by revolution, Gandhi blended the political, social, economic, educational hopes and dreams of India, measuring each by the moral and spiritual values of her ancient heritage. No wonder a government appraisal includes this summary:

His multi-faced personality gave continuity to the religious-rational as well as the politically rebellious trends in our public life. . . . In a very real sense, he made us respect ourselves and stand up as men after centuries of foreign rule. . . . In his vision, the social religious, political and economic did not appear as different aspects. He made a synthetic approach to the problems of life.[15]

To a considerable degree the history of the Indian National Congress after 1920—or even earlier—is the history of the struggle for independence. What social concerns remained after Ranade and Gokhale came from the "enlarged heart" of one man, Mahatma Gandhi. When in the late nineteen-thirties the Congress again placed emphasis on certain social issues (agrarian indebtedness, factory sanitation, illiteracy, the interest rates of money-lenders), they often appeared either to be afterthoughts, almost lost among political reverberations, or to be weapons in the ceaseless pressure against colonial rule. To an outside observer, then, the role of the Indian National Congress in social reform seems disappointingly small. That is not to deny the heroic struggle for political freedom, a struggle which will long remain an epic example to the world. Nor is it to deny the uniquely ethical orientation which Mahatma Gandhi injected into the entire movement. Yet after discovering how early and how positively the issues of social reform—though not the reformers themselves—were rejected by the Congress itself, one feels compelled to look elsewhere for the sources of India's social conscience.

Evidence of that conscience at work can be seen on many sides: in the Constitution of the Republic, in the superabundance of social legislation passed by the Indian Parliament, in the genuine concerns expressed by leaders in India today. But the Mahatma's withdrawal from membership in 1934 and his subsequent refusal to take official place in the Indian National Congress or the Government might be a clue that he himself felt that body represented a narrower outlook and outreach than he—or India—needed. Commenting on this divergence, a Muslim writer makes this assertion:

Gandhiji would have liked to make it [the Congress] primarily an instrument of the moral and spiritual regeneration of India and only secondarily one of her political liberation and economic progress. Jawahar-

lal and other Congressmen with modern education wanted the Congress
to confine its activities to the political and economic field, though they
accepted the Gandhian principle that it would adopt only those means
for achieving its object which were morally pure.[16]

In fact, while Congress leaders began work on a Draft Constitution, Gandhi devoted his time and energy to an "imaginary constitution" which would abandon politics and pledge the new nation to
social service. It was finished the day before he was shot. He had
pleaded in vain with Congress leaders to dispense with party politics and to make the post-Independence Congress an educational
and welfare movement (perhaps along the lines of the Servants of
India Society). "The Congress has yet to win economic freedom, social and moral freedom," he said. "These freedoms are harder than
the political, if only because they are constructive, less exciting
and not spectacular." [17] Louis Fischer once asked the Mahatma
why "constructive work" (Gandhi's term for his social program of
basic education, cottage industries, home spinning, abolishing untouchability, and so forth) could not be carried on by the Congress as a political party, or by the Government under Congress
leadership. " 'Because Congressmen aren't sufficiently interested
in constructive work,' Gandhi replied simply. 'We must recognize
the fact that the social order of our dreams cannot come through
the Congress party of today.' " [18]

In order to pass even superficial judgment on such an assertion,
it is necessary to look not only at Gandhi, but also at Gandhism (or
Gandhianism), at the multifarious ways in which India today inter-
prets and seeks to implement the Mahatma's dreams. In refutation of
his charge, Government leaders would point to the miraculous
changes which have taken place in India's social life during the
past fifteen years of Congress rule, through Community Development, village *panchayats,* legislative reform. In support of Gandhi's
statement opposition parties, right and left, would cite innumerable
failures, moral and social lags, the Government's preoccupation with
political power at the expense of human welfare. Said Frank Anthony, handsome and able spokesman for Anglo-Indians, member
of the Lok Sabha (Lower House) and president of the All-India
Anglo-Indian Association: "Unless we can find a safety valve and a

real alternative democratic policy, people won't accept the Congress Party much longer. They are completely fed up. These people [in Congress] have got power-drunk." [19] Still another segment of India's population would argue that Gandhi's dreams can never be fulfilled in a modern nation state, that rightly or wrongly he envisioned a Utopia quite incompatible with realistic politics or with human nature, that no responsible party or government should be judged by a moral and spiritual ideal.

As long as the common goal of political independence bound the Indian people together, everyone supported the Indian National Congress, however they might differ on tactics. But that focus of unity has been attained. A powerful organization and dynamic leadership, confronted with mass inertia and political ignorance, have naturally carried the Congress Party along on a wave of success. After all, the single party of Ranade and Dadabhai, of Gokhale and Tilak, of Gandhi and Nehru—the party which won freedom from Britain by the sheer weight of mass resolution—can hardly be overthrown. Today the organized political opposition to Congress is numerically, electorally, weak. What becomes increasingly obvious is the divergence of aims and methods and policies within the party itself. Americans occasionally, though not too seriously, express concern about the spectrum of Goldwater to Rockefeller Republicanism, or the uneasy Democratic bedfellows of Eastland and Humphrey. In India a political realignment appears equally desirable—and improbable.[20]

One of the problems confronting the Congress government is an old one in new guise. The early movement split repeatedly over the relative moral values of social reform and political independence. Today the country is divided not only on national goals, but on practical programs for achieving those aims. Freedom has been a cherished but often painful reality for seventeen years. A United Nations survey team has recommended more intensive, concentrated efforts at community development, while the half million villages of India demand more extensive and speedier welfare services. Because state boundaries were redrawn along linguistic lines after Partition, religious and cultural and linguistic groups continue to clamor for "self-determination" and further subdivision. The weight of Chinese Communism on the Tibetan border and of

Western disillusionment and misunderstanding bears heavily on India's vaunted "neutralism."

Can any nation, faced with such desperate poverty and disunity, play a responsible role in world affairs, yet at the same time lift her standards of living and social progress rapidly enough to satisfy four hundred million people? Frustration, discouragement, fatigue, even corruption and cynicism, have crept into the Indian National Congress. In the years ahead it *must* lead the country to *both* political stability and social reform. This time the responsibility is joined. It cannot set up a separate "conference" for social welfare; it cannot expel the advocates of opposing views, or set fire to the common "tent"; it cannot put the blame for failure on colonial rule. Under prodding from minor Opposition parties, and with material aid from more prosperous nations abroad, Congress will have to find herself before she can regain the vitality—and moral integrity—with which she led the Independence movement.

Chapter VIII

Mahatma Gandhi: Ethics in Politics

I hold that democracy cannot be evolved by forceful measures. The spirit of democracy cannot be imposed from without; it has to come from within.

We are all absolutely equal. But equality is of souls and not of bodies. Assumption of superiority by any person over any other is a sin against God and man.

In the midst of humiliation and so-called defeat and a tempestuous life, I am able to retain my peace, because of an underlying faith in God, translated as Truth.

What is true of individuals is true of nations. One cannot forgive too much. The weak can never forgive. Forgiveness is the attribute of the strong.

We can only win over the opponent by love, never by hate.[1]

"Mahatma Gandhi was the spokesman for the conscience of all mankind." This tribute from General George C. Marshall, then

America's Secretary of State, puts Gandhi in the right perspective for
any ethical study. No man in the twentieth century—perhaps in
many centuries—more richly deserves the serious appraisal of the
world. Few recent figures have written and spoken so copiously; India is dotted with public and private foundations dedicated to com-
piling the verbal works of Gandhi. His social and moral and spiritual works can never be compiled. They are scattered through the
most remote villages of his homeland and to unexpected corners
of the earth. As one of his Western adulators put it: "Every reformer, crusader and dictator avows his undying devotion to the
anonymous mass; Gandhi had an apparently endless capacity to
love the individual men, women and children who crowded his
life." [2] For these obvious reasons, a single chapter cannot begin to
do justice to the complexity of the men or even to his transcendent
role in India's social conscience.

Clearly, Gandhi was many things to many people, the more so
since his death. History will continue to ask whether the Mahatma
was fundamentally a politician or a saint, whether (as a recent
American fourth grade quiz posed the question) he should be listed
under "Government" or "Religion." Gandhi himself once "strad-
dled the fence" by saying: "I am not a visionary. I claim to be a
practical idealist." [3] A prominent Muslim college president, who
during student days had had considerable contact with Gandhi,
admitted that he often debated the man's sincerity and basic purpose. "Is this man deliberately doing this or does he seriously believe in it? Even today I cannot answer the question." [4] Confessing
his admiration for both the politician and the ascetic, he concluded
that Gandhi had succeeded in both aims "because to the masses he
became a religious symbol, Mahatma." Sarajini Naidu, a long-time
follower, shed revealing light on the cult of simplicity by remarking
whimsically: "It costs a great deal of money to keep Gandhiji living
in poverty." [5] Although many Western idealists have romanticized
Gandhi, others have painted the picture in cynical, sophisticated
terms:

In the systematic use of his religious hold over the masses for political
purposes, in the grasp of method of extending his religious sway, in his
flair for publicity, and in the use for political and religious purposes of

the technique of commercial salesmanship, he has scarcely a predecessor. He is a kind of Oriental General Booth, and a personality quite like his has not appeared before in Indian history.[6]

Mohandas Karamchand Gandhi (1869–1948) was born in Gujerat, western India, where his father and grandfather had been prime ministers of the state. Here Dayananda Saraswati had left the imprint of religious reform; here Muslims and Parsis and especially Jains (with their basic tenet of *ahimsa,* nonkilling) cast an influence on Hindu society. Louis Fischer notes that Gandhi, the schoolboy, refused to copy from another pupil, even at the urging of his teacher in order to make a perfect record for a visiting inspector.[7] Married at the age of thirteen, he describes in his autobiography his early passion, his later temptations, and his ultimate continence by agreement. "I can see no moral argument," he concluded, "in support of such a preposterously early marriage." [8] When he sailed to England at the age of 18, he was the first of his subcaste to violate the *Code of Manu* by crossing the seas.

In London the young Hindu law student guiltily sampled meat and dancing and other "vices" of Western "civilization." Incredible though it sounds, he read the *Bhagavad-Gita* for the first time and found there, especially in the last nineteen verses, "an infallible code of conduct for me." He dabbled with Leviticus and Numbers (why?) and enjoyed the Prophets and Psalms, but much preferred the New Testament and the Sermon on the Mount, which like the *Gita* "went straight to my heart." In the period when Madame Blavatsky was persuading Annie Besant to go to India, Gandhi met the two women in London, was not won to theosophy, but praised it as "the brotherhood of man" and welcomed their effort to find a substitute for atheism. Thirty years later he renewed his friendship with Mrs. Besant in the Indian National Congress and the Home Rule League.

After revisiting India briefly, the young solicitor set sail for South Africa in 1893, to practice among Indian expatriates, many of whom had been or still were indentured laborers. Soon after his arrival an incident occurred which, more than any other single event, moulded the future career of Mohandas Gandhi. Though holding a first-class ticket, he was ejected as a "colored person" from a first-class car and chose to leave the train rather than accept inferior status. Years later when John R. Mott asked what had been "the most creative experiences" of his life, Gandhi recounted the story of that night in the Maritzburg railroad station.[9] Some Christians still maintain, on rather dubious conjecture, that this one episode decided Gandhi against becoming a Christian. The barriers lay in dogma as well as in Christian practice. Gandhi promised friends in Africa that his search for truth would keep him open to conversion if the inner voice commanded it, but (like many another distinguished and thoughtful Hindu) he could not accept Christianity's *exclusive* claims for its Bible, its ethics, or its way of salvation. Yet he referred to Jesus as "the Prince of Satyagrahis" (practitioners of "truth force") and admitted that he had been fully convinced of its rightness and value by the Sermon on the Mount.[10]

Several Western writings on religion and ethics reached Gandhi in Africa and touched a responsive chord. John Ruskin's *Unto This Last* (Four Essays on the First Principles of Political Economy) "marked the turning point in my life." Gandhi had already been convinced that all vocations should serve others, but he had assumed against the caste background of Hinduism that this equality of purpose justified inequality of status. Ruskin's essay, however, showed him that duty includes the protection and help of the underprivileged by those more fortunate. Later Gandhi commented that Ruskin had been "content to revolutionize his mind" but lacked the strength to change life. Gandhi had the strength and was just beginning to use it in Africa. As Albert Schweitzer put it, "In one corner his world and life affirmation is marked 'Made in England'." [11]

A sense of kinship struck him in prison in 1908, when he read Thoreau's essay on *Civil Disobedience*. Thoreau had been in prison too; Thoreau had read the *Gita* and parts of the *Upanishads;* Thoreau outlined the concept which Gandhi had called *satyagraha* (truth force). Dissatisfied with the English phrase "passive resistance," Gandhi borrowed "civil disobedience" for awhile, but finally adopted "civil resistance" as a more positive term. He also recommended to his followers the essays of Emerson, which "to my mind contain the teaching of Indian wisdom in a Western guru." Still another philosopher whose ideas spoke to the heart of Gandhi was Leo Tolstoy, with his moving assurance, *The Kingdom of God Is Within You*. Through a correspondence of mutual regard the Russian strengthened the Indian's faith in nonviolence, writing, in a final letter received in Africa after his death: "Love . . . is the highest and only law of human life. . . . As soon as force was admitted into love, there was no more and there could be no more love as the law of life." [12] As Fischer wisely notes, the difference lay in the fact that the older man had grown depressed and hopeless, while the younger still had faith in the possibility of change, in the power of love.

Although quick to acknowledge Gokhale as his political *guru* (teacher) and also to praise Gokhale's arch-rival, Tilak, Gandhi in wistful moments confessed that he had never found a religious guide. Perhaps because he himself was so far ahead of his contemporaries in spiritual insight, he never knew the intimate sense of personal trust and companionship. The nearest to such a friend was a Bombay jeweler and poet, Rajchandra (Raychandbhai), a Jain of whom Gandhi wrote:

In my moments of spiritual crisis, he was my refuge. Yet in spite of this regard for him I could not enthrone him in my heart as my Guru. The throne has remained vacant and my search still continues. . . . Only a perfect gnani (seer) deserves to be enthroned as Guru. There must, therefore, be ceaseless striving after perfection. For one gets the Guru that one deserves. Infinite striving after perfection is one's right. It is its own reward. The rest is in the hands of God.[13]

In the pathos of this rare revelation of unfulfilled dependence, Christians would like to believe that this Christ-like little man had so narrowly missed his perfect *guru* because he had refused to enshrine the universal Saviour.

If that is true, however, it is because so many nominal Christians have similarly failed to acknowledge the Lordship of Christ in their daily lives. Repeatedly Gandhi sought to deepen each man's own faith. Asked for a message to a Christian Conference, he once replied: "Just tell them to be better Christians." Asked what was the greatest obstacle Christ had to overcome in India, he answered: "Christians." As Louis Fischer deftly wrote: "Gandhi never tried to convert Christians to Hinduism. . . . Missionaries frequently tried to convert him to Christianity. (He, speaking softly, tried to do the same for them.) " [14] Sometimes in a broader context he would announce that he was a Hindu, a Christian, a Muslim and a Jew. Sometimes he admitted that he would gladly become a Christian—IF he could simply follow the Sermon on the Mount and his own interpretation of it. At still other times, especially in his early days, he proudly proclaimed himself a Hindu because:

I believe in the Vedas, the Upanishads, the Puranas and all that goes by the name of Hindu scriptures, and therefore in *avatars* (incarnations) and rebirth. I believe in the *varnashrama dharma* (law of caste) in a sense, in my opinion strictly Vedic, but not its present popular and crude sense. I believe in the protection of the cow in its much larger sense than the popular. I do not disbelieve in idol-worship. [15]

It is time to examine some of Gandhi's beliefs more fully, as they relate to social and ethical activities. Moral authority, for the Mahatma, is not dependent on or derived from the sacredness of scriptures. It comes instead from the still, small voice of conscience, from the Inner Light, from the conviction of Truth. Gandhi would emphatically deny that the Vedas are *more* divinely inspired than the Bible, the Quran, the Zend Avesta, the Granth Sahib, or that any of these possessed verbal infallibility. So it is with his attitude toward *karma,* rebirth and salvation. He once wrote that his loyalty to Hinduism was like his feeling for his wife, despite her faults. "I am a reformer through and through. But my zeal never takes me to the rejection of the essential things in Hinduism." [16] Again he testified, still in the early days of his leadership in India: "Hinduism as I know it entirely satisfies my soul, fills my whole being, and I find a solace in the Bhagavadgita and the *Upanishads* that I miss even in the Sermon on the Mount." [17] At the same time he granted equal validity to every other viewpoint. If there is only one God, Louis Fischer inquired, why should there not be one religion? "A tree has a million leaves," Gandhi answered; "there are as many religions as there are men and women, but they are all rooted in God." [18]

What, then, is God? How does the Mahatma, the Great Soul, understand the Supreme Soul, the Brahman-Atman? Like every seeker, every theologian, he has used myriad terms: "an indefinable mysterious power which pervades everything . . . that holds all together, that creates, dissolves, and recreates . . . unalterable law . . . Life, Truth, and Love . . . the supreme God . . ." [19] From all these definitions Gandhi long ago selected Truth as most inclusive, most comprehensive. However even the minimal statement "God is Truth," seemed to him too narrow, for it implies an impression or an initial assumption about God. So he turned the phrase around: "Truth is God," since "even atheists do not doubt the necessity of truth." [20] Pyarelal Nayar, Gandhi's official biographer, referred in personal conversation to a "Dialogue with an Atheist" in which Mahatma asked: "Do you feel a pang at the suffering of others? . . . Then that is enough. . . . Do you believe in Truth? . . . Then that is enough, for Truth is God." [21]

This is not the truth of factual knowledge, correspondence with a "real" world. It is more than a universal idea or a natural law. It is the practical activity which St. Paul had in mind when he spoke of "doing the truth." In *Harijan*, Gandhi's publication which followed *Young India*, the Mahatma wrote: "There are eternal principles which admit of no compromise and one must be prepared to lay down one's life in the *practice* of them." [22] Notice that he calls for sacrifice not for abstract theories or dogmatic creeds, but for vibrant reality. As Pyarelal expressed it: Gandiji did not claim to bring any new truth but "to make what was old new and to make it live. His essential contribution was that he took us out of the realm of contemplation into the plane of action. . . . Abstract truth took body in his hands. He taught us to live truth." [23]

In order to "live truth" another ingredient must be added, another attribute must be recognized as God. "He is love. He is the supreme Good. . . . The safest course is to believe in the moral government of the world and therefore in the supremacy of the moral law, the law of truth and love." [24] Whatever the commands of duty in ancient Hinduism, whatever the element of compassion introduced by Buddhism, Gandhi's insistence on positive, dynamic love brought a new quality into Hindu ethics. Although missionaries have frequently claimed credit (too often for themselves rather than for their Lord), grateful Indians as well acknowledge Gandhi's indebtedness—and theirs. A Hindu writer quotes the Mahatma's own assertion that Christianity's greatest contribution to the world has been "active love. No other religion says so firmly that God is love." [25]

At this point, Gandhiji recognized a distinction which many Christians have been unwilling to make. That is, he realized that God cannot readily be defined as Truth and Love and at the same time described in personal terms. "I do not regard God as a person," he admitted. "Truth for me is God, and God's law and God are not different things or facts in the sense that an earthly king and his law are different. He and his law abide everywhere and govern everything." [26] To some readers this implies a touch of pantheism; to others it indicates an ultimate philosophical idealism. Yet one wonders whether such a distinction, between God as person and God as value or power, can be maintained in spiritual experience, however clear it may be to rational examination. Repeatedly in his autobiography Gandhi refers to occasions when "God saved me," [27] from temptations, or God guided him in crucial decisions. To the All-India Congress Committee in 1946 he said, "In God's world unmixed evil never prospers. God rules even where Satan holds sway because the latter exists only on His sufferance." [28] At the hour of prayer, in the very act of greeting and benediction, the frail old man crumpled under an assassin's bullets with the final whisper: "Hé, Ram!" (Oh, God!). It would be easy to dismiss such phrases from some men as blasphemy, from others as instinctive surprise or dismay. From Mahatma Gandhi they seem far more personal, more intimate, than "Oh, Truth!" or "Truth saved me" or even "Oh, Lord!"

Despite this problem, so familiar to all religious experience, Gandhi's theology was extremely personal in quite a different sense. God, the Ultimate Reality, was for him inseparable from mankind. "I know I cannot find Him apart from humanity. . . . They are my first care and my last because I recognize no God except that God that is found in the hearts of the dumb millions." [29] Writing in *Harijan,* the Mahatma declared: "I am a part and parcel of the whole, and I cannot find Him apart from the rest of humanity." [30] Even an evaluation of the political philosophy of Mahatma Gandhi recognizes this cardinal identification, as follows: "The immediate service of human beings becomes a necessary part of his endeavour, because the only way to find God is to see Him in His creation and to be one with it." [31]

Here lies the basis for Gandhiji's dedication to service. At its root it reflects the classical Hindu view that every soul (*atman*) is a spark of the Divine (Brahman-Atman). But where Hinduism in the past had been content to regard this as a theoretical doctrine, or to apply it only toward one's immediate family or caste, Gandhi gave it universal scope and dynamic relevance. "Religion," he said, "which takes no account of practical affairs and does not help to solve them, is no religion." [32] Thus he fitted individual morality into a "social gospel" by demonstrating the responsibility for human welfare implicit in ontological brotherhood. As Schweitzer put it, "Gandhi continues what Buddha began. In the Buddha the spirit of love set itself the task of creating different spiritual conditions in the world; in Gandhi it undertakes to transform *all* worldly conditions." To illustrate, the great Western exponent of "Reverence for Life" cites Gandhi's transmutation of *ahimsa* (an essentially spiritual, nonworldly attitude) to "passive resistance" (a practical, worldly policy). Passive resistance, Schweitzer adds, is *ahimsa* put to the direct service of world affirmation and material activity, "a non-violent use of force" whose distinction from active resistance is "only quite relative." [33] Yet this very metamorphosis may be Gandhiji's most creative contribution to social ethics.

What, then, were the social issues to which Gandhiji turned his profoundly spiritual ethics? In Africa the young solicitor identified himself from the start with the problems of indentured labor: virtually slave wages, taxes which imposed permanent serfdom, the pass system, often a ban on voting or owning land. But he was equally critical of his own people, urging them as well as white employers to improve sanitation. "Leaving nightsoil, cleaning the nose, or spitting on the road is a sin against God and humanity," he told his Tolstoy Farm community outside Johannesburg in 1910, and he felt strongly about smoking and drinking. When Gandhi consulted Ranade about the mistreatment of Indians in Africa, the elder reformer reminded the younger of the evils of caste and untouchability in their homeland. Even before that, however, in his first public speech in Pretoria, Gandhi had urged the Indians to forget caste and religious divisions and form a united, cooperative community.

In later years, back in India, the Mahatma devoted himself to all manner of causes, too numerous to detail here. He sought legislative and social protection for lepers and child widows. He worked strenuously to combat illiteracy, child marriage, dowries and the barter of brides. He demanded laws to enforce prohibition, woman suffrage and village sanitation, yet he knew full well that no laws would be effective without mass education. For the most part, he addressed himself to problems as they arose. Yet he often declared that his Constructive Program had five fingers: the removal of untouchability, home spinning, sobriety, Hindu-Muslim friendship and equality for women. The wrist of this hand, he would say, the base which holds all five fingers in strength and unity, is *ahimsa* (nonviolence) or *satyagraha* (truth force).

It has often been claimed that Gandhi's greatest contribution to social reform was his attack on untouchability. Nevertheless Gandhiji's attitudes and actions in regard to the caste problem need to be examined carefully and honestly. Even those who regard the Mahatma as a moral prophet unique in the history of the world must recognize that to gloss over the difficulties and discrepancies would be as unfair to him as to an objective study of Indian social ethics.

In the first place, Gandhi did not often condemn the caste system as such. For the most part (though he himself admitted that "consistency is a hobgoblin"), he accepted the traditional divisions into vocational categories. "There should be four such big castes so that we may reproduce the old system of four varnas," he wrote in 1925.[34] Moreover, they should include adherence to hereditary occupations "to prevent competition" based on birth, although in rare instances an individual might display talents appropriate to some other caste. "Every child has a natural capacity for his hereditary occupation, and should take it up, unless he discovers in himself an exceptional aptitude for another." [35] This attitude, of course, ignores the influence of environment in contrast to heredity, and the right of every individual to a "higher," better, freer environment in which to develop other capacities. In evidence for the thesis that Gandhi clung to a conservative position one can cite the impatient criticism by Nehru: "For years I have puzzled over this problem:

why with all his love and solicitude for the underdog he yet supports a system which inevitably produces it and crushes it." [36]

Furthermore, the "early Gandhi" defended some of the social consequences of caste. For example, he did not always favor free entry into temples, having once said: "How is it possible that the Antyajas (untouchables) should have the right to enter all the existing temples? As long as the law of caste and ashram has the chief place in Hindu Religion, to say that every Hindu can enter every temple is a thing that is not possible today." [37] Yet near the close of his life he led groups of outcastes defiantly into orthodox temples. To take another illustration, Gandhi wrote in 1921: "Hinduism does most emphatically discourage interdining and intermarriage between divisions. . . . Prohibition against intermarriage and interdining is essential for the rapid evolution of the soul." [38] Yet eleven years later Gandhi insisted that "restriction on intercaste dining and intercaste marriage is no part of the Hindu religion. It crept into Hinduism when perhaps it was in its decline, and was then probably meant to be a temporary protection against the disintegration of Hindu society. Today those two prohibitions are weakening Hindu society." [39] The following year he allowed his son to marry the daughter of a distinguished Brahmin, Chakravarti Rajagopalachari, and by 1946 he was urging intercaste marriages in his ashram at Sevagram. During the last two years of his life he chose to make his headquarters in Bombay and Delhi among the *Harijans* —though he died at the home of one of India's wealthiest families. Thus the first criticisms of Gandhi's position must yield to acknowledgment that he grew in wisdom and in moral stature, even in the final decades of his life.

Gandhi has also been charged with a condescending approach to the so-called Untouchables. In 1931 he adopted the word, *Harijans,* or Children of God, as an alternative to "outcaste," and by his example led all India to use this designation—except where the legal term, Scheduled Castes, is in order. Now this is a noble title, a name which speaks of the brotherhood of man under the fatherhood of God, especially when it comes from the Great Soul of Gandhi. But it may also imply paternalism, a sort of trusteeship over the innocent and immature. This became all too apparent when the

Harijan Sevak Sangh (formerly the All-India Anti-Untouchability
League, then Servants of the Untouchables Society) was formed in
1933. Its concerns were scholarships and schools (sometimes segregated), new or reconstructed wells (sometimes segregated), cooperatives and other economic assistance. When B. R. Ambedkar,
leader and spokesman for the Untouchables, requested further representation on the board of Harijan Sevak Sangh, Gandhi at first refused. Ambedkar and the other outcaste members therefore resigned, in protest against a society which appeared to offer charity
for the *Harijans,* but not in association *with* them or *by* them.

Not even a sensitive spirit like the Mahatma's can readily understand how acutely persecuted minorities suspect and resent any
tinge of condescension when a privileged person tries to work with
or for a victim of prejudice and discrimination. But complete understanding, perfect sympathy, would not eliminate sincere disagreement as to methods. In 1923 the Congress Working Committee referred the problem of "so-called Untouchables" to the All-India
Hindu Mahasabha. As Ambedkar rightly complains, there could
hardly be a less satisfactory agency than this reactionary, communal
body, later suspected with its militant auxiliary, the Rashtriya Swayamsevak Sangh, of complicity in Gandhi's assassination. On the
other hand, the *Harijan* demand not only for a separate but for a
double ballot, to vote in *both* general and Scheduled Caste elector-
ates, appears preposterous. Gandhi's compromise for Reserved Seats
(a kind of proportional representation for outcastes and Muslims
and Anglo-Indians) in the Legislative Assembly and the subsequent
Parliament makes more political sense. Yet it was ironical that
Gandhi should threaten a fast to the death not for broader rights for
Untouchables, but to prevent their securing a separate vote. Even
Prime Minister Ramsay MacDonald wrote to the Mahatma with undisguised pique:

As I understand your attitude, you propose to adopt the extreme course
of starving yourself to death not in order to secure that the Depressed
Classes should have joint electorate with other Hindus, because that is
already provided, nor to maintain the unity of Hindus, which is also
provided, but solely to prevent the Depressed Classes, who admittedly
suffer from terrible disabilities to-day, from being able to secure a limited number of representatives of their own choosing to speak on their

behalf in the legislatures which will have a dominating influence over their future.[40]

Gandhiji himself had affirmed from jail to Sir Samuel Hoare, then Secretary of State for India, that his political concern in this matter "dwindles into insignificance compared to the moral and religious issue." [41] That moral and religious issue boiled down to whether Hinduism (meaning, in effect, the dominant caste majority) should and could and would settle the problems of the outcastes without giving them or the British Government an independent voice. In the Congress Gandhi referred the matter of untouchability to the Mahasabha because it "concerns the Hindu community particularly." He opposed a separate vote for Untouchables because he felt that all Hindus should take responsibility for giving justice to the outcastes.

This position rested in turn on two prior convictions. First, that caste Hindus should acknowledge guilt and penitence for the "canker eating at the vitals of Hinduism." Way back in 1921 he had written: "Swaraj (self-government) is a meaningless term if we desire to keep a fifth of India under perpetual subjection. . . . Inhuman ourselves, we may not plead before the Throne for deliverance from the inhumanity of others." [42] Second, that untouchability was a superficial accretion which Hindus themselves could readily eradicate. In one of the earliest issues of *Young India,* Gandhi wrote:

If the inhuman treatment of the Panchamas were a part of Hinduism, its rejection would be a paramount duty both for them and for those like me who would not make a fetish even of religion and condone every evil in its sacred name. But I believe that untouchability is no part of Hinduism. It is rather its excrescence to be removed by every effort.[43]

"If it was proved to me that it is an essential part of Hinduism," Fischer quotes him as saying, "I for one would declare myself an open rebel against Hinduism itself." [44] Yet, as Fischer goes on to point out, "God-fearing Hindus were content to see the 'children of God' in degrading isolation." Penance and moral resolution are essential ingredients for social reform. But they are not substitutes for legal justice and practical remedies. This Gandhi knew and applied in other ethical areas. This many American Christians fail to recognize in their problem of segregation.

A few other specific issues merit attention here. One is *ahimsa,* nonviolence. Observers may trace Gandhiji's "reverence for life" to Buddha or Mahavira, Tolstoy or Thoreau, Jesus and the Sermon on the Mount. It is difficult for a Westerner to find nonviolence in the *Bhagavad-Gita,* where Arjuna is persuaded to wage war, even against friends and kinsmen, so long as he does it with detachment and a sense of duty. Yet Gandhi's attitude toward killing has caused much controversy and much confusion. During the Boer War, he volunteered for ambulance service in Africa, and when he reached London just at the outbreak of war in 1914, he offered to recruit an Indian ambulance unit. But he also supported military recruitment in India the following year. His explanation reflected something of Gokhale's faith in British integrity and foreshadowed Gandhi's own realism toward Poland and Kashmir. "I discovered that the British Empire had certain ideals with which I had fallen in love," he confessed, "and one of these ideals is that every subject of the British Empire has the freest scope possible for his energy and honour and whatever he thinks is due to his conscience." [45]

By the Second World War he had lost confidence that the British would reward faithful service with Independence; he had gained the conviction that force is always wrong when its use is imposed from without. Yet many of his disciples, especially in the West, ignore or disbelieve his approval—contained ironically in a Christmas Day broadcast—of India's despatch of troops to drive Pakistani tribesmen out of Kashmir in 1947.[46] Because he believed that *satyagraha* is a positive force, Gandhiji realized it could not be employed effectively by those who lacked the indispensable virtues of faith, courage and love. It was better to resist evil with violence, he maintained, if one lacked the courage or strength to resist it by other methods. He showed himself indifferent to defeat; true detachment disregards the consequences of an act if the intention has ethical roots. But "where there is only a choice between cowardice and violence," he wrote in *Young India* as far back as 1920, "I would advise violence." [47]

Always Gandhiji judged the morality of the subject rather than the object. In 1938, after Munich he advocated the use of nonviolent resistance by the Czechs against the German invasion. When the leading statesmen of the Christian world met in Madras that winter for the International Missionary Council, John R. Mott, William Paton and others called on Gandhi and tried to convince him that Nazis and Fascists were incapable of ethical reactions and must be treated accordingly. Gandhi's answer was a single sentence sermon on the Gospel of Jesus Christ: "Your argument presupposes that the dictators like Mussolini and Hitler are beyond redemption." [48] Would the Mahatma today recommend military resistance against Chinese Communist encroachments on the Indian border? Wishful and wistful admirers tend to doubt it, though many Indian "realists" are claiming that he would. But if he did, it would represent a moral judgment on India far more than on China.

The same subtle reasoning—mixed with emotion and "spiritual-ity"—guided other ethical choices. Gandhi has said that "the cow is a poem of pity," [49] that "the central fact of Hinduism is cow pro-tection. She is the mother to millions of Indian mankind. Man through the cow is enjoined to realize his identity with all that lives." [50] While modern Hindus deny the "worship" of the "sacred" cow, their attitude borders on it. Not even Gandhi dared advocate the killing of aged, decrepit cattle, though the economic burden weighs heavily on a destitute people. Yet he realized that the in-humane neglect of such cows was "eloquent of our irreligion rather than of religion." [51] The Mahatma did justify the slaughter of suf-fering animals, and he himself once poisoned a calf which was dy-ing in agony.[52] Furthermore, he modified *ahimsa* to allow the kill-ing of mad dogs, venomous snakes, and even marauding monkeys, thus forfeiting the Jainist label which some would give him. On one occasion, when nurses in his ashram at Sevagran protested the class dissection of a frog as a violation of *ahimsa*, Bapuji (the affection-ate term which his disciples used for "Honored Father") ruled: "Dissect the frog of that is the only way to explain the heart-beat." [53] Again Gandhiji's position must be described in positive terms in-stead of prohibitions. "Complete Nonviolence," he wrote in *Young India*, "is complete absence of ill will against all that lives . . . in its active form good will toward all life. It is pure Love. I read it in the Hindu scriptures, in the Bible, in the Koran." [54]

If some of Gandhi's followers have been dismayed by his appar-

ent exceptions to *ahimsa,* others have been baffled by his attitude
toward science and technology and government. Once he escaped
from the ill-fitting externals of Western civilization in London, he
absorbed from Rousseau, Ruskin and Tolstoy some of their hostility
to scientific and industrial society. In a *Confession of Faith* written
in Africa in 1909 Gandhiji recommended that India should forget
the past fifty years and let all railways, telegraphs, hospitals, doctors, and lawyers (!) disappear. As a defender of aryavedic medi-
cine against modern science, he acknowledged a sense of guilt about
accepting an appendectomy himself, though with typical honesty
he admitted a selfish desire to go on living.[55] His extreme stand
against science and technology had to be abandoned, for political
and practical reasons, when he assumed leadership in India, but he
softened his retraction by declaring that the people were not yet
ready for this "higher simplicity and renunciation." "Ideally, however, I would rule out machinery, even as I would reject this very
body, which is not helpful to salvation, and seek the absolute liberation of the soul. From this point of view I would reject all machinery, but machines will remain, because, like the body, they are
inevitable." [56]

Although he later modified his judgment that machinery was "a
great sin," [57] Gandhi devoted a large share of his Constructive Program to encouraging local handicrafts and especially the use of the
home *charka* (spinning wheel). His motives were many. At the
highest religious level he spoke of spinning as a sacrament, an act
to turn the mind toward God, like using a rosary. More often he
stressed its importance as a moral duty, a personal discipline, to use
time and resources creatively. Politically Gandhiji saw the *charka* as
a symbol of national unity, a weapon which the humblest Indian
could wield peacefully and voluntarily, regardless of caste or creed
or class. Economically the home spinning movement could represent a supplement to the meager income of peasants during their
long idle season, and a simultaneous blow at British textile factories
on behalf of *swadeshi* (home products). Yet with all these purposes—and who can say which was dominant?—Gandhiji regarded
village industry as but one facet in his program. K. M. Panikkar put
it this way: "In his constructive work he knew that without a revolution in rural life Indian development would not be satisfactory,

but he was too big to think that merely by turning the *charka* villages would be improved." [58]

Because Family Planning has become such a vital issue in Indian life, brief mention should be made of Gandhi's attitude toward birth control. For him the solution seemed very simple. "Propagation of the race rabbit-wise must undoubtedly be stopped, but not so as to bring greater evils in its train. It should be stopped by methods which in themselves ennoble the race . . . the sovereign remedy of self-control." [59] This solution represented a double rejection of science (which might almost be defined by Gandhiji as artificial, unnatural) and of government interference in private life. It represented a reaffirmation of traditional Hindu ideals: self-restraint at all times and voluntary chastity, which Gandhi himself practiced, for the latter half of life. It represented, finally, a narrower view of man's biological nature. "Sex urge is a fine and noble thing," Gandhi said. "There is nothing to be ashamed of in it. But it is meant only for the act of creation. Any other use of it is a sin against God and humanity." [60] The Mahatma, after an admittedly passionate youth, advocated self-discipline and renunciation as prerequisites for the spiritual life.

Whether one agrees or disagrees, follows or opposes, Gandhiji's particular moral stands, he must recognize their powerful influence on India—and the world—for generations to come. It is easy for a modern Westerner to criticize, and many Indians join in, especially when Gandhian proof-texts can be cited on both sides of most social and ethical problems. The suggestion that hand-crafts are more essential than literacy may seriously obstruct the mass education program. Gandhiji's attack on secularism and technology has at least indirectly undermined liberal scientific education. His demand for religious instruction is received in some quarters as reactionary in a secular age. As a socialistic sociologist, A. R. Desai complains that Gandhi's personal, moral approach ignores the social and political forces at work and attributes all evil, injustice and exploitation to "man's weak ethical nature":

Instead of a radical transformation of the social structure as the solution of the world's ills, he gave the receipe (sic) of the "change of heart" theory as the panacea of those ills. Not that the social system should be changed but the human heart must experience a fundamental moral transformation. Instead of working for a programme of substituting socialist social relations in place of capitalist social relations, he strove for humanizing capitalist social relations.[61]

Schuster and Wint have collected a list of criticisms against the Mahatma's total social impact.[62] Because they contain some thought-provoking validity, they are worth repeating here, even though there are mitigating factors for some and convincing rejoinders to others. (1) The religious "revivalism" is destructive of certain positive secular values. (2) It encourages India to look backward instead of forward in the twentieth century. (3) Such pietism sets false and unrealistic economic and political goals for the country. (4) It stimulates irresponsible political activity by untutored masses. (5) Gandhi was never specific about the positive institutions he wished to create. (6) His dramatic fasts, imprisonments and personal sacrifice were used as substitutes for serious intellectual leadership. (7) "His zeal for removing the worst disabilities of the untouchables is a bid to win back the untouchables to Hinduism and end the danger of their conversion to Christianity or Islam." (8) "Mr. Gandhi's caution in condemning the caste structure root and branch masks a belief that caste is divinely ordained." (9) His stress on the Hindu heritage helped alienate and separate the Muslims. "Indeed the tragedy of the Mahatma's career is that while his main object in life is the unity of India, his actions have so often tended to cause disunity."

Whatever the practical consequences of this man's teachings may be in the past or present or future, he has left a priceless legacy to the world in the moral realm. It can be summarized in three fundamental principles: the inseparability of means and ends, of rights and duties, of politics and ethics.

Not that Gandhi believed means and end to be identical. On the contrary, he asserted that man always has the choice and control of means which he employs, while the end result (as distinct from the intention) rests in the hands of God. For this reason he took a stand diametrically opposed to Marxian ethics, maintaining that the end does not justify the means, that the means must be compatible or consistent with the end, and even that the nature of the means often determines the quality of the end. It is an easy step for Gandhi—and for disciples like Martin Luther King, Jr.—to insist that the morality of means is essential to the morality of the act as a whole. It is a dangerous fallacy to assume further that the morality of the means *guarantees* the morality of the end. Nonviolence, however noble a method (and this of course is also open to debate), may be used for ignoble, immoral goals.

"The true source of rights is duty," Gandhi wrote. "Action is duty, fruit is the right." [63] The Mahatma who devoted his life to enhancing, uplifting, hallowing human rights as a whole was sharply critical of any demand for particular rights. He spoke not of the rights of women, but of the duties of men and women toward society. He spoke not of the rights of *Harijans,* but of the duties of upper castes to treat all peoples with justice and love. If this approach seems to encourage "a feudal paternalistic attitude on the part of the higher castes," even that was less serious for the Mahatma than the selfish consequences of claiming rights. Emphasis on rights divides men, he believed, whereas emphasis on duties unites them.

To speak of the unity of politics and ethics is to include all fields of social activity. Rajkumari Amrit Kaur, a Christian who served as the Mahatma's secretary from 1932 to his death in 1948, explained this view in blunt terms: "Gandhi maintained to his dying day that politics need not be a dirty game, but that it will be a dirty game as long as people separate it from religion. . . . It [religion?] is not a personal thing between you and your God as far as your life and your daily behavior is concerned." [64] Means and ends are inseparable because they are one in the moral view, in the metaphysical concept of God. Rights and duties are inseparable because human life is inseparable, and duties stretch the individual's thought and energy beyond himself. Politics and ethics are inseparable because life is a whole and religion is its unifying element. "Gandhi enriched politics with ethics. He found each morning's issues in the light of eternal and universal values." [65] The fragmentized, atomized, compartmentalized outlook of the West does violence to the ultimate monism of Indian thought.

For this very reason it may be irrelevant and inappropriate to have asked whether Gandhi was more of a saint or a politician. The fact that he drafted no blueprint of government for a nonviolent society, or formulated no economic system which would operate on "truth-force," has led some observers to conclude that "he was not a social or political theorist, but a moral and spiritual reformer." [66] If the aggressively nonviolent reformer had abruptly withdrawn from politics in his later years (like Aurobindo or Tagore, or like Jayaprakash Narayan today), he would have fulfilled the traditional Hindu sequence of responsible action and pious meditation. But Gandhiji did not. Way back in South Africa he had told a friend: "Men say I am a saint losing myself in politics. The fact is that I am a politician trying my hardest to be a saint." [67]

This is the humblest, the fairest, and probably the truest assessment to be made. Apart from the price of egoism—as soon as a man thinks himself a saint he ceases to be one!—Gandhi's position offers greater scope for growth and service. A saint who was trying to be a politician would not, on the canvas of history, have led India to freedom from Great Britain, or have persuaded an inchoate mass of caste-ridden people to renounce (even in theory) the prejudices and social structures of millennia.

A politician—or a doctor or an engineer or a sweeper or a priest—can try to be a saint. He will make mistakes—as Gandhiji did—for human beings do make mistakes, even if they represent sparks of the Divine. But he can learn, he can try again, he can demonstrate by his own life and spirit that human and Divine do meet. Perhaps no finer tribute has been paid the Mahatma than the simple words of Rabindranath Tagore, before Gandhi had won either his political victory or his martyrdom: "Perhaps he will fail as the Buddha failed and as Christ failed to wean men from their iniquities, but he will always be remembered as one who made his life a lesson for all ages to come." [68]

Chapter IX

The Constitution of India

We, THE PEOPLE OF INDIA, having solemnly resolved to constitute India into a SOVEREIGN DEMOCRATIC REPUBLIC and to secure to all citizens:

JUSTICE, social, economic and political;

LIBERTY of thought, expression, belief, faith and worship;

EQUALITY of status and of opportunity; and to promote among them all

FRATERNITY assuring the dignity of the individual and the unity of the Nation;

IN OUR CONSTITUENT ASSEMBLY this twenty-sixth day of November, 1949, do HEREBY ADOPT, ENACT AND GIVE TO OURSELVES THIS CONSTITUTION.[1]

In few countries of the world are the social ideals and moral principles of a people so clearly and deliberately written into a political document. Unlike many other new republics, India had long experience under British constitutional law, a century and a half of indoctrination with Western political philosophy. Eight months before Independence a distinguished body of men and women commenced their three-year task of drafting a charter of government for an infant nation four thousand years old, an Asian civilization moulded into a British pattern.

The scholars and statesmen, lawyers and politicians, who formed the Constituent Assembly included the outstanding names of India—then and now. A large number had recently emerged from British prisons. Mahatma Gandhi declined to participate in these deliberations, but his spirit was omnipresent. On Friday the Thirteenth (of December, 1946) Jawaharlal Nehru delivered the keynote address as he presented the Resolution on Aims and Objects. In it he summoned his colleagues to draft a constitution—

. . . wherein shall be guaranteed and secured to all the people of India justice, social, economic, and political; equality of status, of opportunity, and before the law; freedom of thought, expression, belief, faith, worship, vocation, association and action, subject to law and public morality.[2]

And he urged that this all-encompassing purpose might be, for every member of the Assembly, "a resolution . . . a declaration . . . a pledge . . . an undertaking . . . and I hope a dedication."[3]

The result proved to be an enormous document of 395 articles, plus eight additional "schedules" of definition and interpretation (with a ninth schedule and seven composite amendments totaling thirty-eight pages added in the first eight years). Based on the Government of India Act of 1935, this charter draws its emphasis on civil rights from Roman Catholic philosophy by way of the Eire Constitution (1922) and Republican Spain, its power of judicial review from the United States, its inclusion of economic goals from Soviet Russia, and surprisingly little or nothing from ancient Hindu law or culture.

In the debate on the Third Reading of the Draft Constitution, one speaker proudly declared that "the Adi Vakya (Preamble) contains the whole gist of the Constitution:" democracy, justice, liberty, equality, fraternity. He went on to claim that "in our country justice has always been given the first place. . . . All is of no worth without liberty. . . . No social structure can beget happiness without mutual love." [4] It is noteworthy, against the background of Hindu society, that he mentioned equality only in economic terms. Pandit Govind Malviya called for inclusion in the Preamble of some reference—

. . . to the Supreme Power which guides the destinies of the whole world. . . . I am certain that more than 90% of our people, if not more, will be staunch believers in God Almighty. . . . We shall be failing in our duty to our people and to our country whom we represent if we do not bring that into the Preamble. . . . The great point about our culture . . . our philosophy . . . our social structure has been that, while we have with complete tolerance allowed unmolested place in society to every school of thought . . . we have always had a strong and fervent belief in the Higher Power which guides us. [5]

When this proposal was defeated, when the name of the Supreme Being was deliberately omitted, Father Jerome D'Souza, a brilliant Jesuit scholar and social reformer, quoted the judgment of Mahatma Gandhi on a purely secular document: "You may keep out the Name, but you will not keep out the Thing from that Constitution." [6]

In such a study as this, an analysis of the entire Constitution would be impossible and inappropriate. But two highly controversial sections, Fundamental Rights and Directive Principles of State Policy, deserve examination and comment from an ethical perspective. B. R. Ambedkar, "outcaste" chairman of the Drafting Committee, referred to the Rights as "the most criticized part of the Draft Constitution." [7] Insisting that social democracy must go hand-in-hand with political democracy ("To divorce one from the other is to defeat the very purpose of democracy"), he charged that Indian society critically lacks two things—equality and fraternity—and that the new Constitution could only encourage, not create, these values. [8]

Fundamental Rights

A fundamental right is inviolable; that is, it may not be infringed by law or custom or usage or administrative order. On the other hand, it is not an absolute right, for the state must place limitations on its exercise in order to protect the equal rights of all. A constitutional analyst explains that "in a Welfare State with a socialistic pattern of society as the ideal, individual rights should, to some extent, be subordinated to the good of society and therefore the state as a whole." [9] Freedoms of speech, religion, the use of property and the like may be restricted for the public good, but whereas the United States has left to the courts the determination of necesary limits, the Constitution of India endeavors to spell out some of these qualifications. In the initial debate one delegate urged that this section should be entitled "Fundamental Rights and Obligations of the State and the Citizens," not only because his phrase more accurately represents the responsibility of government, but also because in terms of reciprocal duties "the Constitution seems to leave out completely the Obligation side of human behavior." [10]

When many sections of the United States are debating the validity of trespass laws as applied to private businesses, it is of interest to note the detailed assurances of the Indian Constitution:

ARTICLE 15: The State shall not discriminate against any citizen on grounds only of religion, race, caste, sex, place of birth or any of them. No citizen shall, on grounds only of religion, race, caste, sex, place of birth or any of them, be subject to any disability, liability, restriction or condition with regard to (a) access to shops, public restaurants, hotels and places of public entertainment; or (b) the use of wells, tanks, bathing ghats, roads and places of public resort maintained wholly or partly out of State funds or dedicated to the use of the general public.

However, this does not preclude religious discrimination at religious sites; such exclusion can be maintained—or rejected—only by the internal ethics of the faith itself. An attempt to specify areas "like schools, colleges, libraries, temples, hospitals, hotels, restaurants, theatres, concert halls, parks, gardens, museums, roads, wells, tanks, canals, bridges, posts and telegraphs, railways, tramways, bus services and the like was negatived." [11] This article also emphasized that it is not designed to prevent special concessions for women and children or (by the First Amendment of 1951) for socially and educationally backward classes or Scheduled (outcaste) Castes and Tribes. The same general provisions were directed toward equal opportunity for "any employment or office under the State."

Recognizing that India's social tradition required even more explicit revision, the Assembly adopted as Article 17 the assertion that " 'Untouchability' is abolished and its practice in any form is forbidden. The enforcement of any disability arising out of 'Untouchability' shall be an offense punishable in accordance with law." For many people this represents the most radical and sweeping assertion of the entire Constitution. To the complaint that the key word "untouchability" has been placed in quotation marks and never defined, the retort came short and sharp: "Indians and Hindus know what it is." [12] The need for special caste reservations (in employment, in government, and in education) was blamed on "the evil effects of foreign rule in our country," when opportunities for development had been denied for one hundred and fifty years. No one mentioned in this connection the inequalities and injustices of Hindu society over many centuries.

Nevertheless, a thrilling aspect of the debate proved to be the number of "untouchables" (outcastes or *Harijans*) who were delegates to the Assembly and who spoke appreciatively of this "liberation," which frees one sixth of the population from "perpetual subjugation and despair, perpetual humiliation and disgrace." [13] One such spokesman called for establishment of a special enforcement agency, but instead this was left to the Penal Code (notably the Untouchability Offences Act XXII of 1955) to "put teeth" into this constitutional protection. This law specifies that when discrimination can be shown against members of a Scheduled Caste, the presumption is warranted that the real ground is "untouchability." In the United States, on the contrary, the plaintiff in each individual case of segregation or denial of civil rights must prove beyond question that racial prejudice is the determining factor. And the Act of 1955 spells out six significant areas of enforcement:

(1) places of worship and prayers and ceremonial bathing must be open to all members of the same religion;

(2) access to all shops, restaurants, hotels, and places of entertainment is guaranteed, including the use of all equipment and facilities, in schools and hospitals, for example;

(3) no Indian, of whatever profession, may refuse goods or services to a customer on grounds of "untouchability";

(4) all watering places, burial grounds, sanitary conveniences, roads, etc., must be open to unsegregated use;

(5) all castes and classes must be free to ride on public conveyances and to construct, acquire, and occupy any residence;

(6) no social or religious custom, usage, ceremony, procession, or the like may discriminate on caste lines.[14]

However hotly the debate may rage between Indian and American *practice* of equality, the Indian laws are certainly more explicit and unequivocal.

In hailing this great emancipation—and the once-outcaste Drafting Committee chairman—Seth Govind Das, an able and ardent nationalist from Jabalpur, referred to Ambedkar as the Manu of the present age, adding: "If there be any one here who desires that the India of the Rigveda should exist again today in our country, such a one cherishes but a forlorn hope, a hope which can never be fulfilled."[15] Yet today Govind Das refuses to use English in public discourse, and in the Assembly debate he reminded his colleagues that India's civilization and culture must be preserved in the face of, and in spite of, such radical social change. Perhaps he recalled the words of another delegate nearly three years earlier: "I do not understand how you can abolish untouchability without abolishing the very caste system. Untouchability is nothing but the symptom of the disease, namely, the caste system."[16] Yet in Article 17 India boldly and explicitly renounced a social structure and a way of life thousands of years old. It took courage, faith and social conscience.

Article 17 deals with constitutional freedoms of speech, assembly, movement, residence, property ownership and occupation. Yet these are immediately qualified by safeguards on behalf of public order, morality, general interest or professional qualifications. Some Assemblymen felt that individual liberty had been sacrificed to social order. Others argued that "personal freedom has to be curtailed if the menace of capitalism . . . the parasitical class that thrives on profit and exploitation is to be liquidated and the communists are to be checked from endangering the safety and existence of all the institutions of our modern life." [17] The prevailing ideology was vigorously expressed in these words:

The doctrines of Mill and Spencer have become thoroughly unrelated to the needs and demands of the age. It is the society and not the individual which has become the object of primary concern and loyalty, both of political theorists and actual administrators. . . . Individual freedom is risky in a community where more than 80% of the people are sunk in the lowest depths of poverty, illiteracy, communalism, and provincialism.

This same speaker went on to voice a rejection of religion which sounds strange in India, and a confidence that collective society can preserve individual liberty: "It is only with the decline of the forces of organized religions, and the establishment of a world State based on the ideals of economic equality and political liberty that men will be able to achieve the content of personal freedom." [18]

In the Assembly debates some crucial particulars were probed. Would the "public interest" prohibit sweepers from leaving their jobs (as social custom still does in many villages)? Would begging or the selling of liquor, or even prostitution, deserve immunity under the "right of occupation"? Would "personal law" (i.e. sectarian religious practice) be curtailed by "public law and morality"? Does the right to hold property stand in the way of socialism? When the tumult subsided, T. T. Krishnamachari (later Finance Minister) summed up the sentiment of the Assembly thus:

There can be no absolute right and every right has got to be abridged in some manner. . . . Most of us envisage that the future will be . . . where the State is going to interfere more and more in the economic life of the people, not for the purpose of abridgment of rights of individuals, but for the purpose of bettering the lot of individuals. . . . The Drafting Committee has chosen the golden mean of providing . . . those rights that are considered essential for the individual, and at the same time . . . such checks . . . as will ensure that the State and the Constitution . . . will continue unhampered and flourish.[19]

Begar (forced labor without payment) and child labor (under the age of fourteen) are drastically restricted by Articles 23 and 24.

Delegates promptly began naming other types of involuntary service which might or might not be covered by these provisions: women in mines or on night shifts, prostitutes, *Harijans* who must immediately tan the leather when a cow dies, *devadasis* (the temple dancers, slaves and sometimes prostitutes) "which preserve our national art and music from time immemorial." [20] As several speakers pointed out, the victims of such exploitation as *begar* and child labor are the very ones who have neither financial resources nor influence to secure their rights under this constitutional protection.

The definition of religious freedom and the problem of religious education perplex the leaders of India as they do the people of many lands. Despite expressed resentment against certain methods of proselytizing, the majority in the Constituent Assembly agreed that religious liberty must include not only freedom of conscience (as in the Russian Constitution), but "the right freely to profess, practice, and propagate religion." These rights are subject, first of all, to "public order, morality and health and to the other provisions of this Part." They are subject, secondly, to sectarian definitions and explanations. The Sikh, Buddhist and Jain religions are placed explicitly under Hindu controls.

The question of religious instruction in a secular and pluralistic state was referred at least twice to subcommittees. A woman delegate declared that "education given by the State should have the teaching of moral and spiritual values; it cannot by the very nature of the State be of a denominational religious character." Another urged an amendment which would permit the teaching of "the elementary philosophy of comparative religions calculated to broaden the pupils' minds rather than such as will foster sectarian exclusiveness," but this was rejected as too fine a line to draw. Dr. Radhakrishnan, the future President, warned that denominational instruction would violate the principle of a secular state and that freedom to refuse religion must be protected along with freedom of religion.

In protesting such restrictions, a Muslim member of the Assembly charged that the Government would thus be set against religious instruction even for the Hindu majority. As Ambedkar summarized the debate, three positions emerged: (1) no religious instruction at all in any educational institution; (2) no such instruction in State-aided or supported schools; (3) full freedom of religious instruction but no compulsion to attend. The first group argued that "your educational institutions will be converted into a menagerie of faiths," that some teachers (especially dogmatic Muslims and Christians) would impose antisocial, divisive doctrines on their pupils. Those who took the second position pointed out that Article 27 relieves any person of paying taxes which are used "for the promotion or maintenance of any particular religion," but that a complete ban would violate the liberty guaranteed to minority groups. The third faction defended some form of religious training as essential for the welfare of society.

What is wanted for the stability of society as well as the State is moral grounding, moral background, and the only way to give this moral background is through religion . . . [if we want to avoid] all the distressing experiences of the West. (Muslim)

Not even members in charge of the Government have lost faith in religion. . . . We all believe in the existence of one God, in prayer, in meditation, and so on. We all believe in the ultimate surrender to Him and that by sacrifice and service alone can we hope to realize Godhead. (Hindu)

What is wrong with religion is not the religion itself but its wrong propagation or its propagation by inefficient or undesirable persons. Religion as such is the basis of all morality, all social and ethical values, and all human institutions. (Hindu)

The sacredness of the individual personality, the claims of his conscience, are . . . based upon a philosophy, an outlook on life, which are essentially spiritual. It is because we believe that the fullest and the most integral definition of democracy includes and is based upon this sacredness of the individual, of his personality and the claims of his conscience, that we have framed these rights. (Christian) [21]

With these affirmations of faith in religion, the drafters of a predominantly secular Constitution incorporated freedom to "profess, practise and propagate religion" (Article 25), to offer voluntary religious instruction in aided but not wholly State-supported schools (Article 28), and to operate sectarian institutions, with or without

State aid (Article 30). Even more significant, the Ministry of Education has asked a Christian agency to draft an eleven-year curriculum for moral instruction in the Indian schools.

Directive Principles of State Policy

The Fundamental Rights discussed above reveal some of the tension and ambiguity which characterize the Indian mind as it moves from an ancient, spiritual tradition into a modern, secular society. Even more is this true of the Directive Principles. Ambedkar described them as an Instrument of Instructions to whatever government is in power.[22] Prime Minister Nehru made this distinction: "The Directive Principles of State Policy represent a dynamic move towards a certain objective. The Fundamental Rights represent something static, to preserve certain rights which exist."[23] And K. M. Munshi observes, with a hint of disapproval: "The doctrine which dominates at present, therefore, is that the justiciable rights must subserve the swift realization of the directive principles."[24]

To those who dismiss these articles as "pious declarations without binding force," the Constitution specifies clearly that they "shall not be enforceable by any court but . . . are nonetheless fundamental in the governance of the country and it shall be the duty of the State to apply these principles in making laws" (Article 37). Officials insist that these goals do stand as guideposts and standards against which government agencies do actually measure their policies and programs. In reality they are steps toward the full implementation of the Preamble, "middle axioms" expressing "the hopes and aspirations of those who framed it."

There are sixteen of these in the Constitution, much briefer than the Fundamental Rights, since, being nonjusticable, they need no reservations. When the future Prime Minister Jawaharlal Nehru addressed the Constituent Assembly on its Aims and Objects, he had frankly declared: "I stand for Socialism, and I hope India will stand for Socialism and that India will go toward the Constitution of a Socialist State, and I do believe that the whole world will have to go that way."[25] Despite such pressure, the pluralistic Assembly refused to commit the Constitution to any single economic system.

Article 38 seeks, "for the welfare of the people . . . a social order in which justice, social, economic and political, shall inform all the institutions of the national life." On the whole, Indian socialism—like its British sources a half century ago—has shown greater concern for socialistic distribution of wealth than for socialistic production.

The following article looks *toward* the time, but does not guarantee, that all citizens shall have an adequate means of livelihood, equal pay for equal work, protection of health and of children. More broadly it seeks a society in which "the ownership and control of the material resources of the community are so distributed as best to subserve the common good . . . [and in which] the operation of the economic system does not result in the concentration of wealth and mean of production to the common detriment." To those who charged that this article involved a socialist state, Ambedkar replied that "our ideal is economic democracy," but that such a goal could be attained by individualism, socialism or communism.

India's Constituent Assembly raised no ideological opposition whatever to such "social security" goals as the right to work, universal education, insurance benefits for unemployment, old age, sickness, and "other cases of undeserved want." The country may wait a long time for the capital resources and administrative machinery necessary. The State shall also endeavor to secure, "by suitable legislation or economic organization or in any other way," a living wage, a decent standard of life and full enjoyment of leisure and social and cultural opportunities.

In most countries the aim of a uniform civil code would be taken for granted. Not so in the United States, which seeks to preserve a modicum of states' rights. Not so in India, where the conflict is religious rather than political or regional. Muslims in particular, whose social as well as religious life is regulated by Islamic law, remain fearful that any revision of the pluralistic pattern accepted by the British will in fact jeopardize their "personal laws." For example, a Muslim pointed out that Hindus regard marriage as a sacrament, Europeans as a status (!), and Muslims as a contract according to the Quran. Others protested a uniform code in the following terms:

People seem to think that under a secular State, there must be a common law observed by its citizens in all matters, including matters of their daily life, their language, their culture, their personal laws. That is not the correct way to look at this secular State. In a secular State, citizens belonging to different communities must have the freedom to practice their own religion, observe their own life, and their personal laws should be applied to them. . . .

What is the purpose served by this uniformity except to murder the consciences of the people and make them feel that they are being trampled upon as regards their religious rights and practices? . . . In a democracy, as I take it, it is the duty of the majority to secure the sacred rights of every member.[26]

The issue, still so crucial in Indian life, drew forth a vigorous rebuttal from K. M. Munshi, who argued that rights of inheritance, marriage laws and so forth should *not* be included under religious freedom or "personal law."

. . . We are in a stage where we must unify and consolidate the nation by every means without interfering with religious practices. If, however, the religious practices of the past have been so construed as to cover the whole field of life, we have reached a point where we must put our foot down and say that these matters are not religion, they are purely matters for secular legislation. . . . Religion must be restricted to spheres which legitimately appertain to religion.[27]

Only because these provisions are Directive Principles and not fundamental laws could the majority have overridden Muslim protests, amid charges that the Congress Whip had coerced party votes. What was significant is the fact that so soon after the bitter bloodshed of 1947 Muslims could freely voice their communal concerns.

The goal of free and compulsory schooling for all children through fourteen years of age was far from achievement at the end of ten years, and the date was extended another decade to 1970. Not only will such universal education demand enormous expenditures beyond the power of India today, but a roughly estimated increase of 500,000 qualified teachers. Yet hopeless as the task may appear, its undeniable importance and the admirable progress already made would suggest that this might well represent a worthy project for foreign aid.

To the article calling for higher nutritional levels and the improvement of public health, the Assembly added a clause in favor of prohibition, "except for medicinal purposes, of intoxicating drinks and of drugs which are injurious to health." The transcript of debates covers fourteen pages, as compared with two on education. Advocates of prohibition argued that the national economy would save four times what liquor revenue might produce, that individual liberty should not include the freedom to commit suicide or destroy the moral sense, that suttee and human sacrifice had been abolished by law, and that Americans "have gone on too long imbibing the poison, and it is too late for them to go back." One delegate quoted K. C. Sen, nineteenth-century leader of the Brahmo Samaj, as having once said that the two great gifts of the British to India were the Bible and the bottle, that the Bible was such a great book the country as a whole would have put faith in it if the British had not brought the bottle too.

Earnest Gandhians insisted that prohibition was the Mahatma's great legacy to his people and must not be surrendered. Another speaker replied that Gandhi wanted individuals to find the truth for themselves, not follow blindly in the path of restrictive legislation. "The essence of Gandhism," he said, "is love, toleration; its essence is non-violence, search for truth and all these important things. The externals of Gandhism or the outward trappings of Gandhism are *khaddar* (homespun cloth) and prohibition." On the Third Reading of the Draft Constitution months later, Frank Anthony, leader of the Anglo-Indian community, added a question popular among American segregationists today: "Can you create morality through legislation?" Although certain states and cities have adopted "dry laws" restricting importation and sale, these are frequently ignored, and copious exemptions or evasions are available for foreign residents and those in Western-educated society.

Similarly, under the aim of improving agriculture and animal husbandry the Assembly added the goal of "prohibiting the slaughter of cows and calves and other milch draught cattle." Again the debate clearly revealed the schizophrenic temper of modern India in doing homage—not to the "sacred cow" but to the emotional pedestal on which the cow stands. Not merely a harmless religious prejudice, cow protection has become in a poverty-stricken land a costly economic burden, even a social and hygienic problem. Estimates number Indian cattle at 200,000,000, one-half of the human population. An Assembly speaker reported that where India has fifty cows per hundred people, America has seventy-one and New Zealand a hundred and fifty. This comparison fails to consider, however, the relative quality or the consumption of beef in the West, whereas a shockingly high proportion of Indian cattle are of no economic value, even as draught animals. It has been claimed that India has more "rest homes" and benevolent associations for cows than for persons.[28]

Difficult though it is for Western readers to comprehend, the fervor of the Hindu position must be recognized.

The cow is the symbol of that oneness of life (summed up in *ahimsa*). . . . The killing of the learned man, the scientist, the philosopher or the sage, and the killing of the cow are on a par. The cow takes precedence over the children of the family, because she is the mother of the individual, she is the mother of the nation. . . .

It is not the crumbs, the loaves and fishes that we are fighting for. [!] . . . We want that India should declare today that the whole human world as well as the whole animal world is free today and will be protected.[29]

A shrewd debater explained that this clause should not be misconstrued as bestowing any special privilege on the cow. Rather, as protecting one's mother is not primarily the right of the mother but one's own right to protect his mother, so this article affirms India's right to protect the cow—or the peepul tree, or the peacock, or the *shaliagram* (touchstone). The debate exposed a high degree of national and communal pride and defensiveness, the more so when Hindus, defending their right to protect the cow on religious grounds, held that the Muslim sacrifice of cows on the festival of Bakrid was *not* a required ritual.

The economic theme was played heavily also. How could India improve its health without milk and grain, without the manure and labor and nourishment obtained from cattle? A learned professor claimed that one half the nation's income is derived from cattle wealth, that the manure alone is worth more than the total cost of upkeep. He began his statement with the conviction that "religion itself sanctifies what is economically good." Claims that 90 per cent of currently useless cattle could be salvaged by proper feeding and treatment were interspersed with reverent references to Kam-Dehmi (the legendary Cow-Mother, "fulfiller of all wants") and to Krishna, the most beloved Hindu deity, who spent his amorous youth as a cowherd with thousands of milkmaids.

When the article came up for its Third Reading, proponents reiterated that "it is a religious sentiment that the cow must be preserved," and that cow killing should have been made a crime (presumably under Fundamental Rights instead of Directive Principles). Ironically, the Assembly which spent thirteen pages (of recorded debates) [30] seeking to protect the nation's cows had required but two pages to decide that India could *not,* in its present condition, dispense with capital punishment for humans, since "society does not consist of unmixed good elements only." [31] Then Frank Anthony arose to assert courageously that religious protection of the cow might be tolerable for a predominantly Hindu land, but that any economic justification should be recognized as an indirect, hypocritical afterthought (another delegate called it "subterfuge"). In a nation which has the largest cattle population in the world *and* the lowest per capita milch and draught output, Anthony said, "the preservation of cattle wealth and the preservation of the best interests of the country would have required not the banning of cattle slaughtering, but the slaughtering of over half of your present cattle population in this country." [32] Mr. Anthony was outvoted.

The final article of the Directive Principles seeks, as one delegate put it, "to embody the characteristics of the Gandhian ideology" in international affairs. To another, it represents "the mighty intellectual and moral influence of a Tagore and a Gandhi, who taught nothing short of international amity"; thus it serves notice to the world that "we belong to no bloc."

ARTICLE 51: The State shall endeavour to—(a) promote international peace and security; (b) maintain just and honourable relations between nations; (c) foster respect for international law and treaty obligations in the dealings of organized peoples with one another; (d) encourage settlement of international disputes by arbitration.

In further elaboration of this point, B. H. Khardekar proposed a more specific confrontation of the giants in the Cold War:

Those who are friends of all sometimes have no friend at all. . . . To Russia we may and should say, 'We accept and we appreciate your aims and ideals, but your means are rather crude; sometimes they are very doubtful.' To England and to America, we must say: 'We have very many misgivings about your aims and ideals. Your means are very very polished, very very civilised.' [33]

When the Assembly moved the addition of the fourth clause regarding international arbitration, only one serious objection was raised. Perhaps conscious of India's reluctance to submit the Kashmir dispute to arbitration or to plebiscite, one member warned that such a device often proves dishonest, weighted and unacceptable. "Sir, I prefer war in such a case," he affirmed. But Article 51, with the addition of Clause (d), stands as the Constitutional basis for India's highly debated neutralism, and for the *Panchshila* (Five Principles) adopted by the Afro-Asian Conference at Bandung. That it was disregarded in Goa in 1961, and apparently in regard to Kashmir, reveals the triumph of *realpolitik,* of impatience and emotions, over Gandhian idealism.

Admittedly the Fundamental Rights of the individual are often circumscribed by the State in the Indian Constitution. Admittedly many Directive Principles of State Policy lack the general will for implementation, as well as the financial resources required. In his first presentation of the Draft Constitution, Ambedkar had said that India needed to cultivate "constitutional morality" because its people do have a reverence for forms and authority. "Democracy in India," he said, "is only a top-dressing on Indian soil, which is essentially undemocratic." [34] He spoke as an "outcaste" who had risen to the top of the legal profession, who knew both the misery of India's traditional social structure and the importance of law—and morality—in overcoming that heritage of discrimination.

No document will of itself create social change. In summing up the achievements of the Consituent Assembly, its chairman, Rajendra Prasad, declared: "It is not possible to devise any yard-stick for measuring the moral qualities of a man, and so long as that is not possible, our Constitution will remain defective." Yet the country must move forward boldly in its democratic experiment, he concluded, "with confidence, with truth and non-violence, and above all with heart within and God over head." [35] In this spirit and with this faith, the Constitution of India stands as a beacon for Asia and the world. Whatever their deficiencies, the inclusion of twenty-four Fundamental Rights and sixteen Directive Principles of State Policy has served notice to all peoples that democratic India has a social conscience, and intends to fulfill these goals to the best of her ability.

Chapter X

Jawaharlal Nehru: Scientific Humanism

"Someone has said that Nehru is by birth a Hindu, by culture a Muslim, by ethics a Christian, but still an avowed pagan. He is the great man of India today." [1] The first quadruple statement may be a provocative, inaccurate generalization; the second sentence—despite his death—is likely to be incontrovertible for many years to come. The world will remember Jawaharlal Nehru as an influential statesman, sometimes a bit aloof, making pronouncements on international affairs which often seemed to disregard not only logic but the ethics they claimed to serve. Residents of New Delhi—and millions of India's peasant masses—knew him as a ubiquitous (and seemingly omniscient) personage of indescribable charm.

Born on November 14, 1889, the son of a well-to-do Brahmin lawyer in Allahabad, Jawaharlal had every educational advantage. An Irish tutor, F. T. Brooks, instilled in him an early appreciation of Western literature and science. Impressed by this Theosophist teacher and the speeches of Annie Besant, young Nehru joined the Theosophical Society at the age of thirteen, but soon lost interest—

though much later he was to work with Mrs. Besant in the Home Rule League and the All-India Congress Committee. In 1904 Jawaharlal, not quite fifteen, sailed for Harrow School in England, where he spent three years before going up to Cambridge. These were days of nationalistic fervor, even among Indian students in England, most of whom (as Nehru himself observed) were "Tilakites or Extremists." Jawaharlal studied natural science and law, was admitted to the London bar in 1912, and returned immediately to India.

He carried with him more than a Cantabrigian degree and a license for the bar. In England he had absorbed the Fabian Socialism of Sidney and Beatrice Webb, a position which demanded social and economic as well as political freedom. He began friendships with Labor Party leaders which continued right up to his death. Above all, he developed a humanistic outlook clearly reflecting a Western orientation, yet rooted in Eastern faith and intuition more than scientific observation and experiment. Thirty years later, in prison, he described this unwavering perspective as follows: "The modern mind, that is to say the better type of modern mind, is practical and pragmatic, ethical and social, altruistic and humanitarian. It is governed by a practical idealism for social betterment. Humanity is its God and social service its religion." [2]

By 1918 Nehru had become secretary of the Home Rule League and converted his father, Motilal, to the independence movement. By 1923, after serving the first of nine terms in British jails in India, he became secretary of the All-India Congress Committee, and was to preside at least five times over the Indian National Congress. At the end of the Second World War he emerged from his longest term of imprisonment, mostly in his own home town, to assume unquestioned political leadership in the final phase of the Independence struggle: as Vice-President and Member for External Affairs in the Interim Government of 1946, and then as Prime Minister and Minister for External Affairs and Commonwealth Relations. Occasional efforts to step down from office provoked nation-wide protest, as friend and foe alike trembled to think of India without Panditji (the affectionate term for Beloved Sage). Apparently Nehru himself became convinced that no one else could inspire India to that unity and strength so vital during that time of crisis. When Pandit Pant died in 1961, the subordinate struggle for power was resolved by the appointment of two Deputy Prime Ministers. Yet Indians themselves frequently quoted, with undisguised concern, the ancient proverb that no new plant life grows in the shade of a giant banyan tree.

"By birth a Hindu." A Brahmin remains a Brahmin, even in modern India, especially when that title signifies educational and financial privilege, as well as social status. The fact that the Nehru family claims roots in Kashmir three centuries or more ago undoubtedly accounted for Jawaharlal's stubborn refusal to accept arbitration or a plebiscite in that incomparable paradise. Whatever the legal, political and military facts may be (and they appear to many observers the obverse of Hyderabad, where a Hindu population under Muslim rulers acceded to India under pressure), some Indians acknowledge that Nehru's feeling for justice, logic and negotiation were all obscured by emotion when it came to Kashmir. Likewise, whatever the Western-educated rationalist-humanist might have believed about the unscientific nature of caste and its damage to political unity, the Brahmin could not escape a consciousness of being "born to the purple." When one stood in the presence of Pandit Nehru—gracious, intelligent, cultured, poised—and realized that "philosopher-kings" are born as well as made, whether they were "born of the spirit" or of a regal caste became an insignificant, semantic question.

Nevertheless, it is difficult for any non-Indian to define what it means to be "by birth a Hindu." Some Westerners identify Hinduism with the social structure, but millions of modern Indians reject caste discriminations, yet proudly claim to be Hindus. Peoples of the subcontinent have intermingled for too many centuries to retain racial lines of Hinduism. With forty million Muslims, ten million Christians, ten million Sikhs and numerous other sects and tribal groups within the country, "Hindu" cannot be equated with Indian nationhood, though Buddhists and Jains are becoming absorbed constitutionally into Hinduism under the present secular state. Any effort to describe a religion of the Hindus encounters so many contradictions and obfuscations that it appears meaningless. Nehru himself wrote: "Hinduism, as a faith, is vague, amorphous, many-sided, all things to all men. It is hardly possible to define it, or indeed to say definitely whether it is a religion or not. . . . It embraces many beliefs and practices from the highest to the lowest, often opposed to or contradicting each other." [3]

Probably not even Nehru knew what it meant to call him a Hindu. If—as capital gossip reported—the Prime Minister still stood on his head ten minutes a day at the age of seventy, and invited his personal *yogi* to the airport when President Eisenhower departed, he was probably more interested in physical benefits than spiritual. In his understanding of Hindu philosophy he emphatically rejected other-worldliness, the concept of *maya* as illusion, the negation of life. He never went to a Hindu temple, unless it were for some civil occasion. Pyarelal Nayar stated bluntly that the Prime Minister was not a man of prayer. And Nehru himself remarked, in a conversation about "dogmas of religion" (which he abhorred):

Fortunately Indian thought, philosophy, can be easily separated from the superstitious and dogmatic part. They are not inextricably intertwined, though for many people they might be. It is not as if you must accept a basic dogma if you are to remain true to your faith. No such thing in India. You can discard every dogma and yet be true to your religion.[4]

"By culture a Muslim." Islam was—and still is—numerically, culturally, and politically strong in the vicinity of Allahabad. Nehru received a broad and tolerant education. Across the plains of northern India stretch the masterpieces of Mogul architecture: the Taj Mahal, the Red Fort, Humayun's Tomb, Fatehpur Sikri—a Muslim heritage which has become an Indian heritage to all but the most bigoted Hindus. Nehru's deepest appreciation for Muslim culture—as an integral part of India's culture—apparently came in prison during World War II, when his "discovery of India" included the wise and patient guidance of Maulana Abul Kalam Azad, later to serve as Nehru's Minister of Education. Yet the Prime Minister said he did not understand the terms "Hindu culture and Muslim culture and Christian culture" as applied to the influence of religious movement. "If I look at India," he wrote, "I find the gradual growth of a composite culture of the Indian people."[5]

Neither the environment nor the historical insights of Azad

could give Panditji an appreciation of Islam sufficient to overcome his political prejudices. For Nehru, the secular humanist, religious divisions were important only as they threatened—and ultimately destroyed—the unity of India, and "personal laws" pertaining to religious groups should be transcended by universal civil laws. Rightly or wrongly, Azad charged in his posthumously published memoirs, *India Wins Freedom,* that the impatience and stubbornness and misunderstanding of Nehru helped to force the tragic partition of India and Pakistan. Likewise, in a personal interview Vice-Chancellor Mujeeb, speaking for millions of "national Muslims" who chose to remain in India, regretted that the Prime Minister had utterly failed to appreciate the religious problem or mitigate the dangers of increasing communalism because he saw the issue only in political, rather than personal terms.

Nehru is so completely a secular person that he does not want to hear of these things. Gandhi was different. He wanted to hear about points of view that rational people will ignore. Panditji is temperamentally incapable of treating this as a problem worthy of attention.[6]

"By ethics a Christian." That is the most extreme distortion in the glib generalization which introduces this chapter. For Jawaharlal was in no conscious sense a Christian, and to give that label to his lofty moral integrity does even greater injustice to Hinduism than in the case of Gandhi or Radhakrishnan, both of whom acknowledge the saintliness and ethical superiority of Jesus Christ and would even concede his divinity in the Hindu sense in which all good men are divine. Nehru would not go that far. Asked point blank about Louis Fischer's statement that the Prime Minister had said in 1948 he was drawing closer to Buddha and Christ,[7] Panditji laughed—that quick, boyish laugh which displayed his irresistible charm. "Did I say that?" he retorted. Then the smile faded to sober thoughtfulness as he replied:

Buddha has always appealed to me. Christ has appealed in a somewhat different way, as a very magnificent person. Buddha appeals to me in that way—plus: his thoroughly undogmatic way of approaching questions, his almost scientific way; and his normal advice to his followers was: "Don't accept anything that I say. Experiment. Find out for yourselves." [8]

Reading between the lines, one can discern at least three typical emphases. First is the adroit evasion of the influence of Christ, the shift to the more familiar, more tolerant, more Indian Buddha. Second is the deep, underlying resentment of most Hindus against dogmatic, exclusive, arrogant claims of Christianity. Third is the insistence on a rationalistic, scientific approach even to spiritual questions. When the probing was put another way, Nehru's answer varied little if any. Does his own sense of ethics come from European philosophers or from Hinduism? "I don't know," he responded candidly.

I can't say about European philosophers, but in regard to the Indian roots, I am attracted to the Vedanta philosophy of the Hindus. If you ask me to give you an account of it, I might find it difficult. . . . In my mind it is some kind of a scientific approach; it is an approach which tries to appeal towards reason—not normal reason, but reason you can get by further experience.

Again the dismissal of European as well as Christian sources, whether from a dislike of metaphysical debate or from a reluctance to acknowledge Western influence. Again the "retreat" to the safer ground of Indian values. Again the rapid transition from religious to scientific and rational norms.

In *The Discovery of India* Nehru expressed interest in Reinhold Niebuhr's *Moral Man and Immoral Society,* which he read during his last and longest prison term. "That book interested me greatly," he said, "because it put rather concisely some problems which very greatly were troubling me." What problems, specifically? The frank and heart-wrung confession revealed the greatness of Nehru's soul and the sensitivity that distinguishes a statesman from a mere politician:

The major problem that I have had to deal with—or any person in a position of authority or leadership—is not his own problem (though that is there) but how to make others function. The conflict between the morality of the individual and how the same individual in the mass tends to become very much less moral. It shocks me how good people as individuals behave very badly in the mass, as a group.

In other words, Nehru was impressed by the Niebuhrian concern for a universal problem of human nature. He made no reference to a Christian solution. If "by ethics a Christian" one refers to "human conduct as determined by divine conduct" (Emil Brunner) revealed in Jesus as the Son of God, this Nehru would never admit. If one implies *simply* the humanistic dignity and equality of man, as proclaimed in the Enlightenment and professed in democracy, this clearly represents an inadequate concept of Christian ethics.

"But still an avowed pagan." In defining this phrase, and in seeking for the ethical heritage of Jawaharlal Nehru, it is necessary to look more closely at the affirmative stance, and particularly at his attitude toward the master of political morality, Mahatma Gandhi. In response to personal praise for the Prime Minister's practice of ethics in politics, he explained modestly: "After all, after about thirty years [the association] with Mr. Gandhi has produced that powerful impression upon me and moulded my general reactions to life." The primary conviction which Gandhiji left with Nehru might be simply put as the relevance, the necessity, of morality in political life. The second fundamental lesson the Prime Minister expressed in these words:

I think if one can put his (Gandhiji's) basic contribution—though I hesitate to do so—it is a question of means and ends. You should never adopt wrong means to attain even what you consider desirable ends. Gandhi, even more than the old philosophers, believed in detachment: to work hard with an objective, yet not to be swept away by it.

But Nehru was not temperamentally fitted for detachment. He differed strenuously with the Mahatma on numerous practical and theoretical issues. He could neither appreciate nor fully understand asceticism and mysticism. He believed that Gandhiji's rejection of industrialism, science and technology would be as absurd as it would be disastrous to India's progress. Even where he accepted Gandhi's program—of civil disobedience, the use of the spinning-wheel, decentralization of industry—his motive was invariably pragmatic, a conviction of strategic effectiveness, rather than spiritual value. As Husain wrote in his comparison of the two men: "Religion and morality do not have the same place in their scheme of things. For Gandhiji they are the whole of life, for Nehru only a part, though a very important part. . . . Gandhiji represents the religious mind and Nehru the secular mind of India." [9]

More specifically, however, Panditji distrusted the consequences of religion—in the narrow sense which he more often used. For one thing, he believed that "religious outlook does not help, and even hinders, the moral and spiritual progress of the people . . . [because] the religious man is concerned far more with his own salvation than with the good of society." [10] Secondly, he regarded religion as "the enemy of clear thought, for it is based not only on the acceptance without demur of certain unalterable theories and dogmas, but also on sentiment and emotion and passion." [11] Furthermore, Nehru feared that the religious emphasis, however universal and ethical it might be in Gandhiji, could easily intensify reactionary revivalism among the masses[12] and thus jeopardize India's hard-won unity and freedom. Finally, he doubted the sincerity and efficacy of *maulvis, priests, swamis*, and so on, whose vested interests he felt would tend to dominate their social concern. When even the Mahatma seemed diverted from his political goal by moralistic considerations, as in the fast of 1932, Nehru grew angry and impatient, and denied that the nation could ever be trained—or freed—by pious faith in God.[13]

Like many an adherent of other religions—or none—Nehru was clearer about what religion is *not* than what it *is*. It is not belief in any personal deity. "What the mysterious is I do not know. I do not call it God because God has come to mean much that I do not believe in. I find myself incapable of thinking of a deity or of any unknown supreme power in anthropomorphic terms, and . . . any idea of a personal God seems very odd to me." [14] It is not belief in immortality. "Essentially I am interested in this world, in this life, not in some other world or a future life. Whether there is such a thing as a soul, or whether there is a survival after death or not, I do not know; and important as these questions are, they do not trouble me in the least." [15] Religion is not prayer or temple attendance; these would be as unscientific and superstitious for Nehru as for a confirmed Marxist. It is not traditional dogmas: *atman, karma,* future life, reincarnation. In his later years (of war-time imprisonment) he expressed himself as "favorably disposed" toward these ideas as assumptions or intellectual speculations, but "they do not affect my life," he declared.[16]

Those who made any of these beliefs into absolute creeds became sectarian and hence divisive, in Nehru's view. The true inner spiritual values could not be imposed on another individual or on society, though they should motivate each genuinely "religious" person. The most we can say, from an orthodox standpoint, is that Jawaharlal was a man of *dharma,* and this traditional Hindu concept he defined in an inclusive manner:

Dharma really means something more than religion. It is from a root word which means to hold together; it is the inmost constitution of a thing, the law of its inner being. It is an ethical concept which includes the moral code, righteousness, and the whole range of man's duties and responsibilities.[17]

What, then, were the Prime Minister's social ethics? They rested primarily on humanism. "No," he declared in *The Discovery of India,* "one may not lose faith in Man. God we may deny, but what hope is there for us if we deny Man and thus reduce everything to futility." [18] His ethics rested, secondly, on man within the group. Admitting that in the Vedas "probably the ethic of individual perfection was overemphasized and hence the social outlook suffered," Nehru preferred to quote the *Mahabharata* to the effect that "the whole world of mortals is an interdependent organism." [19] Later in the same volume he discussed the fascinating paradox that Indian metaphysics has been predominantly individualistic, a search for inner perfection and personal salvation from the cycle of rebirth, while the Indian social philosophy has been primarily communal, concerned almost exclusively with relationships and duties toward the group.[20]

But that very individualism led them [Hindus] to attach little importance to the social aspect of man, of man's duty to society. For each person life was divided and fixed up, a bundle of duties and responsibilities within his narrow sphere in the graded hierarchy. He had no duty to, or conception of, society as a whole, and no attempt was made to make him feel his solidarity with it. This idea is perhaps largely a modern development, and cannot be found in any ancient society. It is unreasonable, therefore, to expect it in ancient India. Still the emphasis on individualism, or exclusiveness, or graded castes is much more evident in India.[21]

It is significant that Nehru went on to give religion credit for keeping windows open for the individual soul through centuries of communal conformity and social pressure. Not only because "religious thought and spiritual seeking have always emphasized the individual," but also because the outstanding critics of caste and other social evils were usually religious reformers, Panditji paid tribute to this moral and spiritual purification. But he too, like social philosophers of the West, confronted the dilemma of the individual versus society, with all its ramifications. If R. H. Tawney and Max Weber are correct, Protestantism has given rise to the spirit of capitalism and free enterprise, the maximum rights of the individual. Democracy, too, implies the freedom of each person—or at least the equal rights of each citizen. Socialism, on the other hand, represents the collective good, ownership of productive property by the community, service for the general welfare rather than the profit motive.

Yet here is Prime Minister Nehru, trying to reconcile individualistic and collective elements in Indian tradition in order to build a socialistic democracy in the modern world. No wonder he said: "The conflict is between two approaches to the problem of social organization which are diametrically opposed to each other: the old Hindu conception of the group being the basic unit of organization, and the excessive individualism of the West, emphasizing the individual above the group." [22] These approaches may be "diametrically opposed" but they are also inseparable. One may say, with some oversimplification, that early Christendom sought individual salvation through the corporate agency of the Church, as Hinduism sought individual salvation through the social cohesiveness of caste and family. But subsequently Protestantism and rationalism have swung half circle to lift up the individual as the basic unity of society, while at the same time reconstructing collective theories of nationalism, the Church, communism, group dynamics, socialism, organization man, world brotherhood. In a speech in January 1956, Nehru declared: "How to reconcile this inevitable centralization with individual freedom is the problem of modern civilization." [23]

In economic terms India has made a clear-cut choice for social-ism—although its ideological base is now being challenged by the Swatantra Party. What has emerged in the past seventeen years is obviously a "mixed economy" in which the Private Sector retains control over certain industries, while others are reserved exclusively for the Public Sector. In firm contrast to Mahatma Gandhi—and to Jayaprakash Narayan and other Sarvodayans today—Nehru not only believed in the necessity for rapid industrialization in India, but he rejected the notion that this process could emerge from the "grass roots" of *panchayat-raj* (local self-government).

Furthermore, he differed from many Western socialists—and here came closer to Communist practice—in resisting the growth of trade unions and other independent organs within society. Pre-sumably the Prime Minister felt that such pluralism weakened the body politic and delayed the achievement of state socialism. There is no question but what Jawaharlal had subjected Marxism to crit-ical examination. "The theory and philosophy of Marxism light-ened up many a dark corner of my mind," he wrote.[24] He admired Marx's social insights, if not his moral values. But he instinctively rejected not only the dogmatism and regimentation of Commu-nism, but also what he considered metaphysical and pseudo-scien-tific. Here was a mind, as he himself admitted, "too much influenced by the humanist liberal tradition to get out of it completely."

Our final aim can only be a classless society with equal economic justice and opportunity for all, a society organized on a planned basis for raising of mankind to higher material and cultural levels, to a cul-tivation of spiritual values, of cooperation, unselfishness, the spirit of service, the desire to do right, goodwill and love—ultimately a world order.[25]

As Husain notes, this was the glorious goal of *Ramrajya* (the Kingdom of God) without the high standard of *ahimsa* (nonvio-lence). For Nehru acknowledged, as Gandhi did not (though his nonviolent methods included many forms of coercion), that in a world like this some pressures are needed to achieve even the most lofty aims. Where the Mahatma possessed boundless faith in the goodness of man, the Prime Minister (with or without the influence of Reinhold Niebuhr) knew that man's tendency to abuse his most precious freedoms requires restrictions, restraints and sometimes forceful controls. A wise statesman, Anup Singh (member of the upper house in Parliament, spokesman for India in Washington during World War II, representative of the United Nations in Korea), commented simply: "Gandhi's role ended as soon as India was free." [26] In other words, the spiritual leadership which had won Independence must yield to pragmatic programs for the government of a modern, industrialized state.

The most conspicuous test of Nehru's ethics was in the realm of foreign policy. Here he was most often misunderstood and maligned in the West, yet here he achieved and maintained his leadership of the uncommitted nations in the East. The *Panchshila* (Five Principles) of neutralism first appeared in the preamble to the Sino-Indian agreement on trade with Tibet in April 1954, and were reiterated in a joint statement by Nehru and Chou En-lai two months later. Briefly summarized, they include: mutual respect for each other's territory and sovereignty, nonaggression, noninterference in each other's internal affairs, equality and mutual advantage, peaceful coexistence and economic cooperation. Their adoption by the Bandung Conference of Afro-Asian nations at the end of that year gave added strength to their inherent moral value. The irony of Chinese Communist repression in Tibet and incursions over the Indian border led many cynics to conclude that *Panchshila* had been shattered beyond recognition. But one of the characteristics of Hindu detachment is that practical failure does not nullify morality.

Nehru, the realistic statesman, recognized the political and military threat which hung over the Himalayas. Although he must have known the circumstances for months or even years, he was obviously cut to the quick when the full extent of Chinese occupation of Indian territory was first revealed to the nation and the world in 1959. Not only his neighbors but his Five Principles had seemingly betrayed him. Hostile critics—in India as well as the West—accused him of cowardice for not trying to regain occupied terrain by military force. Nehru was no more of a coward than Mahatma

Gandhi. But he did have the political responsibility of trying to maintain a *modus vivendi* with Communist China. Furthermore, he realized full well that a minor skirmish or even a major mobilization could be the decisive straw that broke the back of India's hard-won but precarious economic progress. "Peace is our passion," he said on his arrival in Washington on November 7, 1961, "essential for our growth." When critics urged him to join the military alliance of SEATO or to risk major war in the confidence that Great Britain and the United States would have to come to India's aid even without a treaty, Panditji knew that this too would be ruinous to his country's unity, economy, freedom and spirit. "Just when you are in reach—not of heaven, but of a much better world," he told the Indian Council of World Affairs on April 5, 1960, there emerge new problems and the threat of atomic annihilation. "It is not a pleasant thought that indefinitely this frontier is likely to be a dangerous frontier—for either country." In the same speech he went on to assert the Gandhian approach in these words:

While you must never give in to what you consider wrong, you do not think wrong of the wrong-doer. . . . It may be an idealistic way of approaching world problems, and yet this is not only an idealistic way, but in the circumstances of the world today, I would submit, the only practical way. . . . It avoids the closing of doors, no matter how much we may be angry. . . . It was not a policy—as some people would criticize—of weakness or of bargaining. . . . It doesn't involve surrendering any vital interest.

The West, so little concerned about India's own moral or territorial problems, sharply criticized the Prime Minister for his stand on numerous international issues. Nehru was quick to condemn British and French attacks in the Suez area, extremely mild and belated in deploring Russian intervention in Hungary. The Western world was surprised and shocked that Nehru (and the other uncommitted nations meeting in Belgrade) merely expressed "surprise and shock" at Russia's resumption of atomic testing in the atmosphere instead of adopting a strenuous denunciation. This may be due to caution. It also can be argued with some justification that India judges the United States more harshly than Russia precisely because she expects a higher degree of morality from the

West than from the Soviet Union. Furthermore it is natural for newly independent nations of Asia and Africa to fear a return at least of economic and military colonialism by European powers who have ruled them in the past, more than they fear a still uncertain Communist domination. Yet Nehru spoke frankly of "old imperialisms and new imperialisms coming into the picture." (At the same time his government dealt firmly with domestic disorder and subversion, so that it has been said India has more Communists in prison than any other country—except the Soviet Union!)

Behind these practical, realistic motives, Panditji still leaned on the ethics of Mahatma Gandhi. "There is no possibility of solving the world's problems by threats or coercion or war," he told the Indian Council of World Affairs. This area of foreign policy highlights the dialectic tension that was so characteristic of the Prime Minister. In a "Critical Look at the New Neutralism" [27] Hans Morgenthau identified Nehru as "the most eminent champion" of a type of neutralism which he calls "moral indifference." Even after the invasion of Goa, this appears to be a misreading of Nehru and of India. On the contrary, the Prime Minister was convinced that nonalignment represented the greatest use of moral freedom in international affairs. Alliances, he said in effect, commit a people to supporting one side or the other regardless of the ethical issues in any particular situation. Nonalignment, on the other hand, enables uncommitted nations to pronounce moral judgments on both Suez and Hungary, on provocative acts by either side in Berlin or in atomic testing.

Although Nehru himself declared in 1960, "We don't for a moment regard ourselves as more right or morally superior to others," a number of perceptive Indians recognized the danger of self-righteousness in India's neutralism. Other critics, perhaps even more pragmatic and less ethically conscious than the late Prime Minister, echoed the sentiments of V.K.R.V. Rao, former Vice-Chancellor of Delhi University. At the close of Nehru's address on foreign policy (quoted above) Rao exercised an old Indian prerogative of replying (often in extended oration) to an already long and significant speech. After ten years of effective nonalignment, Rao said, "The Prime Minister [not India, notice—CL] is passing through a second important phase of foreign policy. . . . The world is watching to see if our policy is based on fear and weakness." Patriotic citizens, he added, must offer an appeal and a challenge to Nehru, as Minister for External Affairs, "to hold fast to the policy which has given India distinction and yet not give away any of India's vital interests." The political dilemma which confronts every statesman in the world today finds complications as well as wider dimensions in the moral stance of Pandit Nehru and his ethical *guru,* Mahatma Gandhi. Initial evidence suggests that Prime Minister Shastri may follow similar policies but with greater firmness than his predecessor.

Nehru had very little to say about specific social reforms. Yet every so often his indignation grew hot and spilled forth in fiery condemnation. In *The Discovery of India* he praised the idea of ceremonial purity in traditional Hinduism, not for its spiritual value but for its "one good consequence" of bodily cleanliness. The habit of a daily bath, he claimed, spread from India to England, and destitute peasants could take pride in their shiny pots and pans. Then he lashed out in bitter frustration and shame for the way in which religion once more proved a cloak for unscientific, antisocial behavior:

This sense of cleanliness is not scientific, and the man who bathes twice a day will unhesitatingly drink water that is unclean and full of germs. Nor is it corporate, at any rate now. The individual will keep his own hut fairly clean but throw all the rubbish in the village street in front of his neighbor's house. The village is usually very dirty and full of garbage heaps. It is also noticeable that cleanliness is not thought of as such, but as a consequence of some religious sanction. When that religious sanction goes, there is marked deterioration in the standards of cleanliness. The evil consequence of ceremonial purity was a growth of exclusiveness, touch-me-notism, and of not eating and drinking with people of other castes. This grew to fantastic lengths unknown in any other part of the world.[28]

Or again, before the Subjects Committee of the Indian National Congress, meeting in Bangalore in 1960, the Prime Minister deplored the condition of cattle in India, where they receive the greatest respect in the world and the worst neglect, often becoming an economic burden and sometimes a serious menace to crops and people. "Yet nothing tangible could be done against their depredations," he complained, "because of the oldworld ideas and prejudices about cattle. . . . We want to keep our old prejudices and old thoughts and we also want to be in the new world. This always created difficulties." [29]

Acknowledging the problem of modernizing India without loosening its roots in the cultural past, Nehru warned the Congress and the people that they would have to choose between progress and certain social customs. As a scientific pragmatist, he was confident that the right choice would be made when conservative peasants are shown the usefulness of new ways. Years earlier, writing of Gandhi's indirect attacks on the caste system, Panditiji concluded: "But an even greater power than he is at work: the conditions of modern life—and it seems that at last this hoary and tenacious relic of past times must die." [30] In short, practical, economic, realistic pressures could be counted on to transform India. "There is no visible limit to the advance of science, if it is given the chance to advance," he said. Then, with a wistful gesture toward the confident spiritual faith of Mahatma Gandhi, he added: "Yet it may be that the scientific method of observation is not always applicable to all the varieties of human experiences. . . . And when both science and philosophy fail us, we shall have to rely on such other powers of apprehension as we may possess." [31]

Where did this fascinating man draw his reserves of strength and moral integrity? Over and over during his administration I asked people in India how Panditji attains such high ethical values without religious sanctions. Anup Singh drew a striking contrast: "Gandhi could not conceive of any ethical values without unshaken belief in the omnipotence of God as the central entity about which everything revolved," but Nehru represents instead the average Hindu, "always—though he may not pray and go to the temples—convinced that the whole universe is run by some inscrutable Power." [32] Vice-Chancellor Mujeeb, speaking for orthodox Muslims with a more religious viewpoint, reversed the uniqueness in these words: "Nehru is one of the very rare persons—they are very, very rare—who does not need any authority for holding his particular views, so far as I can understand them. . . . The Mahatma's personality was more in line with the Hindu genius; the Prime

Minister stands by himself." [33] And K. M. Munshi, former Food
Minister in Nehru's Cabinet, now active in the Swatantra Party,
summed up the Prime Minister thus:

Western in outlook, and partly Marxian (especially in slogans), his
outlook is economic interpretation of life—I will not call it materialistic. . . . He has wrenched the moral, ethical, and spiritual revolution
into exclusively socio-economic lines. He has not a faith in God; he
makes no bones about it. . . . Everybody can't do that [i.e. retain ethics without religious foundations]. . . . He is the product of the
Bhagavad-Gita without knowing it.[34]

Nehru himself wrestled with the question of his own inner
sources and resources. Unable to adapt to the primitive life and
outlook of Gandhi, he often felt himself divorced from his surroundings. In his autobiography he wrote frankly:

I have become a queer mixture of the East and the West, out of place
everywhere, at home nowhere. Perhaps my thoughts and approach to
life are more akin to what is called Western than Eastern, but India clings
to me. . . . I am a stranger and alien in the West. I cannot be of it. But
in my own country also, sometimes I have an exile's feeling.[35]

From observations during a year in the capital, and from personal
conversations with the Prime Minister, it seems to this writer that
Panditji, in his last years, drew vastly closer to his Indian heritage
than he was when he wrote those words, or even at the time of Independence. Some people attribute this to the pressures of the freedom struggle, the extension of cultural roots as a consequence of
external storms. Some, concentrating on his historical pilgrimage
within war-time prison walls, credit *The Discovery of India* to that
intensive study and the profound influence of companions like
Maulana Azad. Some see the natural return of an old man to the
faith and dreams of his forefathers, regardless of how far the youth
may have strayed. Still others charge Nehru with an assumed patriotism, an artificial adoption of Hindu tradition and attitude for the
sake of effective political leadership.

On the whole it seems more likely that all these explanations
may be overshadowed by a deeper, sincerer growth; namely, that

the responsibility for governing over four hundred million people forced the Prime Minister not only to travel into every corner of India, and become involved with every human need and problem, but also to seek earnestly for the unshakable foundations—historical, psychological, social, moral, spiritual—on which a new India can be built. As one of his family wrote:

His personality today strikes deeper roots into the ancient soil and draws increasing sustenance from the rich past. The peace of mind and lack of bitterness that he has in spite of many a disillusionment are truly Indian. In him the East and the West have blended, the former to show him the way of life to give him a wider understanding of the impulses that move the destinies of man . . .[36]

If the land of India is infinitely complex, so too was its Prime Minister. A man of many moods, he never achieved the complete peace of mind some admirers claimed for him. New Delhi was full of gossip and of more reliable reports of Panditji's tempestuous outbursts. He would come from Parliament, after delivering a suave, irenic speech in the midst of a Tibetan border crisis, and swear violently, in rage and frustration against the Chinese who not only violated his territory but shook his confidence in *Panchshila*, the principles of neutralism and moral suasion. He would greet a Christian delegation from abroad most graciously, then sternly rebuke a Cabinet minister for wasting his time on such "trash" as an anniversary observance of Christianity's arrival in India. He undoubtedly had frequent moments of utter discouragement and hopelessness as he faced the task of lifting India's masses from their depths of prejudice, poverty, and inertia. "I prefer the open sea, with all its storms and tempests," he confessed in his autobiography.[37]

This mercurial temperament contributed to his charm. Yet the man who swayed millions by his oratory and magnetic power, and who appeared to respond vibrantly to the stimulus of crowds, remained nonetheless aloof and even ill at ease among strangers and masses. Hardly a person who met Nehru failed to comment on the gentle smile which revealed at the same time serenity and sadness, weariness and wisdom. The Prime Minister was a dedicated man. Even before his death he had already given his life for India—not for the India which is past (with all its bitterness of subjugation, personal humiliation, bloody partition) not even for India today (with its magnitudinous problems of communalism, destitution and revolutionary change). Nehru gave his life for the India of tomorrow, the India he was confident could emerge not only to world influence, but—as the Mahatma repeatedly insisted —to world service.

A man of peace and non-violence, of suffering and humility, a follower of Christ's "Sermon on the Mount," Gandhi was revered, even worshipped. Exuberant and excitable, youthful and active, vehement and dashing, Nehru is only loved. The highest adoration has gone to Gandhi, who has completely quelled aggression. He is the Mahatma. However heroic Nehru might be, he is yet human, with the faults and weaknesses of a mortal.[38]

This was the man who led India through seventeen tumultuous years of freedom. By his frankness and independence of spirit, he antagonized partisans on both sides of the Cold War. By rejecting formal religion as a prerequisite for the highest ethical integrity, he forced theists to look further for the springs of conscience. By combining acute wisdom with obvious blind spots in public policy, he demonstrated his kinship with all of fallible mankind. Yet by his gracious charm and heartfelt sympathy he identified himself not only with the masses of India, but with the hopes and ideals of the world.

He is human like the rest of us and has weaknesses that most human beings have. Only where the majority succumbs he does not; hence his greatness. If India idolizes Jawahar today it is not for his virtues and strength and courage alone but for his very human qualities.[39]

Chapter XI

Opposition: Right and Left

"If ultimately we have to choose the lesser evil, we must take the free way of life as preferable. . . . Socialism ignores the truth, binds human incentive, and binds freedom." [1] In the fateful year of 1959, a little man with a long name and towering fame launched a new party of protest into the stormy seas of Indian politics. Thus far, the new movement has been slow to gain strength at the polls or among the masses. But Swatantra (generally called the Freedom Party) represents the first significant ideological challenge to the dominant Indian National Congress. Without conceding that the Congress or the late Prime Minister followed the Marxist "party line," one must recognize that their economic policies have been sufficiently socialistic to blunt any incisive opposition from either the Communists or the Praja Socialists. On the right wing, the Jana Sangh (People's Group) and the Mahasabha (with its militant ally, the Rashtriya Swayamsevak Sangh) have been too obsessed with Hindu nationalism to offer a constructive political program.

189

Swatantra was born on August 1, 1959, at the very moment when President Prasad imposed Central Government rule in the disordered Communist state of Kerala. More than a thousand delegates met in Bombay, under portraits of Lokamanya Tilak, the violent freedom fighter; Mahatma Gandhi, the gentle Father of Independence; and Sardar Patel, late bulwark of conservatism. Among the distinguished participants were K. M. Munshi, former Governor of Uttar Pradesh; M. R. Masani, former Mayor of Bombay; N. G. Ranga, recently General Secretary of the Congress Parliamentary Party; and the Raja of Ramgahr (Bihar). Overshadowing them all stood the "Founding Father," Chakravarti Rajagopalachari, known to newspaper headlines as "C. R." and to affectionate admirers as "Rajaji." India has had many beloved elder statesmen; Rajaji deserves the title today. He served as first Indian Governor-General, then as Chief Minister of Madras. His daughter married the lower-caste son of Mahatma Gandhi. According to Frank Moraes, he was Nehru's choice for President of India,[2] yet he has emerged from retirement to lead a vigorous crusade against his former colleague. Recalling that he joined Gandhi's noncooperation movement at the age of forty, Rajagopalachari told the Bombay delegates—and the nation:

Now when I am twice that age, I am leading the revolt against what I have come to believe to be a fatally wrong direction taken by the Indian National Congress in the governance of this great country . . . against this misconceived progress of the Congress towards what will finally end in the suppression of individual liberty and the development of the State into a true leviathan.[3]

In a twenty-one-point program the new Swatantra Party affirmed the need for increasing food production by encouraging the "self-employed peasant proprietor" and for raising industrial production by competitive enterprise. The statement advocated assistance to agriculture, protection of labor, decentralization of industry, and "education without discrimination." It condemned bureaucracy, crippling taxation, State compulsion and the acceptance of foreign loans "beyond the capacity of the country to repay." Reflecting more socialistic elements than many Western conservatives would accept, the platform would employ State enterprise wherever it "must supplement private enterprise," in such national services as railways, and in initiating pioneer projects difficult for private capital to undertake. It also called for government aid in irrigation, farm credits, marketing facilities and other areas which would not jeopardize the "ownership, management and cultivation of land."

Interspersed with this economic program ran a clear-cut moral and social philosophy:

(1) The Swatantra Party is pledged to social justice and equality of opportunity for all people without distinction of religion, caste, occupation, or political affiliation.

(2) . . . The progress, welfare, and happiness of the people depend on individual incentive, enterprise and energy . . . maximum freedom for the individual and minimum interference by the State. . . .

(3) . . . The state should foster and utilize the sense of moral obligation, the pride, satisfaction, and fulfilment felt by individuals in serving others, which are inherent in our tradition. . . .

(5) The Party stands for every effort being made to foster and maintain spiritual values and preserve what is good in our culture and tradition, and avoid the dominance of a purely materialist philosophy of life. . . .[4]

Optimistically the party aimed at a million members by the end of its first year. Its problem was one of organization—and of convincing sympathizers that it promised sufficient strength and stability to justify a shift of political allegiance. One news commentator pointed out that its principles should appeal to

. . . the so-called intelligentsia . . . to those who are more conservative or who still believe in the verities of democratic life even though of the outmoded liberal kind . . . to traditionalists of many varieties . . . and to Gandhians whose interpretation of life is not materialistic but ethical.[5]

Many followers were attracted to the Swatantra Party by the venerable wisdom of its leading spokesmen. Rajagopalachari has stated his aims in clear and succinct terms:

The philosophy behind my present work is that we should have minimum government, and that socialism inevitably leads to totalitarian

regulation, whether they want it—as the Communists do—from the outset, or whether they don't want it but have drifted to it—as is the case
with our government.[6]

In other words, the former Governor-General is convinced that
State power invariably sacrifices not only the freedom of the individual, but "the soul of these things." And he defends the necessity
of the profit motive as well as private property. "Unless the fruits of
labor are protected and insured," he insisted, "incentives will van-
ish."

Furthermore, like conservatives elsewhere, Rajaji is convinced
that religious motivation and religious sanction can succeed in stimulating progress where compulsion is bound to fail. Yet he acknowledged with equal fervor that reform—and even social ethics
—will come in part from fear of socialism. "Yes," he conceded,
"social and political conditions will have their effect upon character
and morality." At the same time, he rejects vehemently the contention that Hinduism is focused on individual salvation, with little interest in social welfare.

That is not correct! That is a misunderstanding! If you take the Scriptures and draw conclusions, you can come to that conclusion. But if you
see the people at work, you will not come to that conclusion. Helping
others is fundamental in Hinduism, not contemplation. The *Gita* stresses
not one's own salvation but service. Inquiring into the nature of the
soul should not be equated as the whole of our religion. Our religion
gives very great importance to helping others.[7]

This explanation illustrates several significant attitudes. Obviously the speaker recognized that the traditional picture of Hinduism features contemplation, "inquiring into the nature of the soul."
He acknowledged that the scriptures—apart from the beloved
Bhagavad-Gita—might seem to indicate a strictly personal religion.
He implied, further, that the real ethics of Hinduism are to be found
in popular practice rather than Vedantic lore. This contrasts with
more conventional responses, which point to the social concern
of India's ancient writings, while ruefully admitting the anti-social
deviations that have grown up around caste, human sacrifice, the
status of women, and so on.

In a speech near Madras the former Governor-General said that no economic Five-Year Plan could succeed without *dharma* and God, that the Swatantra Party had come into existence to remind the Congress of *dharma*. "We say that the individual needs freedom and happiness because he has a soul." [8] When N. G. Goray, a leader of the Praja Socialist Party, taunted that this moral basis of Swatantra was "the old wine of *laissez-faire* in the new bottle of *dharma*," "C.R." sharply denied that his party wanted to maintain the *status quo*, adding that *dharma* was a very old bottle.[9] Indeed it is. Elusive yet indispensable, it implies integrity, the rule of moral law, deep-rooted in nature and in human nature. Rajaji called it "virtue" and is himself the personification of *noblesse oblige*.

Another distinguished elder statesman who has cast his lot with the Swatantra Party is K.M. Munshi, whose colorful career in government and literature has been marked by political deviations and courageously independent thought. As a young man he studied English literature under Aurobindo Ghose, and worked for Independence at the side of Tilak, Jinnah and Annie Besant—all in their respective ways reactionary nationalists. Originally disillusioned with Gandhi as "revolutionary, impractical, understandable," [10] Munshi resigned from the Congress in 1919, but returned eleven years later. As an eminent lawyer, Home Minister of Bombay State, a conspicuous leader in the Constituent Assembly, Food Minister in Nehru's Cabinet from 1952 to 1957, and revered Governor of Uttar Pradesh, he exerted a decisive influence on the New India. The purpose of the Bhavan Book University, a publishing series which he inaugurated in 1951, expresses his philosophy in these words:

We seek the dignity of man, which necessarily implies the creation of social conditions which would allow him freedom to evolve along the lines of his own temperament and capacities; we seek the harmony of individual efforts and social relations, not in any make-shift way, but within the frame-work of the Moral Order; we seek the creative art of life, by the alchemy of which human limitations are progressively transmuted, so that man may become the instrument of God, and is able to see Him in all and all in Him.

Munshi's own springs of ethical thought are not Roy and the Westernized reformers, but Ramakrishna, Dayananda, Tilak and Ghose, religious nationalists who put Independence ahead of social reform. And what he fears for India is the materialism and moral decline he has observed in the West. Though he paid courteous, even undeserved, tribute to the moral standards of American homes and universities, and to those ethical and spiritual traditions which survive in the (Protestant) Anglo-Saxon community, he emphasized that "the difference between this country [India] and some of the European countries is that in the West the religious moorings have more or less disappeared." [11] And he added that "Hollywood does more damage to your country and the world than any one factor in this country, by its glorification of crime and sex." But America's crowning virtue, he implied, is the perpetuation of individualism: political, economic, cultural. "The dominant idea in America," Munshi remarked, "is that the individual should be left free to do as he likes," but if such influential groups as universities and Protestant churches should abandon this basic idea, he warned, American culture itself will die.

"Every generation has to recapture the values of its culture," Munshi asserted; "Christianity today is not the Christianity of the eighteenth century. In recapturing it goes on reinterpreting the values." This progressive, even radical, concession appeared surprising, even inconsistent. Can such reinterpretation of traditional values be accomplished without losing the support of the conservative masses? Munshi's reply was aristocratic, almost feudal, in its import: "The vast majority of masses don't count, to my mind. It is the 'dominant minority,' the best man, when he tries to live up to the dominant central idea of that culture." Apparently conservatism holds the same fundamental attitudes in every land and in every age, however different the cultural guise may be. Thus his decision to oppose his former colleagues by joining the Swatantra Party grew painfully out of this same apprehension.

Always I have fought for freedom, for independence, and if I am truly convinced that the present government is introducing Marxist devices, [I must oppose them]. . . . I was one of the framers of the Constitution, but I find year after year it is being converted into a totalitarian state.

Munshi went on to interpret his political ethics within the framework of his understanding of traditional Hinduism. First, "your *raison-d'être* is your duty to others—not a right. The emphasis on rights is all wrong. My right is to perform my duty to the best of my ability." And second, "when I have got my duty to perform, I disregard what is going to be the consequences so far as I am concerned. . . . The whole modern civilization—thanks to the West—has been based on magnifying all three [wrath, attachments and fear]." The only solution to this modern malaise, he concluded, is "by seeing all in God and God in all . . . by believing that we are all part of the same God . . . [that] there is moral order, a law or moral causation."

In general it is true of Indian politicians today, as of those who struggled for power fifty or a hundred years ago, that conservative leaders seek religious sanctions in the ancient past, whereas social reformers lean toward religious liberalism. Minocher Rustom Masani represents a different breed, perhaps because he has swung the wide arc from "fellow-traveling" (though never a Communist Party member), through the socialist wing of the Congress, to the conservative Swatantra Party secretaryship. But he rejects that designation in declaring: "We do not want conservatism but true liberalism. . . . Parliamentary democracy can only thrive if economic freedom is restored, freedom from the state. Our definition of economic democracy is just the reverse of the Marxists'." [12]

Paradoxically, Masani characterizes the labor platform, which he wrote for the Swatantra Party, as "very pro-labor," and counts on "enlightened labor support" for the new movement. The basis for this program is the conviction that centralized socialistic industrialization can employ only one quarter of the hundred million surplus people on the land, so rural crafts and industries will have to be expanded. In this respect he joins forces with Narayan and the Sarvodayans to preserve rural family life and agrarian values. Furthermore, Masani asserts emphatically that the most neglected segment of Indian society today is the small landowner, who outnumbers the landless peasant five to one, but sees his precarious independence threatened by socialism.

Does this mean that Masani (and his Swatantra colleagues) would sacrifice equality for freedom? "Of course," he responded frankly, and then elaborated his statement, as follows:

> I would even go so far as to say that equality is Utopian. It is reactionary in the present situation. . . . [It may be an ultimate goal]; in a world of plenty there will be rough equality. . . . [but] I don't think equality in the economic sense has any meaning today. . . . [Of course we would eliminate any] grotesque inequality, and we all very vigorously stand for equality of status. . . . [But economic] equality is an existential fact of backwardness. . . . If you work for liberty, you get equality as a by-product. . . . [For example, America's economic differentials are far lower than in India or in the Soviet Union.] . . . What I am arguing is liberal economics. I understand our part to be a projection of liberal thought.[13]

Significantly, Masani's viewpoint disclaims the religious base so crucial for Rajagopalachari and Munshi. As an avowed agnostic who does not "understand about these things," Minoo acknowledged some ideological relationship between Swatantra and traditional religion in that "the conservative Hindu is naturally anti-Marxist and anti-Communist." Admitting that "Munshi in a way represents the reasonably conservative Hindu" and that Rajaji puts great emphasis on *dharma,* he deplored their Gandhian views against birth control and in favor of prohibition.

The future of the Swatantra Party is still problematic. That it has widespread ideological support few would deny. That it has fearless and forthright leadership is still more obvious. It remains to be seen whether conservatism truly represents the wave of the future, whether free enterprise and individual initiative could carry the masses of India forward rapidly enough to meet economic needs and create social change. Still more basic, it remains to be seen whether conservative religious sanctions can preserve and stabilize the ethical foundations of a developing nation, or whether an impatient secularistic society will rush unheeding into a moral vacuum.

It is even more difficult to identify the ethical sources of left-wing movements in India. Although the Congress Party today covers a broad ideological spectrum (as do both major parties in the United States), its focal point is so far to the left in its socialistic philosophy that even the Communists have little room for maneuvering except in foreign affairs. This means that the Praja Socialist Party perches precariously on a narrow ledge between the massive wall of Congress and the deep abyss of Communism. True, some Socialists have reached their present political alignment from still farther to the left, but more of them have been active members of the Indian National Congress, and a few are drifting back into the dominant party in the hope of wielding greater influence.

The Praja Socialists comprise a young, composite and very vocal party. Acharya J. B. Kripalani founded the Kisan (Peasants') Mazdoor Party in 1951 and led it for a year before joining with the Socialist Party. The merger resolution announced as its aim: "to achieve through peaceful means a democratic socialist society free from social, political and economic exploitation. . . . Free India faces many tasks. Among them is the evolution of a social philosophy that would give the people an unwavering sense of direction." In his presidential address Kripalani complained that Congress saw Independence solely in political terms and neglected such social issues as untouchability, women's rights, decentralization and local autonomy, even though "Gandhiji made social and economic reform an integral part of the political movement."

Over the past decade at least four of the ablest minds and most dynamic figures in Indian politics have been associated with the P.S.P., but the party has lacked the organization and the following to make effective use of such leadership. Acharya Kripalani fought a good fight in vain against Krishna Menon in the Bombay elections of 1962, only to have his victorious rival deposed as Minister of Defense during the Chinese invasion that same year. Shrimati Kripalani had already rejoined the Congress Party. Jayaprakash Narayan, hailed in the mid-fifties as the most likely successor to Prime Minister Nehru, withdrew from politics and joined Vinoba Bhave's Bhoodan movement to work for village betterment and a kind of grass-roots socialism. Asoka Mehta, elected chairman of the Praja Socialists in 1959, suffered a serious automobile accident which made him inactive for months, and in recent years has stood almost alone as a brilliant spokesman for the non-Communist left.

Kripalani's chief difference with the Sarvodayans has been his insistence on strong government action. As Chairman of the Congress Party in the first year of Independence, he had gone with others to Gandhi only a month before the Mahatma's assassination, pleading that "Constructive Workers" should be drawn into government development programs. Gandhi said No! He believed that his Sarvodayans (service volunteers) should abstain from political conflicts and exert their moral and social influence in public and private reforms. Frank Moraes claimed that the Prime Minister favored Kripalani as Congress President again in 1950, but did not openly support him against the "old-school Hindu revivalist" candidate backed by conservative Vallabhbhai Patel.[14]

Like his right-wing opponents previously quoted, Kripalani fears that "too much emphasis on power—whether of science or politics or society—will destroy values." [15] But he acknowledges that "power can work for good or evil; it is morally neutral." Kripalani himself would wholeheartedly endorse Gandhi's use of moral power, of nonviolence, but he believes that this can be done only by actively attacking the injustices and inequalities of society. Insisting that Gandhian democracy, as opposed to centralization, is the only true socialism, Kripalani declared: "Gandhi's socialism was based on moral values, and therefore differed from Marx's, which was based on material values only!"

As Rajagopalachari has his agnostic Masani, so Kripalani has his Mehta. One of the youngest political figures in India today (born 1911), Asoka Mehta attended a mission school, worked as an active trade unionist, helped to found the Congress Socialist Party, and then resigned in 1939 (with Minoo Masani) in protest against Communist infiltration. As General Secretary and then Chairman of the P.S.P., he has written regular newspaper columns of economic and social analysis, and frankly criticizes the "marked decline in our political standards."

More perceptively than most leaders, Mehta grapples with the problem of "how to communicate to this vast mass" of Indian people, whose roots are in mythology, religious history and social tradition. "You cannot talk to them in modern terms," he explained; "there is constant need for translation from one idiom to another."

On the other hand, he recognized, one cannot disregard his myth and his religion. "It is that which makes India one, with all its divergent languages—a cultural community of minds, which is ultimately rooted in religion." Not a temple-goer himself, Mehta nonetheless appreciates the necessity for respecting and preserving this tradition rather than encouraging conflict between religion and society.

If you become modern in that sense, you snap your contact completely with the people. It is not necessary to go to temples. But there is a certain understanding and responsiveness to the deep-seated heritage of the Indian people, which is primarily shaped by the religion of the people. It is like an iceberg, largely below the surface. Even the Communist Party dare not say anything about religion. It is an inarticulate major premise, an assumption [underlying all] oral propaganda.[16]

Thus Mehta sees clearly the chasm between the two Indias: the educated élite and the traditional masses. He sees also that this chasm cannot be bridged by government action from the top. Both Congress and Swatantra, he believes, have sharpened the gulf and increased the danger of polarization, whereas "we had to modify our socialism in terms of the conditions in the country . . . to acclimatize socialistic ideas to the Indian climate." The earlier social issues of untouchability and the status of women are being dealt with, slowly but adequately, in Mehta's view. "Today the main problem in India is social mobility, the capacity of people to move up and down. A stratified society can never be a free and equal society." Such a goal, he affirmed, cannot be achieved by any great movement or by abrupt legislation, but only "by a gradual development of social concerns of some of the people, by the assertion of rights on the part of these deprived of them, and by a willingness to meet them halfway. I believe that is the genius of India, and we will continue in that way."

Despite the Western image of Communism as dogmatic and inflexible, Indian Marxists have shown a remarkable—and apparently sincere—measure of adaptability within their history and culture. In some instances this may represent reluctant acquiescence to the sheer weight of tradition. A national oratorical contest held in the capital in 1960 took as its topic for debate: "Resolved:

that Communism is *not* suited to the soil of India." The first speaker, an attractive and fluent college student, began with these words: "I am a Communist—but . . ." He went on to expound his thesis that the Marxist ideology he favored is unsuited psychologically, sociologically or economically to Indian life. For one thing, "religion is an integral part of Indian society," and Communism rejects belief in God. In the second place, "we have never believed in equality for everyone," either in the family or in the caste system. Thirdly, "we are too traditional; our eyes have been to the past and not to the future," and India therefore remains unprepared for rapid or drastic social change. For these reasons, "our preserved culture is the greatest stumbling block to Communism." Thus he reached his conclusion, "although I firmly believe that the salvation of India lies in Communism," that its ideology and social principles are alien to Indian religious and cultural traditions. Succeeding orators echoed, less bluntly and personally, some of the same ideas. Said one: "It is undeniably true that the people of India are intensely religious." A spirited girl student argued that "India requires a complete overhauling in its social structure."

This tension between Communism and Hindu society is not new. M. N. Roy, the pioneer of Indian Communism, a member of the Presidium of the International with Lenin and Trotsky, had criticized the religious "ideas, ideals, institutions, and traditions" of his country as unscientific and socially backward. But Roy quarreled with Stalin and was expelled from the International in 1929, presumably because he opposed its condemnation of the Gandhian movement. Years later he declared in a speech on "Radical Democracy of New Humanism": "I have never been an orthodox Marxist." [17] He then went on to uphold views which sound more like India than Russia, more like Hinduism than Communism. Roy asserted individual freedom as the supreme value, rather than the individual for society. He criticized materialism, the class struggle and state power, appealing instead for harmony and cooperation. In tones like those of Gandhi himself, Vinoba Bhave, or Jayaprakash Narayan (a former Marxist), Roy judged heavy industry unsuitable for India, warned against the party rule inherent in Parliamentary democracy, and advocated decentralization of government power into the hands of village *panchayats* (councils).

To the thesis of the student orator, that Communism is not suited to Indian life, Minoo Masani of the Swatantra Party replied: "Yes, I agree. Temperamentally we are not made for it. We are lazy and incompetent and undisciplined, etc. But for that very reason dictatorship becomes natural and acceptable to the people." From a very different perspective, Saunders Redding, Negro ambassador of goodwill from the United States, concurred with the judgment: "Communism's rival for power in India is not democracy, or even socialism, but traditional Hinduism, which is also bitterly inimical to the West." [18]

Neither Communism past nor Communism present—much less the unknown future—can be dismissed so lightly. Lenin's famous dictum that "the road to Paris lies through Pekin and Delhi" has given India top priority ever since the Bolshevik Revolution. In 1920 the First World Congress of the Comintern adopted a resolution which misjudged the loyalties of the Indian masses and laid the foundation for a tactical error in Communist policy:

Tendencies like Gandhism in India, thoroughly imbued with religious conceptions, idealize the most backward and economically most reactionary forms of social life, see the solution of the social problem not in proletarian socialism but in a reversion to these backward forms, preach passivity and repudiate the class struggle, and in the process of the development of the revolution become transformed into an openly reactionary force. Gandhism is more and more becoming an ideology directed against mass revolution. It must be strongly combated by Communism.[19]

The Communist Party of India came into existence in 1924 as a branch of the Communist International, and Stalin, grasping for power at Lenin's death, expressed the hope—or confidence—that in India "the imperialist chain may break earlier than in other countries." During the next few years the C.P.I. won some support from labor unions, whose earlier leaders—drawn from such idealistic groups as the Servants of India and the Theosophical Society—had been genuinely concerned with wages, welfare and col-

lective bargaining. Before long the British Government, fearing violent revolution against colonial rule, arrested thirty-one Communist leaders and ten months later sentenced twenty-seven of them to
prison terms. This famous Meerut Conspiracy Case attracted not
only widespread sympathy for the defendants, but also a distinguished corps of defense lawyers—including Jawaharlal Nehru.

Even this opportunity for cementing a nationalist-Communist
alliance fell victim to Moscow's ideological blindness. Instead of supporting *swadeshi* (native products) and boycotting British goods,
Indian Communists wore foreign clothes to demonstrate solidarity with British workers, at the same time that they advocated violent world revolution instead of nonviolent Indian independence.
The party platform of 1930, as published in Pravda, proclaimed:

The greatest threat to the victory of the Indian revolution is the fact that
great masses of our people still harbour illusions about the National
Congress and have not realized that it represents a class organization of
the capitalists working against the fundamental interests of the toiling
masses of our country. . . . The most harmful and dangerous obstacle to victory of the Indian revolution is the agitation carried on by the
"left" elements of the National Congress led by Jawaharlal Nehru.[20]

The Communist press around the world launched a more explicit
attack, which was translated into Urdu and other Indian languages,
as follows:

The policy of Gandhism, on which the programme of the Congress is
founded, uses a cloak of vague talk about love, meekness, modest and
hard-working existence, lightening the burden of the peasantry, national unity, the special historic mission of Hindustan, etc., but under this
cloak it preaches and defends the interests of the Indian capitalists, the
inevitability and the wisdom of the division of society into rich and poor,
eternal social inequality and exploitation.[21]

The Comintern and the C.P.I. learned too late that attacks on
Gandhi and the Congress decisively precluded any substantial influence on the Indian people, that a repetitious theme of violent
revolution could not compete with the spiritual power of a "little
brown man in loin-cloth." The Hitler-Stalin Pact of 1939, followed
by the outbreak of war in Europe, bewildered the Communist Party

in India as elsewhere. It recovered more readily, however, since now, for the first time, it found itself in tune with the Congress and the Congress Socialist Party, condemning Britain as an imperialist warmonger and organizing strikes in Bombay and elsewhere.

When Hitler attacked Russia, the C.P.I. reversed itself again to support the "People's War" against Fascism, by *opposing* strikes and aiding the British war effort. In gratified surprise the British Government released Communists from prison in India, lifted the ban against the party (imposed in 1934), and even provided newspaper facilities. Such are the exigencies—and ethics—of war! In return the Communists fostered disunity between Hindus and Muslims by favoring the idea of Partition, encouraged further linguistic dismemberment or "Balkanization" of India, and gave limited acceptance to the Cripps mission rejected by the National Congress. With such a record it is little wonder that leaders and populace rejected Marxist policies, or that Nehru should refer to the Communist Party of India as "the most stupid among the Communist parties of the world." [22]

Nevertheless, as Independence failed to bring immediate prosperity and the Cold War sharpened ideological conflicts, Communism made some headway among labor unions in poverty-ridden Calcutta and among "white-collar unemployed" in Kerala State. Having failed to revive a United Front in 1950-1951, the Party renewed its attacks on Prime Minister Nehru, on parliamentary government, on the power of landlords and capitalists, on foreign investments in India. The Communist program at this time was noteworthy for its minimal social concerns: a living wage, an eight-hour day, a forty-hour week; freedom of conscience, speech, press, assembly and strike; and the confiscation of land without compensation, for distribution to peasants. Most of its aims showed political overtones: regional and "national" self-determination, separation from the Commonwealth, replacement of police by a "people's militia," protection against foreign imports and investments, an alignment with "peace-loving countries" to stop "flirting" with the United States, and—*mirabile dictu*—an alliance with Pakistan!

Later on, a Draft Program demanded the use of regional languages in schools and public institutions (rather than Hindi or

English); free and compulsory primary education to the age of
fourteen; the establishment of a network of hospitals and medical
centers to form a "people's health service"; the separation of the
secular State from all religious institutions. Not only did these ob-
jectives represent a rare concern for social welfare on the part of
Communists, but they closely paralleled provisions already adopted
as Directive Principles in the Constitution and as national goals by
the Congress Party. Concluding his study of *The Communist Party
of India,* Masani reiterates the natural hostility between Marxism
and religion and deplores the failure of most religious groups (such
as the Hindu Mahasabha, Jana Sangh, Muslims or Christians) to
emphasize the Communist threat. Two exceptions are cited, however: the Catholics, whose organized opposition "shows a high degree of awareness and sophistication," and the abiding influence
of Gandhi, who still speaks to the Indian people "of non-material
values like God, Love, Truth, Human Brotherhood, and the Equality of the untouchable Harijan and the proud Brahmin." [23]

Anti-Communists around the world have been appalled by the
strength of Marxism in the southwestern state of Kerala, often interpreting it as typical of India. They have alternated between
equally unwarranted gloom and glee as they have watched "the
world's only democratic election of a Communist regime" (in
1957), its dismissal by the Central Government under Constitutional provisions (in 1959), and its acclaimed "defeat" at the
polls (in 1960). It is true that the Indian state with the highest educational level and the highest proportion of Christians (though still,
of course, a small minority) did elect a Communist government
in 1957, not by a majority but as the largest plurality over disorganized and divided opposition. (It is also true that Communists
represent the largest single opposition bloc in the national Parliament.) It is true that Chief Minister E. M. S. Namboodiripad and
his cabinet tried to move too swiftly in confiscating and redistribut-
ing land, in seizing control of parochial schools, in consolidating
the perquisites of office into Communist hands. The riots and demonstrations of protest in the spring and summer of 1959 led to
the assumption of power by the Central Government under Presidential Proclamation on August 1. It is *not* true that the subsequent
elections in February 1960 resulted in a resounding defeat for the

Reds. The Communists actually increased their minority percentage to secure the largest single party vote, and only the united opposition of all other parties succeeded in installing a coalition, a coalition so shaky and jealous of one another that few observers expected it to last.

Like other countries, India has her Communist intellectuals, more open and articulate than the professional party organizers. Professor Hirendra Nath Mukerjee was educated at Presidency College, Calcutta, and at Oxford and Lincoln's Inn. After serving on the All-India Congress Committee in the late thirties, he joined the Bengal Communist Party soon after World War II, and now serves as a Communist Member of Parliament, as well as professor of history at Surendranath College, Calcutta. His sympathetic study of Gandhiji[24] praises the Mahatma's social reforms but deplores his "obvious superstitions" and his "impractical" answers, which produced "a sublime touch, but also, in terms of real life, an element of futility and failure." The volume ends with a denial that Marxism, unlike Gandhism, is indifferent to means; on the contrary, the author asserts, Communists are morally serious people.

This quiet scholar puts emphasis on individual values of truth and selflessness which Westerners find difficult to reconcile with stereotyped concepts. "No Communist society," Professor Mukerjee declared, "can afford to minimize this stress on ethical conduct in individuals. This is something which we have inherited from the past." [25] But he acknowledged that Communism approaches the problem of ends and means from different perspectives. For one thing, if Gandhi's methods have not achieved even the universally accepted goals, they will have to be re-examined, he suggested. Secondly, "a Communist society will have to see that the largest possible number of individuals in that society behave in what we consider to be an ethical way." Thirdly, "unless the social context is changed we can't get that kind of individual in society." By way of illustration the professor chose sex ethics, a problem requiring not only individual purity, but social programs (homes for rehabilitation, alternative employment, opportunities for wholesome contact between the sexes) and "social reconstruction" (such laws and coercion as Communist China has adopted). Because the whole moral tradition in India is individualistic, despite the communal social organization, Socialists (sic) seek to reconcile the two, since "individual reformation won't go far enough—has not gone far enough—unless we have social reformation."

For Mukerjee "the religious propensity of the Indian mind" need not be a barrier to Communism. Acknowledging that Indian people have "spiritual resources to draw upon along with materialism," he expressed confidence that "communist propaganda . . . will have to be adapted to the Indian scene and the Indian temperament . . . without making any compromises to the fundamentals." At the same time he criticized the "revivalist groups" (communal religious parties), whose financial and political supporters "are hostile to any social program." His criticism of Nehru's Government was based on the "terrible gap between theory and practice," the need for village reconstruction from the *panchayat* up instead of down from the Ministry for Community Development. Repeatedly Mukerjee emphasized not an ideological conflict but a pragmatic failure. Even Gandhiji, he claimed, mourned at the end of his life that there had been no basic change in Indian society. But, this Communist M.P. added: "It is an ethical problem at the same time it is a political problem," a lack "even in our party" (!) of exhilaration, of incentive. If he complains, as a political opponent, that Nehru has failed in that task, he knows as an historian that no Communist has ever come close to the Mahatma in inspiring that kind of moral dedication.

Gandhiji himself had pointedly rejected Marxism on innumerable occasions, primarily because of his faith that no good ends could be attained by violent, immoral means. He proclaimed the supremacy of spirit over dialectical materialism, of universal love over class warfare, of decentralization over collectivism, of the individual over the state, of duties over rights, of service over power. His ascetic disciple, Vinoba Bhave, has often turned his gentle humor against the Communists, according to Hallam Tennyson: "Since our ancient scriptures, has anyone equalled the Communists in their boundless zeal for repetition? . . . Marxist literature is as wide and shoreless as the sea. Only a few dare venture toward the depths of Das Kapital. But most draw back, content with a mere dip in shallower currents of propaganda that flow from Russia. . . .

[or, told that his ideas amounted to Communism without violence]
Perhaps. But then you might say that two people were identical except that one breathed and the other was a corpse." [26]

Prime Minister Nehru often expressed indebtedness to Marxism for insights into history and economic society. But invariably he came back to an "Indian" or even a Gandhian appraisal:

Communism has definitely allied itself to an approach of violence. Even if it does not indulge normally in physical violence, its thought is violent, and it does not seek to change by persuasion or peaceful democratic pressures, but by coercion and, indeed, destruction and extermination.[27]

Marxism . . . proved too narrow a creed and . . . failed to resolve our basic doubts. Life is something more than economic growth, though it is well to realize that economic growth is a basic foundation of life and progress.[28]

The world still wonders anxiously whether India is likely to turn Communist. Frank Anthony answered that question succinctly and convincingly: "My own faith is that Communism is not a threat to India unless the administrative machinery breaks down." [29] In other words, *if* the Congress falls into internecine struggle, *if* the Western world fails to provide the economic aid essential for an industrial "breakthrough," *if* Chinese aggression succeeds in shattering India's precarious progress and stability, *if* communal divisions (regional, linguistic, religious) are allowed to threaten the integral unity of the country, then Communism will be ready, with a highly organized machine, to "pick up the pieces." If democracy, social welfare and economic development make significant advance, then the moral and religious roots of India's heritage may prevail, and the spiritual power—if not the political program—of Mahatma Gandhi may yet triumph over the materialistic might of Karl Marx.

Chapter XII

The Gandhians and Sarvodaya

The first public duty for any distinguished visitor to India is to lay a wreath at Rajghat, the platform where Mahatma Gandhi's body was cremated in January 1948. A few hundred yards from that simple shrine stands the Gandhi Centre, built and maintained by the semi-official Gandhi Memorial Fund. Its quarterly publication, *Gandhi Marg*, bears a quotation: "There is no such thing as Gandhism and I do not want to leave any sect after me." On the wall of the adjacent museum, where mementoes of the Great Soul are rather sparsely displayed, another motto catches the eye: "They might kill me, but they cannot kill Gandhism." Apparently neither Gandhiji nor his public administrators saw any contradiction therein. Likewise, only a few thoughtful, perceptive leaders seem disturbed by the national disposition to render lip-service to the Mahatma while ignoring the practical implications of his program or his ideals.

The Gandhi Smarak Nidhi (Memorial Fund) and the University Grants Commission are constructing Gandhi Centres in all major Indian universities. *The Illustrated Weekly of India* carried a series of articles and correspondence on the topic, "Are We Forgetting the Mahatma?" Indians in all walks of life are discussing the question, whether Gandhiji is being neglected or exploited or sincerely followed. President Prasad, having refused to speculate as to which political party more truly represents Gandhi, did answer this query as follows:

As a matter of fact, all these things are true, that he is neglected and exploited and followed. All these things are going on side by side in this country. . . . To the masses he was a religious man. He was a religious preacher and a religious reformer. And that he is today to the masses. To the sophisticated people like us he was a political leader, and he is a political leader—no more.[1]

"A political leader—no more!" Yet this speaker was the man of whom Nehru once wrote, "Few others, if any, can be said to have imbibed more thoroughly the real message of Gandhiji."[2] In a speech at Bikaner on October 31, 1959, Dr. Radhakrishnan, then Vice-President, deplored the fact that "we have the name of Gandhi on our lips but not in our hearts. We involve his name in any and every connection but do not pause to ask how he would have acted in particular situations." K. M. Munshi expressed the dilemma in sharper terms:

We acclaim Gandhiji as the Father of the Nation, and yet we decline to live accordingly to those standards by which he lived or to try to be an instrument of God as he aspired to be. . . . What is difficult to understand is this craving for [more food, clothing, shelter, happiness, security] without developing the spiritual values by which we can earn them—courage, tenacity, and the will to render life secure.[3]

Since both Communists and Swatantra Party leaders claim to be the true inheritors of Gandhi's dream for India, the quest for "Gandhism" sixteen years after his death offers a fascinating challenge. Certain people might be termed the obvious and influential "professional" Gandhians. One of these is G. Ramachandran, Secretary of the Gandhi Memorial Fund and Peace Foundation. The many facets of interpretation, he explained, are due to the many facets of the Mahatma himself. Among specific contributions, Ramachandran listed the following:[4] Gandhi taught nonviolence not merely as a strategy but as a way of life; he led untouchables into temples and (according to this long-time associate) wanted caste so uprooted that not even research could disclose a man's caste; he laid the foundations for basic education; he drew women into the Independence movement and social service; he purified politics ("despite the claim that one can clean up Hell but never politics"); he "invented" a kind of village latrine and insisted that cleanliness was necessary for true godliness; he concerned himself with diet for the sake of both health and economics, claiming that India could solve her rice shortage if people would substitute some other grain for one meal a day as well as using more vegetables.

Ramachandran vehemently denied any dichotomy between religion and ethics or between religion and politics; for Gandhi, religion *was* ethics, he said. Similarly, politics should be regarded as one expression of the search for Truth. Thus, Nehru, Vinoba, Rajagopalachari and Kripalani could all follow Gandhi despite their divergent political policies, just as Clement Atlee and Winston Churchill both regarded themselves as Christian politicians. Ethical and spiritual sanctions will be preserved, Ramachandran declared, even though temples and temple worship will change with other aspects of society. On the whole, this Memorial Foundation appears to follow a social and secular orientation, interpreting religion in broad ethical terms and avoiding the problem of "religions" as such.

Another "professional" Gandhian is Pyarelal Nayar, long-time companion of the Mahatma, Secretary of the Navajivan Trust (Gandhian publishing agency), and author of *Mahatma Gandhi, The Last Phase,* a two-volume authorized biography. Diversity of perspective is inevitable, he said, pointing to countless men like St. John who have moulded Christianity "according to their own temperament and preconceived ideas and philosophies." It is particularly natural in the case of Mahatma Gandhi, who said: "Nobody would be able to represent me completely, but a part of me will live in many people." This, in fact, was the essence of Gandhi's philosophy, Pyarelal explained:

His special contribution was to allow the utmost freedom of thought to
everybody. He never tried to make anybody conform, but he helped
everybody to grow into the person's own best self. . . . His essential
contribution was that he took us out of the realm of contemplation
into the plane of action. . . . Abstract truth took body in his hands.
He taught us to live truth.[5]

Did the Mahatma feel that religion, in the broad sense, was necessary for ethics? "Spirituality would be a more correct word than
religion," his close companion replied; "a truly spiritual person cannot acquiesce in evil." Returning to the importance of living one's
faith, he added that someone had given him a New Testament
when he entered the university, and he had read it, but it came alive
for him only when he saw it being lived by Gandhiji. "Now,"
Pyarelal testified, "the New Testament is part and parcel of my
being since I saw the truth of it in the life of Mahatma Gandhi."

On the ethics of caste, Nayar echoed the early—and perhaps
the "true"—Gandhi. As an excuse for superiority or persecution,
"it never had any place in Gandhi's thought—at any stage." But
as a vocational distinction, the Mahatma believed that, "other factors
being equal, a person would be best fitted to carry on the vocation
that he was born into . . . if every activity has for its end the goal
of selfless service to society." Gandhiji urged, according to his friend,
that everyone should reduce himself to the level of outcastes, the
servants of all, and then occupational divisions would develop by
the natural laws of heredity and environment.

Pyarelal and other Gandhians feel very deeply the neglect of
Gandhian ideals in present-day society. Although there has been
a reaction against Gandhiji's moral discipline, and "at present
[there are] not many signs of a return of the pendulum . . . if
India is to survive as a nation, unless we retrace our steps, we might
even lose our independence," his biographer asserted. These men,
Pyarelal's sister Sushila (Gandhi's doctor), Rajkumari Amrit Kaur
(his secretary), and other intimate associates, represent a di-
minishing handful of elderly citizens, hugging their memories with
pride and gratitude. Most of them, in diverse ways, are making professional "capital" of their comradeship with Gandhi, occupying
"offices" related to him, living a very different life from what they

knew with him in Sevagram. These faithful "companions of the way" are helping to keep the torch of Gandhi bright, but one needs to look elsewhere for the truly vital signifiance of Gandhism in modern India.

Who best represents Gandhiji's ideas? Over and over again the answer is: the Bhoodan Movement, Vinoba Bhave. A man who had been with Gandhi nearly thirty years, he had emerged from obscurity almost accidentally as a symbol of "spiritual land reform." The son of a Maharastra Brahmin textile technologist, Vinoba thrilled as a youth to a biography of Giuseppe Mazzini, took a vow of celibacy at twelve, earned a university certificate in mathematics and then burned the document, presumably in protest at British rule. Soon after that he adopted Gandhi as his *guru* and joined the "retinue." The Mahatma, who recognized Vinoba's philosophical depths by calling him *Acharya* (teacher or preceptor), assigned him to court the first arrest in the civil disobedience campaign of 1940.

After the assassination of Gandhi in 1948, all attention seemed to focus on his political heir, Jawaharlal Nehru, and the crucial efforts to establish a stable, independent nation. Disillusioned by the apparent neglect of cottage industries, decentralization, nonviolence, and other Gandhian tenets, Vinoba founded the Sarvodaya Samaj (the Society for the Welfare of All or, more simply, the Service Movement). "We do not want the rise of the few," he said, "not even of the many, nor of the greatest number. . . . We can be satisfied with the good of one and all, of the high and low, the strong and the weak, the intelligent as well as the dull. The word Sarvodaya expresses this lofty and all-embracing sentiment." [6] This he believed, was what Gandhi had wanted the Congress to become, a servant of India not her ruler, a community of peace not an instrument of power.

The Bhoodan Movement began by a casual request for land for the landless. Soon it became systematized in its formula to landowners: "If you had five sons, you would divide up your wealth equally between them. Treat me as your sixth son. Give me a share of your land for the sake of *Daridra Narayan*—God revealed in the poor." [7] Still later, Vinobaji gave this campaign a whimsical label: looting with love. He explained it in terms which put a new twist on the Marxian charge that religion is an "opiate of the people," and which give a new incentive to capitalism: "For the poor I am trying to win rights. For the rich I am striving to win moral development. If one grows materially and the other spiritually, who then is the loser? Like air and water, land belongs to ·God. . . . And who can be happy if they oppose his will?" [8] To give landlords this spiritual privilege—and to supplement the slow but coercive processes of democratic socialism—Vinoba set out on foot across India, first through Hyderabad and Uttar Pradesh, less extensively in other provinces. Constantly he has emphasized the moral and social, the spiritual and the practical aspects of his challenge.

Although estimates vary widely, it is probably safe to conclude that in eight years (1951-1959) the Bhoodan Movement elicited some five million acres of land (with a fifty million acre goal), of which one tenth has been redistributed to the poor. Bhave wants local committees set up to handle the distribution of donated land, but often grows impatient when these prove to be inefficient, selfish or even corrupt. Donald Groom, a British volunteer worker, admitted in 1960 that about 40 per cent of the land has been uncultivatable,[9] though he charitably explained this useless land as part of large, irregular holdings, whereas others have suspected deliberate deception by the donors.

Even nearing seventy (he was born September 11, 1895), Vinobaji keeps moving out toward new horizons: physical, social, moral, spiritual. In 1958, in the southwestern province of Kerala, he launched a new technique for the support of his volunteer workers (now numbering some 1500, but with a goal of 70,000). This he calls *sarvodayapatra* (literally *service vessel*), in which he asks the youngest child in each family to place one handful of grain in a pot each day for the *shanti-senaks* (peace army workers). Like Bhoodan, this movement has a spiritual as well as practical purpose: to symbolize a family's concern for the common good, "to stimulate that sense of personal responsibility for your neighbor."

By 1960 Vinoba had turned to other crusades, leaving the actual administration of *Bhoodan-Yagna* to his corps of workers. Recently he has been stressing the abolition of all *religions* (in the narrow sense, including Hinduism) and the development of *spirituality*. Let us take divisive, sectarian, organized religions, he says,

and "give them respectful burial; . . . party politics also must be
given a burial in this modern scientific age. . . . Away with
religion, forward to spiritualism; away with politics, forward to
science." [10] How? By bringing people of diverse viewpoints together
in love instead of dividing society along lines of common ideologies
or group conformities. Asked if Vinoba's movement might be the
long-sought meeting place of East and West, Groom replied: "It
represents a very vital challenge to the whole basis of Hinduism. It
is a reform movement. . . . He has a very definite sense of building up the relationship between East and West in the cultural-reli-
gious field." For example, he speaks of *world* victory rather than
Jai Hind! (Victory to India!)

Still more recently Bhave has embarked on certain specific social—and personal—reforms, with only limited success. One was
to persuade the *dacoits* (bandits) in central India to desist from
their plunder and murder and violence. A second was to mediate on
behalf of the Bengali minority in Assam.[11] For the latter mission
Prime Minister Nehru offered him a government plane, which he
declined in favor of walking the thousand miles or more, at his
steady pace of ten miles a day.

How is one to evaluate such a man? Is his magnetic power a
matter of personality or of direct reliance on God? "He feels that
God is working in the world, and he is just being an instrument of
the Spirit," Groom explained. In fact, the real problem is the reverse: not that he is unaware of dependence on God, but that he is
so absorbed in spiritual life and divine guidance that it is impossible
to predict what he may do next. Like Gandhi, he is "completely un-
attached to results," feeling no responsibility for the consequences
of his actions, and therefore no credit for success. This is the detachment of the *Gita*, but it heightens the difficulties of practical
leadership and administrative details, such as distributing land or
directing personnel. Vinoba wants to develop initiative in others,
but instead overwhelms and "stultifies" it by the sheer power of his
own mind and personality. In other words, he lacks the talent for
strengthening and encouraging others which so characterized the
Mahatma. Vinoba, as did Nehru, consciously but helplessly accepts
the Indian pattern of looking to a leader, failing to see that the move-

ment will not really grow until he is gone and his disciples will
have to diverge from his pattern and find new expressions.

Strangely enough, despite his rejection of mechanical transportation, he sees in the universality of science a powerful ally toward brotherhood and sharing. When this writer inquired about
Vinobaji's social concern, his sense of responsibility for those beyond the family, caste and village, an aide conceded, "This is probably what is new. . . . I think almost every address he makes,
he refers to Jesus in some form. . . . He finds tremendous support
and inspiration from the Bible. . . . He has a very direct sense
that he is speaking and working in the spirit of the Bible." Furthermore, he believes that the concept of nonviolence is derived
from Jesus, and once gave a course on the Christian Gospels. Yet,
when asked if he shared Gandhi's attraction to the personality of
Jesus, Vinoba once replied:

Christ was love personified, no doubt, but I have no tendency to regard
Him as perfection. . . . Even Christ uttered "woe" on the Pharisees
and, according to Matthew, whipped the money-changers from the
Temple. And cannot we criticise Him for it? Cannot we see that such
conduct was more likely to turn the Pharisees and money-changers
into continued enemies rather than convert them? Such an attitude may
make people obstinate as well as wicked. Were all the Pharisees hypo-
crites and liars? [12]

On this same theme, Groom added: "He is very strongly influenced
by Jesus, but I suspect you would not like his attitude to the Church.
He feels the Church has lessened the contribution of Christ. . . .
The only thing he cannot accept is a dogmatic avowal that Truth
is *only* to be found in Jesus."

Vinoba's new emphasis is his blending of science and spirituality. He believes strongly that there is an awakening, the call of
a new age, a "wind of God" throughout the world. What are the
sources of this moral and social reform in India? the present writer
asked Vinobaji. The response was clear and unequivocal:

The basic principle should be that all our actions which are meant for
the service of man should be in our heart of hearts consecrated actions,

devoted to the service of God. Man is the manifestation of God. Therefore all our actions should be devoted to Him. That is the only basic
principle which will cover [the rest]. All other ethical principles will follow from the single devotion to God.[13]

Does one find in India this essential core of religion? Yes, this
"saint on the march" replied, "one does find the spiritual here. Indian character is adequate for my ideas. I am not preaching to
them anything which is not according to their tradition. The things
I am trying to inculcate are basically to be found in the teaching of
our men of old."

Not even Indians themselves are sure whether Vinoba Bhave
represents primarily a social revolution or a spiritual renewal. He
himself would insist that economic and moral concerns of life are
inseparable. Hallam Tennyson calls this program "Communism as
it might still be if we had the courage to grow to spiritual maturity.
Communism plus so many other things, including God, that it
looks remarkably like the society described in the Acts of the
Apostles." [14] But even at the practical level it is not yet clear what
Bhoodan-Yagna has really accomplished. It can be argued that the
movement has aroused false hopes on the part of peasants and
false complacency among landowners, that the wistful piety of this
method will stiffen resistance to the centralized program of Community Development. Devout and illiterate farmers may respond
ecstatically to the appeals of a "Great Soul" or a "Walking Saint,"
but there is little evidence that support for such movements will
outlive their founders. Certainly the problems and areas of India
are too vast to be covered by a "handful of hikers," however successful they may be in setting up local projects. President Radhakrishnan has written:

It is because we cannot make all the people prophets that we have to
depend on legislation to bring about changes in our social order. The
Bhoodan movement acquires great significance in this context of urgent
change. It underlines traditions that are implicit in the Indian way of
life. It recaptures the idea of the social order as the family writ large.
It appeals to our religious instinct that spiritual freedom can be attained only by those who are not attached to material possessions. The
movement started by Acharya Vinoba Bhave is potentially revolu-

tionary in character. The response to his appeal which has come from all levels of the social order shows that the moral reserves of our country are large. The movement is based on an act of faith.[15]

The President has revealed the problem precisely. "Because we cannot make all the people prophets," we must look—even in "god-intoxicated" India—to government programs, to Five-Year Plans for economic growth, to Community Development. Vinoba Bhave is an inspiring, saintly man. The world needs saints, and the West has almost lost the formula. To some degree, Vinobaji personifies the conscience of India today, as Gandhiji once spoke for the conscience of the world. But even that must be qualified, for educated, urban India shrugs off Vinoba Bhave or smiles tolerantly. Campbell says, for example: "Nehru respects Bhave enormously. But Nehru is a practical statesman with a tremendous job to do, and he does not even try to fit Bhave into his plans." [16] For all his peregrinations, Vinobaji can visit only an infinitesimal fraction of India's rural millions; his influence on the rest can be, at best, remote and dilute. As has been indicated, he himself possesses a naively optimistic view of human nature, a naively unrealistic view of social change.

For all his adulation of the "Saint on the March," Hallam Tennyson sees the moral and spiritual dilemma in these terms:

He [Vinoba] is not, like Gandhi, a politician saint, but a saint temporarily on the fringe of politics. "Fire merely burns; it does not worry whether anyone puts a pot on it, fills it with water and puts rice in it to make a meal. It burns, and that is the limit of its duty. It is for others to do theirs." Gandhi the politician succeeded, but Gandhi the saint failed. India was freed but not converted.[17]

Those who want to eat—and this is a basic need of India today—*must* be concerned with finding a pot, filling it with water and rice, and putting it on the stove. The fire is important; pray God, India may never lose her reverence for saints. But "a saint temporarily on the fringe of politics" will have no opportunity to "convert" his people unless he joins hands with equally profound and sincere attempts to feed them—and to lead them.

The one man who could speak effectively within the political

structure on behalf of Gandhian socialism and Sarvodaya has officially "withdrawn" from politics to support Vinoba Bhave's village
reforms. Jayaprakash Narayan (or Jai Prakash Narain) has proclaimed as his creed: "Democracy is good for everyone. What shape
and form should be given to democracy so that it may be suited to
the climate concerned? It is axiomatic for me that democracy is the
only way of life for any people." [18] Yet for this apparently sincere
chameleon, no single definition of democracy has been axiomatic at
any time.

It may be embarrassing to some Americans to learn that "J.P."
is the only important figure on the Indian scene today who received
his education in the United States—on his own initiative in order to
boycott the British scholarship he had won. During the early twen-
ties (he was born in 1902) he studied science and economics in five
different American universities, earning his way by such varied
jobs as waiter, fruit packer, farm laborer, factory worker and sales-
man. More important to his career, he was converted to Marxism
by a Wisconsin professor and had some association with the American Communist Party from 1924 to 1929. On his return to India
he headed the Labor Research Department of the Congress and
served as Acting General Secretary of the Indian National Congress
1932–1933, a post which earned him his first prison term under
the British.

He founded a Railway Workers' Union, a short-lived Socialist
Party, and in 1934 the Congress Socialist Party, which he served as
General Secretary. During the next two decades he displayed a rare
blend of Marxism and Gandhism. In 1942 Fischer included him
among the "political children of Gandhi but recent students of
Karl Marx . . . [who] moved secretly across the land fomenting
rebellion." [19] Minoo Masani, a close personal friend though often
political opponent, says of the Congress Socialist Party: "While,
perhaps, intellectually they accepted the Leninist theory that 'the
end justifies the means,' temperamentally and secretly, honesty and
purity of means attracted them." [20] Early in World War II, perhaps
with the signing or breaking of the Russo-German Pact, Narayan
acknowledged the futility of trying to work with the Communist
Party, but soon after the war he led his followers out of the Con-

gress and merged with Kripalani's group to form the Praja Socialists in 1952.

When he abruptly resigned from active politics and joined the
Bhoodan Movement, many condemned his desertion of the Socialist cause as the only significant rival to Nehru. "Doubtless he will
continue to meditate in a sneering sort of way on the folly and vanity of all human beings save Jaya Prakash Narayan," remarks Alexander Campbell in his own "sneering sort of way." [21] But "J.P."
has had better, more important things on which to meditate. His
"conversion" to *Sarvodaya* appears to be sincere and deep. Tennyson speaks of his quiet manner in contrast to his former fervent oratory, of the passion gone from his "fine, strong face." Of his own
basic faith Narayan says: "My old Socialist comrades tell me that
no change can be brought about without the aid of force or law. But
I tell them that neither force nor law are needed to bring in the age
of love." [22]

The political program for *Sarvodaya* was expounded by Narayan in October 1959, in a thesis entitled, *A Plea for Reconstruction
of Indian Policy*.[23] Negatively, it deplores the cost, competitiveness,
corruption and centralism of parliamentary democracy. Positively,
it appeals for a "communitarian society" based on local economic
and political power. Condemning what he calls the "democratic
oligarchy" of the West, Narayan recognizes three historical but
precarious safeguards for Indian democracy: liberal social and
political traditions inherited from Great Britain, the teachings of
Gandhiji and Vinobaji, and the village autonomy of long ago. Society, he believes, should be reconstructed on the ancient bases of
varna (caste), "in which occupations, professions and functions are
integrated with the community;" the social ethics of *karma;* and
panchayat-raj, rule by local councils *not* administered from above.
He therefore recommends decentralization of police, courts, taxation, social services and planning. Industry as well as government
should stem from community needs, beginning with the village and
moving up to regions, districts, provinces (where there might be
some large-scale industries but no executive ministries), nations
(responsible only for defense, foreign relations, currency, and inter-
provincial coordination and legislation, *not* administration), and "a

day might come when the national communities might federate to form the world community." [24]

On December 28, 1959, he interpreted his position in a public address at Sapru House before the Indian Council of World Affairs. One of his sharpest blasts he aimed at Westerners who assume that democracy is "something which has succeeded in their own country, and they think it will succeed everywhere."

Western society has become an atomized society, a disorganized society. A natural society has been disrupted by the machine, which has become the master of man. What we need today is a human revolution to make man the master of technology instead of technology the master of man. . . . I do not know how the West will unscramble the egg again, will make a community again.

He then paid tribute to experiments in "guided democracy" which he had recently investigated in Pakistan, Yugoslavia and Egypt—none of them countries which the West regards as "typically" democratic. Yet Narayan was convinced that "all Afro-Asian dictators, from Cairo to Jakarta" were genuinely interested in handing over power to the people as early as possible. In fact, his plea for "participating democracy" from the "grass-roots" up is precisely the effort to avoid the alternatives of chaos or Communism. At present, Narayan admits, "there is no initiative in the village today; village democracy is gone." Yet he insists "it is not only possible but desirable and necessary for us to reconstruct these self-governing democracies." For whom? Whence cometh the initiative, the resources, the training, the personnel to reconstruct what is admittedly lacking in the village today?

Because "the most effective party in our country is caste . . . [and] the voters are more anxious to find out the caste of a candidate than his party or his political theories," elections should be abolished. This would circumvent the widespread demagoguery, "unscrupulousness, manipulation (by parties and mass media), and intrigue." "There has been a general deterioration in the moral standards of our people, but the most marked deterioration has been in the political sphere," he declared. Elections are not only costly, but divisive, when what Asia needs most today is unity. The alternative? Narayan cited villages in the north of India where officials are chosen by consensus or by nomination of the village elders, and others in the south where they are picked by lot (with certain qualifications of literacy, property and/or character).

"Narayan's Thesis" became political table-talk everywhere in the capital, discussed in countless groups, with and without its author. In one such informal dinner meeting a high-ranking official of the United States Department of Labor asked whether such singleness of purpose could be achieved in the face of great diversity. "J.P." acknowledged that diversities are inevitable, necessary, even valuable, but he regretted their accentuation in party politics.

Democratic methods should be discovered for the resolution of differences after the community has discussed them. Particularly for a developing country like India, there is more need for common unity of purpose and action than for differences to be emphasized. Democracy may really be in danger if democracy appears to the common people as a sort of debating society.[25]

In this connection he reiterated his hope for representative councils chosen by general agreement, nomination of "umpires" or drawing of lots, rather than by majority victory. "This may be Utopian or idealistic or even foolish, I don't know," he admitted wistfully.

Max Lerner, brilliant columnist and Columbia professor, who was teaching and learning in India that year, inquired: "In avoiding factionalism, aren't you likely to get One Party as the unifying force, as in Egypt, Pakistan, and Yugoslavia?" Narayan merely affirmed his belief that Egypt is trying to build a partyless society from the bottom up, that Pakistan's village democracy is "guided" primarily by magistrates at a district level. Then he spoke of Gandhi's dream that the Congress would dissolve, "commit *harakiri*," convert itself into a Lok Sevak Sangh (Association of Servants of the People). The third facet of reply dealt vaguely with ethical goals. "The economic, social, and moral independence of India has yet to be achieved," "J.P." asserted, though no one quite knew what he meant by "moral independence." Gandhi and Vinoba, he said, have provided "the nonviolent answer to the One-Party system. . . . The next social revolution will have to come from those who are not in parties," and it will be a "moral revolution."

Narayan's plan calls for 60 per cent of industry to be owned

and operated in villages or districts, 25 per cent in the states, and
only 15 per cent on a national basis. Likewise, planning, he said,
must begin from the bottom, for a limited region, instead of the
present "top-down planning," which encourages an attitude of *"we
want*—what others *give us."* In his confidence that such decentralization is practicable, Narayan even denied the necessity of initiative from above. "Using idealistic language," he added, the aim is
"to create a stateless society, or a state which is very much decen-
tralized." Pressed further, he admitted that this is "not fully" a
withering away of the state; "the Center shrinks" but is never completely done away with. The goals he describes more clearly:

The value of sharing, the attitudes of family life applied to the life of
the community, the spirit of a community of belonging to one another,
of concern for one another, so that they all become one family and
join hands together to serve.

A similar group of political and economic experts debated
Narayan's *Plea* . . . under the sponsorship of the India chapter of
the Congress for Cultural Freedom.[26] Gyan Chand, noted econo-
mist, summarized Narayan's chief points as follows:

India's political system has to be related to India's heritage. . . . Any
democracy which is to function properly must be a participating democracy . . . in which the people have a sense of belonging. . . .
Polity and economy must have an ethical basis. . . . Any form which
is divorced from ethics . . . can be neither lasting nor effective. . . .
Industrialization and the centralization which it inevitably involves . . .
are remote from the people and therefore cannot be truly democratic.

In refutation, Chand charged, first of all, that the ancient heritage of India is being idealized and romanticized, that village institutions appropriate to the past have long been stagnant, that there
is no inspiration or incentive in Indian villages today. Secondly, he
said, decentralization is desirable, but so are national unity, international trade, world culture, and the like. To condemn the materialism of both capitalism and communism is to overlook the needs
of men and social institutions, and to see the present crisis solely in
moral and spiritual terms is unjustified and unwarranted.

Thirdly, although parliamentary democracy encounters many

difficulties when transported to Asian soil, the "Communist solution" of indirect elections is not the only alternative, for there may be many forms based on popular consent and public responsibility. Under the faults and failures of the West, he conceded, is a great inner vitality. "The world is on the threshold of a great epoch," Chand concluded; "India has got to be a part of this new world civilization. . . . Most of the problems to which 'J.P.' refers are problems not of India, but of the world."

Others supported Narayan's plea for decentralization, but argued that he neglected problems of leadership and the educational values of elections for stimulating social change. Gunnar Myrdal, distinguished Swedish sociologist, spoke sympathetically for Narayan's concern over great inequality and great poverty. But he too asserted that elections and parties have educational value, and "there is no reason, as we say in Sweden, to 'throw the axe in the lake.' " On the whole, it appeared that Indians showed less patience with the ethical idealism of Jayaprakash than their European colleagues. A specialist in public administration declared: "I don't see how 'J.P.' can idealize the village and at the same time denounce it. . . . I don't believe in decentralization, localism, ancient villages. I disagree root and branch." A philosophy professor questioned the basis of Narayan's ethics as optimistic and undefined, whereas "I take man as fallible, hungry, suffering, tempted." An editor challenged Narayan to stop intellectual debating and prove his program by grass-roots experimentation. " 'J.P.'s' ideas have moved from one philosophical platform to another, always within the ivory tower. I believe this is worth testing."

Max Lerner essayed a searching analysis of Narayan. First, he suggested, "J.P.'s" concern for fragmentation of personality, alienation, and so on, is common to American psychology and sociology, "a philosophy of anxieties" typical of our times. Narayan sounds like Kierkegaard, Lerner said, but instead of Kierkegaard's solution in the individual's relation to God, "J.P." finds his solution in the existential community. In reference to borrowing from the West, Lerner went on to point out:

Efforts to take over political institutions are not so easy, unless you take over a number of the experiences through which the originators of those institutions lived [e.g. civil liberties, judicial review, rule of law, non-partisan administration, etc.]. . . . I find "J.P.'s" thesis a curious misunderstanding of the working of the party system. . . . It is certainly not the American party system. . . . Parties do not create conflicts, though they may exacerbate them.

Then Lerner examined, item by item, what he called Narayan's "cult thinking":

1. The Cult of Primitivism . . . idealizing and abstracting the values of an assumed Golden Age, ignoring its inequalities, corruption, and degradation;

2. The Cult of Localism . . . the assumption that man is naturally and automatically better at the grass-roots than at the top. . . . We have all known idiocy at both levels and also sanity and creativeness, but in America the New Deal came from "the Center" (the federal government).

3. The Cult of Partyless Democracy . . . Narayan's naive disregard of the one-party system which really exists in the countries he cites.

4. The Cult of Consensus . . . the assumption that agreement without vote is always possible and practicable—and democratic.

5. The Cult of the Organic, of the Whole. . . . In his failure to recognize new kinds of organic unity, "J.P." tends to alienate man from the forces of his own day (such as science). The effort to preserve an organic whole makes India static instead of dynamic; it is good to move as well as to have roots. . . . "The problem of power is not to eliminate it, but to use it in creative ways."

Reaction to Narayan's Thesis from the general public was even more hostile. His own Praja Socialist Party analyzed the plan and reported: "Although the executive did not adopt a resolution on the thesis, most of the members are understood to hold the view that Mr. Narain's suggestions are impracticable and too ideal to suit present Indian conditions." [27] A Calcutta professor remarked: "He is a good, sacrificing man, but sometimes he is very muddled, confusing. . . . He is not sufficiently realistic." And a leading editorial demolished the proposal with the comment: "The most hopeful thing about Mr. Narain's thesis is that no politically effective person or party in India today is remotely likely to try it." [28] Perhaps there can be no clearer, more decisive illustration of the gap between Gandhian theory and political practice in India today.

Chapter XIII

Ethics in Practice

One of the chief instruments by which the Indian government seeks to realize the goals of Sarvodaya is the Ministry of Community Development and Cooperation. B. S. Murthy, its Deputy Minister in 1960, has claimed that Community Development is an extension of Gandhiji's Constructive Program, that the Mahatma's cardinal principles of self-reliance and mutual help are "the warp and the woof with which the present fabric of Community Development is being woven." [1] Nevertheless, he and his colleagues took pains to explain that "this is not a religious movement; it is social and economic, more economic." By the end of 1959 the Ministry reported 3,000 Blocks, serving 300,000 out of India's 500,000 villages. When a United Nations survey criticized the program for moving too fast and recommended more intensive rather than extensive coverage, officials replied that neighboring villages see the improvements in one Block and demand similar services immediately.

As in many other parts of India's secular government, Community Development officers draw a sharp distinction between ethics and religion. For example, they said, "Gandhi may have drawn his motivation for social service from his religious faith, but he never insisted that others must do likewise. . . . Gandhi regarded *conscience* as essential . . . the higher moral and spiritual values . . . but not necessarily religion." Only one identified religion with vital social forces under these three headings: the knowledge of good and evil, acceptance of *karma* as ethical duty, and faith in future reincarnation "that has kept us going during centuries of oppression."

Nor do these capital bureaucrats rely on religious sanctions to accomplish their social and economic reform. Unanimously they reported, "Just as religion provides no incentive, so it offers no obstacle to community development." "Religion provides no incentive!" In the land of Buddha and Asoka, of Ranade and Gokhale, of Gandhi and Bhave, is it true that religion has been discarded as a dynamic social force? When the question was pressed, these government officials reiterated their convictions: "Exclusively secular. . . . Social justice is sufficient . . . self-reliance. . . . Today there is no principle [of religious motivation] though it may sometimes be a technique for reaching the people."

On the contrary, Community Development prides itself on bringing various religious groups together for the common good. "Religion and caste have played their part in India," one conceded, but now "this new movement is to by-pass caste and religion and focus the support of people, irrespective of caste and creed, on working for their economic development." Other approaches ranged from the blunt insistence that "there is no support for caste in our religion" to the confidence that smashing indirect barriers, such as segregated wells and schools, will gradually weaken the institution of caste itself. Such frank disavowal of religious concern may seem, to some, as justification for the moral and spiritual protests of Vinobaji or J. P. Narayan. Those who believe that lasting social reform must have ethical roots *and* that ethical roots must be planted in a transcendent faith may well be discouraged.

But there is another side to the picture. Most Westerners, at least, would be unwilling to follow the *Gita* or Gandhi in complete indifference to practical results. And most observers—especially those who knew the India of ten or fifteen years ago—are profoundly impressed by the achievements of Community Development. To be sure, there have been failures—and will be more. The very first C. D. Block established in south-central India, has neat, modern bungalows for the staff, embryonic landscaping, an open-air theater—but on this writer's visit, at least, absolutely no activity going on. The director of a nearby Christian school confessed that, on the occasion of government inspections, he had been asked to lend chickens to the Block to give the appearance of "being in business"; that farmers often grew tired of waiting for Community Development agents to spray their crops, and sent instead for the agricultural extension worker from the mission school.

On the other hand, general activities of Community Development include simple literature on citizenship, nation-wide tours for village representatives to inspire patriotism, films and posters on public works and other national projects, local participation in digging irrigation ditches to link the community with major dams, increasing mobility of the population on better roads and railways. All these help to expand the narrow Hindu sense of duty toward family and caste, to include the community and the nation. In each village of a C. D. Block, three basic social units are set up: the *panchayat* (or council), the cooperative (for economic sharing), and the school. In addition there are community organizations for sports, dramatics, labor, religion, and so on. Block councils receive training in agriculture, health and sanitation. The Ministry estimates that Blocks have achieved a 20 per cent increase in productivity over non-Block regions, and to this must be added immeasurable benefits of more fish and vegetables, better clothes, better homes, better health, better education. The number of children in schools has doubled since the program started; life expectancy has been raised from twenty-three to over forty years.

What are the bottlenecks? Ministry officials listed three: excessive dependence on government credit instead of developing local thrift, the shortage of fertilizers and seeds to meet the demand (though the demand itself is a sign of progress), and "the main bottleneck is shortage of trained personnel." Problems one and three go directly back to motivation, the first in the village itself, the third among the vast reservoir of educated unemployed, who are still unfit—by training or dedication—for the village service their country most needs.

In recognizing this challenge—and the undermining of caste which is "already in the air"—the Ministry's Director of Social Education asserted that "the real praise must go to our national movement and the work of Gandhiji." Hand-in-hand! "Our national movement *and* the work of Gandhiji." Many of the statements of Vinoba Bhave or of J. P. Narayan, many of the blasts from their critics, seem to imply a basic conflict or rivalry between these two approaches. They do appear to have essentially different motivations and orientation, as well as radically opposing concepts of government. Yet the two are not inherently incompatible. In certain situations they have already demonstrated a practical partnership: in Rajasthan and Andhra Pradesh (two of the Indian states), where *panchayat raj* (rule by local councils) has been developed on a state-wide basis, and provincial subsidies have been given without strings to allow the people to decide on their own allocation of funds. S. K. Rey, Minister of Community Development, has declared that the changes encouraged through this village democracy are more significant, more radical, than anything else in the entire program.[2]

These signs of progress indicate the concern of Indian officialdom for greater democracy at the "grass roots," for implementing *some* of the goals of Sarvodaya. Narayan may be right that "without Vinoba's movement this democratic decentralization would not have come," but it is equally clear that Bhoodan and Sarvodaya and "participating democracy" and "communitarianism" will not get far without supporting resources from the Central Government. It may also be true that "Community Development programs are not succeeding because there is not enough enthusiasm for them," although another facet of Narayan's protest is that there is *too* much enthusiasm for *material* advance at the expense of moral and spiritual values. Here in the area of personal commitment—not in the realm of industrial organization or parliamentary democracy—Vinoba's "spirituality" may make its greatest contribution.

To take but one example, in a tiny segment of South India "100 villages, 100,000 people are slowly forming themselves into a cooperative family pattern." Already the majority in 35 of these villages have voluntarily placed their lands in common ownership. One of them decided to give 20 of its precious 250 acres (feeding 60 families) to 10 landless families. Two new high schools have been started in remote districts; a new road is planned in response to the women who demanded a bus route to get more easily to regional meetings. The government (!) has started a Pilot Health Program. The writer goes on to speak of the larger India in exciting terms:

Our rural development program is one of the most extensive in the world. But how much improvement the work and worker needs. Our hope is with the villager himself. Electric light and power are coming to the villages. I marvel how the buses are rapidly creeping into the remotest villages. Rural housing programs are becoming common. Each large town or city has its larger co-operative housing programs. I cannot think of a single aspect of our life that is not changing quickly. . . . We are challenged by the initiation of Panchayat Raj! Government is coming to the people, to our villages! Now to live up to it! [3]

Here is a thrilling testimonial to the teamwork between national government and local peasants. But there is a deeper current of partnership in this particular area and this particular project. For this is an international, interracial, interfaith venture. Its volunteer workers from various religious backgrounds provide a constant reminder of "spiritual" foundations for Community Development. And the American Christian spokesman goes on to say:

If I could tell you the story of changed minds, hearts, and souls, then you would better understand the real revolution taking place. . . . Present-day Christianity, Hinduism, Buddhism, Islam are not enough. Vinobaji calls us to a new "spirituality." I would say a new comprehension of the fullness we have in God, in our traditions, in our heritages— a new comprehension, then a new incarnation for today.

The Status of Women

Another area of vital significance in charting India's social change is the status of women. President Radhakrishnan once asserted that "one of the many causes of India losing its freedom in the past was ill treatment of women, and after achieving Independence it is only fair that we compensate them for that." [4] Although there may once have been a Golden Age of equal rights and honor, ancient proverbs indicate a woman's place more accurately: "Regard not a woman's word. . . . Three are inconstant: woman, wind, and wealth. . . . To educate a woman is like placing a knife in the hands of a monkey. . . . Woman, thou hast three good qualities (to sing, to burn *as a sati,* to produce sons) and 400,000 bad." [5] Over the centuries, with the encouragement of Manu, child marriage, polygyny and supersession increased. Far from being a measure of protection against Muslim violation, as some Hindus still claim, *purdah* can be traced to priestly rules in the *Mahabharata.* If foreign invasions (Turkish, Mogul, Portuguese, Dutch, French, Danish, British) did intensify these restrictions, they certainly did not create them or the need for them.

Under sharply divergent religious customs, Macaulay and other British statesmen found it impossible to adopt a uniform marriage code. Even today there exists a multiplicity of "personal laws" and communal (sectarian) legislation which prove extremely difficult to administer. A nation-wide ban on dowries was adopted on July 1, 1961, over the protest—ironically enough—of certain Christian groups which prefer dowry payments rather than the land fragmentation involved in female inheritance rights. A much-needed tightening and enforcement of the Act of 1956 (For the Suppression of Immoral Traffic in Women and Girls) confronts such ancient obstacles as *devadasis* (temple dancers) and organized slave traffic in some localities, such modern problems as the lack of sex education and of rehabilitation programs. It also encounters the optimistic Hindu view of man, devoid of any doctrine of original sin. An Indian psychoanalyst, well trained also in Christian theology, commented that Hindu social workers would not be fully effective until they learned to face the fact of unethical behavior as a part of human nature.

By Western standards Indian women are still a long way from emancipation. Despite the spectacular achievement of individual leaders, they are often limited as to fields of employment outside of teaching, government and social service. Even among college graduates most marriages are arranged by parents, and many will argue sincerely that this is a wiser and safer basis than romantic but immature attraction. It is better to love the person you marry, some would say, than to marry the person you love. In a passage intended to glorify Hindu womanhood Radhakrishnan declared:

Stable marriages are more numerous, and family affections much stronger than perhaps in any other country. This is due largely to the character of Indian women, who are miracles of dignity, graciousness, and peace. *For many of them the object of life is to endure life.*[6]

There is, of course, high courage and moral grace to be found in patient endurance and quiet—even cheerful—desperation. But what reflects true virtue on the part of Indian womanhood represents a corresponding disgrace to Indian society as a whole. Not infrequently today an Indian wife performs modern suttee by intentionally setting her sari afire or by leaping into a well to escape an intolerable situation.

In recent decades many groups have been concerned to change this situation. One of the oldest is the All-India Women's Conference, founded in 1926 by Rajkumari Amrit Kaur as a voluntary membership organization devoted to social welfare. Its chief focus is education, ranging from the establishment of Lady Irwin College through international relations institutes and social legislation to literacy and family planning classes. It also provides nurseries, medical clinics, hostels for working women and encouragement for feminine careers. Similarly, the most active department in the All-India Congress Committee appears to be that for Women's Work, under the direction of Kumari Mukul Mukherjee, a modest and efficient administrator. Publications and training schools deal not only with political responsibility, but with home economics, sanitation, social education, and community welfare.

It is difficult to overestimate the importance of such a "grassroots" approach—or the enormous gulf which still separates millions of village women from the justice, liberty, equality and fraternity promised by the Constitution. But the measure of social progress can be seen in dazzling terms at another level: the achievement of outstanding women. Since independence, Indian women have occupied posts as President of the United Nations General Assembly, Ambassadress to Russia, High Commissioner at the Court of St. James, President of the Congress Party, Minister of Health, Governor of Uttar Pradesh, Deputy Minister of External Affairs, Deputy Minister of Home Affairs, President of the World Health Organization, Co-President of the World Council of Churches.

Mrs. Indira Gandhi (no relation to the Mahatma) is Prime Minister Nehru's only daughter, a woman of such quiet capability that she had been seriously proposed as her father's successor—with no hint of nepotism. In conversation she displays a remarkable combination of quick comprehension and direct honesty. Asked whether traditional moral and spiritual values may be discarded along with superstitions, she replied, "That has not happened in India," then added with an apologetic laugh, "They are not even discarding the superstitions." Mrs. Gandhi usually wears homespun cloth "out of habit, having done it all my life . . . It does help people to earn extra money, but"—her honesty and realism led her on—"there is a question whether it should be subsidized to the extent that it is, whether the money could be used for better purposes."

With typical frankness and humor, she discussed the "old days" when Congress leaders imitated Gandhiji in his simplicity. "It was all right for him as a saint to say that whoever comes [to see him] must sleep on the floor," but one could not conduct the country or treat foreign visitors in that fashion. (That particular year had seen state visits to the capital by Eisenhower, Khrushchev, Nasser, Chou and others.) Furthermore, Mrs. Gandhi went on with refreshing candor, "I happen to believe that a table and chair lead to greater efficiency than working on the floor." In more serious vein, the late Prime Minister's daughter gave credit to Gandhiji for opening to Indian women the whole range of political activity. And from the freedom movement, she said, came the realization that social change in other areas not only is possible, but depends in large measure on feminine participation.

The first new idea was Independence. They didn't entirely believe that it was possible. Although no extravagant promises were made, gradually Independence became a magic word. When everything [e.g. poverty, caste restrictions, corruptions, etc.] did not automatically go, there was quite a reaction. . . . That change can only come today by the people. This Government or any political party cannot bring it about. The actual work has to be done by the people . . .[7]

Mrs. Lakshmi Menon, Deputy Minister of External Affairs and thus second to Nehru in foreign relations, revealed a sophisticated insight into these moral issues. Asked about the relation of ethics to politics, she countered with the "realistic" query: Can there be ethics in politics?

It is one thing for an individual to try to act according to his moral standards, but it is not easy to apply ethics in the same way to political matters. When a person speaks and acts for a whole nation, he cannot impose his views on the people. Of course we should endeavor to keep moral principles in mind, and to use ethical means for achieving our goals, but in contrast to those who would impose a kind of moralism on the government, I would say that "enlightened self-interest" must be the basis of our decisions.[8]

Mrs. Menon went on to admit that human nature cannot uphold a stress on the "absolute importance" of means, any more than it can support the view that "ends justify means." But she denied that one can fruitfully discuss "Gandhian principles" because the Mahatma evolved particular techniques for particular situations. Thus, *satyagraha* (truth force) succeeded against the centuries of freedom and moral responsibility of Great Britain, but would not have the same effect on France, Russia, China, Japan (or Portugal?).

Rajkumari Amrit Kaur, the only woman to have served in the Indian Cabinet, spoke frankly of discrimination against her sex. "Social custom and usages (both Hindu and Muslim)," she declared, "have dealt harshly with women in India." Too often, she averred, these man-made restrictions on individual rights have had the sanction of institutional religion, including Christianity. But today, the Rajkumari went on, women should neither want nor need privileged positions in society; "they should be willing and able to compete with men on merit and merit alone." She herself had done just that, as a nurse in World War I, as secretary and welfare worker on Gandhi's staff, as a chairman of the national and international Red Cross, past president of the World Health Organization, former Minister of Health and Communications, a member of the Upper House in Parliament until her death in early 1964. Although she fully supported Gandhi's Constructive Program, she realized the importance of government assistance in social service, for India cannot wait until a village can support a school and hospital before establishing them there. "The sick and the illiterate cannot work well enough to become self-sufficient. . . . The villagers want education and health before they ask for fertilizers, etc."

As a Christian, Rajkumariji firmly believed that the great social movements of the nineteenth and twentieth centuries in India were inspired by Christian missions. But she went on to acknowledge the validity of certain criticisms: that recent missionaries have not always lived up to the ideals of their predecessors, they have relied on government patronage, they have alienated converts from their environment, they have engaged in proselyting when "evangelism should now be left to the Indian pastors." Furthermore, "religious leaders often become arrogant in their search after God, but all roads really lead to God. . . . The divisions in your own churches have not been a help in the spread of Christianity in this country." Finally she added:

Why has Christianity not spread in India? Because we are weak interpreters. . . . There is plenty of room for all of you here to join in this social service, to come here not so much as preachers of Christ's Gospels as actors of His Gospel, silent actors. Action is much more powerful than words.[9]

The Ramakrishna Mission

A number of Indians, including some Christians, assured me that the Ramakrishna Mission comes nearer than any other organization to carrying on the welfare services and the social concern which the Christian Church pioneered. Today Vivekananda's organization reaches across the country with a twofold purpose. One branch is the Math (or Order), providing retreats for study and meditation, and in urban centers a weekly discourse which draws the largest "congregations" of any religious function. The other branch is the Mission, which conducts at least ten hospitals, seventy dispensaries, schools and colleges and libraries, famine relief and *Narijan* welfare projects. In addition to his weekly lectures, usually based on the *Bhagavad-Gita*, Swami Ranganathananda in New Delhi is often called upon to speak on social ethics. For example, to the Indian Conference of Social Work he said:

Modern society does not believe in some of the ancient values that we call spiritual values, but they want to fill it up with social work. . . . You can never deal with social work without bringing in the concept of ethics and moral values. . . . When you speak of the ethics of social work, you are speaking of the development of the individual into a new dimension . . . making man of every individual. . . . If ethics is eliminated, it will be an exploitation of the world around for my own self.[10]

In quiet, earnest tones the Swami referred to Jesus' Great Commandment as "the whole scope of religion and ethics . . . [which] has been with us since the Vedic age." He described political unity as the discovery that "the whole world is my neighbor," that "there is no frontier so far as sympathy is concerned—no family, sect, class, nation, etc." Quoting once more from the New Testament, he concluded, "Social work is *the* word for our country today. . . . 'The harvest indeed is plenteous, but the laborers are few.' Anybody who lives for a purpose ceases to be an individual and becomes a force." Yet in private conversation Ranganathananda vehemently refused to give Christianity credit for stimulating social concern. "The chief influence of early Christian teachers was to take on the European vices [drinking, eating beef, etc.]," he said. "Unfortunately most of Christianity came to revile. . . . The preaching of the Gospel to bring humanity back to true life—that nobody will object to," he conceded, but when it was seen to be a Trojan Horse, it was rejected.

The Ramakrishna Mission deplores divisions of caste or creed and helped to relieve Hindu-Muslim tensions during the Partition riots. More specifically, to explain the modern attitude toward social and individual values, Ranganathananda explained:

Society must form into some groups. It is not possible to break down all groups. What we say is, "Make any group you like, but don't be exclusive." Don't put barriers in the way of others. If the old caste has failed to work, new groups will come into being. Whatever the grouping, remember that equality of man to man depends on the integration of every individual. . . . Vedanta is universal . . . not individualistic in that [Western] sense. It emphasizes the importance of the individual in the society, in the group. . . . It recognizes the value of society in the training of the individual and the need for the individual to respond to the social call.[11]

Family Planning

One of the most widely discussed social issues in modern India seems to be Family Planning. In fact, Prime Minister Nehru once remarked: "There is more official talk and action on birth control than in any other country." [12] For some people and nations population growth represents an economic threat, for others a medical problem, for still others a political dilemma. For India it raises deep-seated moral questions as well. Mahatma Gandhi's emphasis on voluntary continence was firm and unequivocal. On one hand, he believed that "union is a crime when desire for progeny is absent," thus rejecting any concept of sex for emotional, psychological or even biological fulfillment. On the other hand, he condemned all forms of artificial contraception as "dangerous to the nervous and moral health of the community." [13] Rajkumari Amrit Kaur, reportedly opposed to contraception (even when she was Minister of Health) as immoral and un-Christian, nevertheless acknowledged that "family planning has been the official policy of the government for many years," and although the desire to limit families exists, there are still "formidable barriers" to be overcome.[14]

Population pressure, however, is a formidable threat to any slowly developing nation. India's annual rate of net increase is approximately 2 per cent (as compared with 1.8 per cent in the

United States), but starting from India's base, this means enough additional humanity to populate a New York City each year, with a conceivable total of one billion by 2000 A.D. The concern of Government leaders is shown in financial appropriations for Family Planning: 6,500,000 rupees during the First Five-Year Plan, 49,-700,000 for the Second, and 250,000,000 for the Third. In 1960 the Ford Foundation contributed $330,000 to a Family Planning Communication and Motivation Action Research Committee. The complex, multifaceted title reflects some of the criticisms leveled at government and private agencies at work in this area: namely, a lack of formulated aim and purpose, a scarcity of educational and contraceptive materials, a failure to recognize the need for private, psychological approach. Too often, it has been charged, the program pushes forward on the single track of reducing population, with insufficient attention to maternal welfare, economic factors, child health and so on.

By and large, rural Indians are not concerned about reducing birth rates. For one thing, the *sine qua non* of a successful marriage is sons, preferably three or more, with daughters not even counted. Several doctors in India reported that they are consulted by more women wanting to have children, seeking fertility counsel and help, than those in need of "family planning." Before long, sanitation and medical care will reduce infant mortality to the point where a mother need not bear six to ten children in order to guarantee the survival of a few. But India's peasant masses are not yet convinced of this. In addition to the personal "obstacles of ignorance, shyness, and customary taboos," investigators discover that contraceptives are too expensive for the average family, that they require a degree of privacy and personal hygiene unavailable in crowded homes. Even the "rhythm method" or the simplest pills depend on keeping records or memories of regular time spans too complicated for illiterate, impatient, indifferent villagers.

Government agents declare that "no fundamental objections of a religious character have been raised," although one Community Development block leader reported that he encountered some fear that restricting conception may be sinful. Meanwhile officials of his own Ministry in New Delhi hopefully announced that the ancient greeting, "May you have more children!" is now being met by the retort, "Enough! I don't want more." Explicitly, however, they claimed only that birth control is being accepted in many *urban middle-class* families, though *very slowly* even there.

Sripati Chandrasekhar, one of the world's outstanding demographers, has appeared on numerous platforms and television programs in the West. He claims to find no moral or cultural barrier to birth control. In fact, he asserts that "when economics knocks at the door, religion jumps out of the window." Asked if this means that Hinduism has no deep-rooted social ethics, he responded: "Yes, I am sorry to say it, but it is true. We have no concern," no responsibility or feeling for others beyond family and caste, only an occasional gesture of charity to beggars as a sort of insurance for our own salvation. This modern, secular, Hindu scientist, disclaiming all traditional religious practices for himself, suggested that the key contribution of Christianity might be summed up in the word, *compassion*.

In countless other spheres of every-day life, one might attempt to appraise the ethics of India in transition. A very ancient civilization is moving forward with jet-age rapidity in certain areas, with glacial inertia in others. Whether Hindu culture can adapt itself sufficiently to provide the essential dynamic for social progress remains to be seen. In practice, as well as in theory, India clings on one hand to a deeply rooted spiritual heritage; on the other hand, she questions "religion" not only in Marxist terms (as an unscientific superstitious obstacle to change), but also as a divisive threat to national unity and freedom. Yet a UNESCO survey in 1953 recognized the continuing importance of the moral and spiritual factor:

Reporting on our impressions of India, we are ready to say that the use of religion in the sense in which we now use it, to mean a deep cosmically oriented concern for the meaning of human life, is one of the fundamental appeals which drive Indian life forward and integrate it with the humanitarianism and idealism of the Western tradition. . . . It can well be argued that religion as an organizing tendency will fade in India under the impact of science and technology. . . . [Nevertheless] in the India of the next decade or two religions, in the sense of reverence for the cosmic drama represented by human life, the inherent divinity and dignity of human personality, the ultimate spiritual sanctions to be found for everyday ethics, is a fundamental factor in guiding the transition toward the elimination of social hostilities and the integration of a national life.[15]

It is this positive factor which Indian leaders are seeking to revive in Hindu culture—in part, at least, because they have seen it, abused and violated but nonetheless present, in Christian communities.

Chapter XIV

Christianity in India Today

When the Prince of Wales visited his mother's empire of India in 1876, Lord Reay, Governor of Bombay, presented to him a group of Indian Christians. "They were doing for India," the Governor observed, "more than all those civilians, soldiers, judges and governors whom Your Highness has met." [1] British officials were not always so appreciative of this minority "sect." Until 1854, just four years before the Crown superseded the East India Company, the Bible had been excluded from libraries in Government schools, and teachers were forbidden to explain Christian references or to answer religious questions in or out of school. Even after such restrictions were lifted, Christianity labored under a number of handicaps whose weight is still felt amid changing circumstances a century later.

Some of these difficulties lay within the faith itself, its institutional forms and its alien representatives. They ranged from superficial cultural blocks to the dogmatic assertion that "there is no other name by which man may be saved" than that of Jesus Christ.

They included the separation of converts from their families and jobs and societies, the adoption of new names, new customs, new ethics. They found focus in "unbrotherly" treatment by many so-called Christians, in the doubtful mores of individuals and nations of Christendom. Some of these difficulties came from Hinduism: vested interests of the priestly caste, national and cultural pride resisting social change, traditional doctrines of inequality, ontological monism and escape. One Roman Catholic priest, disillusioned after working among Hindus for thirty-one years, exclaimed in disgust: "You must erase from the code of the Christian religion the cardinal precept of charity if you are to appeal to these caste-ridden folk." [2] Some obstacles came from a government which wanted no social agitation and required from missionaries a pledge of political "non-involvement" under pain of losing one's residence permit. All of these factors, in varying degrees, remain in the picture today.

Nevertheless the Church has continued to grow—and to serve. Fifty years ago it was probably true that "Christian ideals and principles are supplying the only new and constructive element in the period of religious and social transition through which India is now passing." [3] In those days mission schools provided the finest education in the country (as indicated in the records of most national leaders); mission hospitals offered the most dependable medical care; mission agencies pioneered in concern for orphans, lepers and other neglected groups. To take but one example of social progress, in 1919 it was estimated that 0.4 per cent of Muslim women were literate, 0.8 per cent of Hindu women, and 9.6 per cent of Christian women.[4] Thirty-two years later the over-all literacy rate for India, men and women, was 16.6 per cent, for Christians 28 per cent.[5]

Perhaps the most dramatic contribution of Christianity can be seen in the status of Untouchables. Without a doubt, much of Gandhi's concern for what he called *Harijans* (Children of God) came from observing the transformation which the Church brought to these outcastes: a transformation far deeper than better housing, education, new occupations. Lobo Prabhu, a retired Civil Servant now supporting Swatantra, discusses the approach which Christians have made to Scheduled Tribes in indigenous areas—and even more, in earlier times, among Scheduled Castes. Deploring the "psychological complex, which only missionaries have been able to remove," the writer explains:

The success of the missionaries in changing primitive people is because they give them a purpose in life. . . . Christianity, with its definite classification of right and wrong, reward and punishment, God and the devil, has a simple and direct approach which overcomes superstition. The question is, whether Hinduism can be similarly simplified so that these people have a meaningful life. In a way Hinduism, at least for the better educated and not merely in respect of the marriage law, has become christianized in its ethics. . . . It is unfair to the scheduled sections that a religion which has been given the freedom of the country should be obstructed from removing the chains of fear and frustration.[6]

To be sure, the Christian challenge has not operated only in the moral realm. Both Western and Indian observers recognize that many reforms for the *Harijans* have come from fear and jealousy rather than love. A former missionary to India recalls that as long ago as 1926 a high school debate brought ringing cheers for the argument: "We should treat Untouchables like men. Otherwise they will all become Christian." If it sounds ironical that caste Hindus should be afraid of losing (to Christianity, Islam or Buddhism) any portion of the fifty to eighty million Untouchables, who are not even officially counted within Hinduism, remember that these *Harijans* also represent an increasingly significant electoral bloc of voters.

This social advantage has now been undercut in India. The Constitution not only forbids discrimination along caste lines, but provides "reserved" or allotted seats in Parliament, offices in government, and scholarships in universities, for members of the Scheduled Castes and Tribes. This means that Christian converts—far from receiving special benefits in their new faith—may actually sacrifice educational and vocational opportunities, at least in the higher brackets of society. B. R. Ambedkar, first Law Minister, and Jagjivan Ram, Minister of Railways since Independence and one of Nehru's last two Deputy Prime Ministers, were "outcastes." Only two Christians, Rajkumari Amrit Kaur and John Mathai, have served at Cabinet rank, and comparatively few others occupy top positions in the Indian Government. Furthermore, government and private agencies are rapidly providing competent higher education and medical care. The day may be far distant when such Christian institutions are superfluous, but the day has already come when their uniquely superior functions are questioned or ignored. More and more, they are being surpassed by government services, not only quantitatively, but in some instances qualitatively as well.

This is not to minimize the outstanding exceptions. Christian hospitals at Vellore, Ludhiana, Bareilly, Indore are among the great medical centers of Asia. The spirit and motivation, as well as academic leadership, to be found at Isabella Thoburn, Lucknow Christian College, Baring Union College, Madras Christian College, Women's Christian College of Madras (to name only a few) continue to set a standard for private and government emulation. Nor can one overlook the contributions made to Indian society and economy by Christian social welfare agencies and vocational training programs. They are too numerous to recount here. The witness of Christian converts, mission study materials, any open-minded churchman's travel, can provide convincing evidence of the value of Christian missions in India even today.

There are countless places, for example, where the mission school still represents an oasis of cleanliness, eagerness and that rare combination of security and freedom, in the midst of dirt, degradation, apathy and despair. Take, for example, one school and orphans' home in the midst of a teeming city. Outside were indescribable filth and the incessant din of trams and double-decker buses and ricksha *wallahs;* inside the courtyard the laughter and shouts of children at play—and a flowering tree in bud in January. Here homeless, destitute, abandoned youngsters found food and shelter and education, plus that priceless commodity of "tender, loving care." All in the name and spirit and service of Jesus Christ. The value of each individual transformed life few Hindus or Christians would deny. Yet many such institutions—and, be it reluctantly added, the interpretations of the Christian Gospel taught therein—appear as remote and irrelevant for the surrounding metropolis as if they were located in the high Himalayas fifty years ago.

That school—warm and friendly within, yet literally barricaded against the dangers and evils and sin of the world around it—remains a symbol of the Church in India. With conspicuous exceptions the Christian Church has become an ingrown, self-protective clique—a caste of its own with relatively little social or evangelistic outreach. The real tragedy of the situation lies in the fact that the Church as a whole does not know that it has become irrelevant. The clearest evidence for such a devastating charge will be the chorus of indignant protests from the Church itself, even though many missionaries as well as outside observers corroborate the view. Or take the word of Indian Christians instead of an American visitor:

Today . . . there is a noticeable lack of enthusiasm, a failure of nerve, which gives the impression of a tragic apathy in the vast majority of Indian Christians. . . . The Indian Christian, by and large, is no longer in the swim of things. He is not aware of the swift currents of the social revolution that are sweeping over the country, unconcerned and indifferent. Perhaps this description is overdrawn, but none of us Indian Christians dare deny that there is enough truth in the caricature to sting.[7]

Before this statement is taken as unfair, uninformed condemnation instead of genuine concern, two things should be kept in mind. The first is Jesus' admonition: "Let him who is without sin among you cast the first stone."

The second qualification must be a sympathetic understanding of historical causes. For one thing, the earliest form of Christianity in India (the Syrian Jacobites, claiming their origin from St. Thomas in 54 A.D.) possesses—like its Eastern Orthodox cousins —no tradition of missionary zeal or social responsibility. In the second place, for the sake of any evangelistic success whatever among caste-bound Hindus, the earliest "modern" missionaries (Xavier and de Nobili, Roman Catholics in the sixteenth century, or Ziegenbalg and Schwartz, Protestants in the eighteenth century) accepted the stratified Indian society and established separate congregations or even divergent methods for the various castes or sub-castes. Thirdly, passing reference has been made to the lack of encouragement, even to outright opposition, which the Christian cause usually received from the East India Company. Even after

1858, what tolerance or help the British rulers did give rested on the condition that missionaries and Indian converts refrain from "rocking the boat" with agitation for social change. Finally, and most important, the overwhelming accession of Christian converts during the nineteenth and early twentieth centuries came from the "untouchable" group.

After all, privileged Brahmins had nothing tangible to gain and much prestige and position to lose by deserting their ancient cultural heritage. On the other hand, outcastes who had no status, no freedom, no individuality at all within the Hindu structure heard for the first time—not from Gandhi, but from Christian missionaries—that they were "children of God." They came to the Church by the thousands.[8] Some may have been "rice Christians" in the narrow, derogatory sense of self-seeking opportunists intent on the physical benefits dispensed by Christians. Others welcomed the nonmaterial advantages of education, self-respect, dignity. Many found a deeper gift: a sincere faith in a loving Father, in forgiveness and redemption from sin, and in the assurance of salvation more immediate and profound than *karma, samsara* and *nirvana*. This meant, however, that the Church was made up of the "lowest" element in society, those with the least background of culture, incentive, initiative, creativity, leadership. (One can believe completely in equal inherent potential among races and peoples, yet recognize that generations may be needed to transcend social and cultural handicaps.)

Thus the Christian Church in India moves into the new day of Independence with great gifts and great limitations. It remains a tiny minority (roughly ten million Catholics and Protestants combined, or 2.3 per cent) amid sometimes hostile Hinduism. Furthermore, it remains not only a widely scattered minority, diffused over the entire country with concentrations in the south and on the Gangetic plain, but a critically divided minority. Sobering accounts are all too plentiful about major subcastes or regional groups ready to move *en masse* into the Christian Church, until the denominational fragmentation looms large, and potential converts turn sadly back to the relative unity of Hinduism in preference to the obvious disunity of Christianity. To overcome this situation, as well as to fulfill the prayer of Christ "that all may be one," the Church of

South India in 1947 took a giant step forward in organic interdenominational union, and major bodies in the north are approaching a similar consummation.

Socially, adoption of Christianity has given individuals status and opportunity *within* the Christian community but not outside. Partly because so many converts came from outcaste families (still recognized in spite of altered names and ways of living), partly because conversion appears to be a rejection of Indian customs and social unity, Christians find little acceptance among the population as a whole. Liberal urban centers of course represent an exception. Economically, the advantages of education are gradually overcoming the barriers to employment and raising the living standards of the group as a whole. However, from "outcaste" levels this naturally takes three or four generations, and when it is realized that the vast majority of converts still occupy the lowest place in village society, that many a pastor receives a monthly salary of fifty rupees (ten dollars, the wage of unskilled laborers in cities), it can be seen that self-support for local churches and Christian institutions poses a major problem.

Politically, the Church and its members still suffer intermittent persecution. The most noteworthy recent example was the inquiry by the conservative state of Madhya Pradesh into the activities of Christian missions. Principal charges were that the Church's aims are not spiritual but socially disruptive; that foreign funds are used extensively for nonreligious (government) purposes such as education and orphanages; that Christian institutions exert undue (and unconstitutional) pressures toward conversion in schools and hospitals. Although national leaders generally repudiated the charges, reaffirming the constitutional freedom to preach, practice, and propagate religion, and no major demonstrations have arisen since, one should not discount the likelihood of such recurrences. Sometimes these are deliberately incited by ultranationalistic Hindu groups. The inescapable fact remains that the Christian Church in India depends largely—and for some time to come—on financial support and personnel from abroad, and this situation is bound to stimulate opposition in this period of self-conscious nationalism. Government officers entrusted with the issuance of visas to incoming missionaries protest that there are al-

ready more Christian workers from abroad than there were under
the British. Therefore, as guiding principles, no additional missionaries should be admitted except to replace those departing;
should be admitted for the primary purpose of evangelizing or
proselytizing; none should be admitted for jobs which qualified
Indians could fill. Nevertheless, each application is considered individually, and the door has not closed as tightly on missionaries or
mission work as many feared five years ago.

On several occasions Christians in government or other public
service were asked whether they felt any discrimination on account
of their faith. Those who had firmly "arrived" invariably answered
in the negative. They conceded that where qualifications were
practically identical for a specific job, a Christian (or other minority applicant) might be rejected. But they added that in many instances Christians grumbled about discrimination when, in reality,
their qualifications were inferior. In effect, then, conspicuously able
Christians can usually achieve recognition and status, but in a predominantly Hindu state there is always room for real or fancied
prejudice to operate, despite constitutional guarantees. Thus many
Christians have a psychological block, a sensitivity or suspicion,
which drives them still further into the shelter of their own community. When the Indian Constitution was adopted, the Christians—
like the Parsis and unlike the Muslims—chose deliberately *not* to
request special status, reserved seats in government, proportional
representation. On one hand, this undoubtedly represented a genuine patriotism, a readiness to cast their lot as loyal citizens with
the New India and to trust the promises and principles of a "secular"
state to preserve minority rights. On the other hand, this also reflected a typical caution, defensiveness, retreat, a desire not to do
anything which would call attention to them as a distinct group or
intensify the resentment of the Hindu majority.

All of these factors help to explain why the Church in India has
become encysted, self-protective, ingrown, looking to the strengthening and service of its own members rather than to the society in
which it lives. Many devout Christians would add a further, theological dimension: namely, the danger of syncretism, absorption,
dilution. So insidious is the all-embracing "tolerance" of Hinduism, so heavy the weight of its ancient social structure, that the

Church must be constantly on the alert to avoid being swallowed slowly and subtly. The same culture which has punished nonconformity so cruelly in the past can also speak with seductive siren-voice about its reverence for the moral and spiritual perfection of Jesus—if only Christians would not insist so arrogantly and dogmatically on the exclusive claim of Christ. The temptation is there, to be sure. But the Church cannot live its life in a ghetto—in India or anywhere else. For over a century Christianity has been fearful of its pagan environment. It has isolated its converts from their culture and insulated them from knowledge of other faiths with a great wall of protective prejudice.

Paul David Devanandan, former director of the Christian Institute for the Study of Religion and Society, was a pioneer who not only saw over that wall, but climbed over it before his sudden death in 1962. That fear of syncretism, he admitted, was necessary and justified in the Church's infancy. But now, in its teen-age adolescence, the Church of Jesus Christ must seize and exercise the freedom to participate actively and fully in the life of India, to find its place—and its power—in social and political movements around it, to converse intelligently and courageously with Hinduism, Islam and other non-Christian faiths. When Vinoba Bhave says that "because Jesus Christ is our own" and his teachings "are familiar food to every Hindu," Christians should join in the *fuller* life of the "indigenous" religion,[9] Christians in turn should be able to show proudly and confidently how their faith and life represent the supreme fulfillment of God's love.

That demonstration will not convince a Hindu or Buddhist or Muslim on the creedal level of doctrinal affirmation. By and large, the Indian mind does not work that way; it is convinced that all such formulations are transitory and inadequate to describe a transcendent deity. Nor will the Indian accept the testimony of any mystical introspection, for he and his race have infinitely more— and probably more profound—experience at this than the West. The fact of incarnation will attract no notice; India has dozens. The superior character of the Christian Incarnation and of the Christian Scriptures will have to be shown in Christian ethics. This does not mean simply the goodness and purity of Jesus Christ; India sees and admires this. Parimal Das, a brilliant Christian woman who has served with UNESCO in Paris and Community Development in New Delhi, estimates that "perhaps sixty to seventy per cent of them [top-notch people] revere Christ as one of the greatest figures in the religious world, to the point of just falling short of the last step, in that they are not baptized Christians." It does not mean only the moral insights of the Sermon on the Mount; India honors these, relates them to the Buddha and to many *rishis,* and sometimes seeks to practice them. But India will accept the *unique* divinity of Christ only when it is convinced that his followers somehow share in it. Instead they point, not so much with scorn as with disappointment, to the history of Western war, to the acceptance of slavery in Christendom for over eighteen hundred years, to Dachau and Hiroshima and Birmingham.

Unfortunately, this challenge is still heeded by the Indian Church—as in parts of the West—in pietistic, individualistic terms. The lepers do need care; outcaste boys must be freed from the chains of village prejudice; a railway clerk may overcome the temptations of his job by the New Birth he has found in Christ. But this is not enough, not in the twentieth century, not in Independent India. Listen to the words of a distinguished Indian Christian, former East Asia Secretary for the World Council of Churches, now a Lutheran Bishop:

While Christians have done much in the way of social service, they have not, on the whole, seriously considered the larger questions of social, economic, and political order which face the entire nation. They have trained men to be honest, considerate and just in personal relationships, but they have not usually thought through the consequences of this for political life. Out of love and obedience to Christ they have helped greatly to heal the bodies of men and to check the spread of disease, but they have not examined seriously the resulting economic problem of over-population with which countries like India and Japan are faced today. They have taught tenant farmers to take better care of the soil and to produce more food, but they have not encouraged these same farmers to challenge the feudal landholding system which deprives them of so much that they produce. As a result, those who are concerned with social justice look to movements other than Christianity for the insights and principles which the Church has failed to declare.[10]

What, then, should be the contribution of the Christian Church to India? First in order of priority for most Christians, but last in the eyes of the government or the Hindu population, the continual proffering of the Gospel of Jesus Christ as the ultimate pathway to individual salvation, a witness to God's redeeming love as supremely revealed in Jesus Christ, a gathering of those who fully accept this love into the fellowship of the Church. As one seminary professor described his own pilgrimage: "From this individual experience, Christianity leads me to, and points to a social goal, the Kingdom of God. Popular Hinduism seems to be exactly the opposite of this, namely, a corporate religious experience leading to the goal of individual salvation." [11]

Secondly, the operation of educational, medical and social institutions just as long as they are needed for the upbuilding of modern India *and* as long as their motivation and atmosphere remain distinctively Christian. This does not mean, as some Christians maintain, that the Christian mission includes service only as an instrument of evangelism. It does mean that the Church has better things to do than support public institutions which are so circumscribed by government regulations, financial dependence or personal apathy that they no longer represent religious freedom or manifest love. One of the finest younger Church leaders, Chandran Devanesan, recently named Principal of Madras Christian College, expressed this perspective in an address to the Synod of the Church of South India in 1960:

Should we not look upon the emergence of a welfare state in India with relief because some of our resources and energies can be channelled now into church-building activities like theological education and Sunday Schools? Will it not enable the Church to be less of an employment agency and more truly the Body of Christ? [12]

The answer to the final question is Yes, providing the Body of Christ gives itself in sacrificial love for the world, rather than suffering acute hypochondria.

Third, and closely related to the second, the development of more institutions which express the love of Christ through active involvement in the community and in the nation. An extension program which fosters credit cooperatives, lends capital for a leather tanning project, or enables the teachers' wives to become literate, may not be "building the Kingdom of God," but it is certainly in a better position to witness to "the whole Gospel for the whole man in the whole world." An agricultural worker who wades creeks in order to spray an infested field, without inquiring caste or financial affluence, can speak to farmers about One who came "that they might have life and have it more abundantly." A mud hut in an out-caste village, whitewashed by its Christian occupants, may be a nobler edifice in the Kingdom of God than a brick cottage behind virgin compound walls. A college laboratory where Indian girls are testing guinea pigs to devise more adequate diets for rural people might be more truly the Church than a chaste chapel bright with stained glass windows and spotless *saris*.

Fourth, as Manikam suggested, Indian Christians must show more active concern for political and social currents moving in the land. The most significant venture in this direction is the Christian Institute for the Study of Religion and Society, with headquarters in Bangalore and affiliates in Dehru Dun, Kerala, and wherever M. M. Thomas and P. D. Devanandan have itinerated. In every major state regional conferences have been held for Christian leaders and occasional non-Christian experts in sociology or economics or agriculture or population, to appraise the needs of the area and the possible contributions of the Christian Church. For example, in 1959 the C.I.S.R.S. and the National Christian Council of India convened a national study conference on "Christians and Indian Foreign Policy," where key men from major Protestant communions carefully and prayerfully analyzed their country's international relations—and bravely put the spotlight of transcendent love on such issues as Kashmir (the majority supported India's present policy) and the dangers of self-righteousness in nonalignment.

The literary output of Devanandan and Thomas has been tremendous (the former delivered one of the keynote addresses at the World Council of Churches' Assembly in New Delhi in 1961). Not relying on their own scholarship alone, they have solicited cooperation from Roman Catholic, Muslim and Hindu *pandits* as they seek to broaden the Church's understanding of religion and society. Space forbids any extensive evaluation here. Suffice it to say, with sincere regret, that this Institute and any Indians or missionaries associated with it are misunderstood and unjustly criticized in many quarters. Idealistic, political meddling, utterly unrelated to the Church (by which was meant the narrow, individualistic, local or denominational church)—these were some of the comments heard from Indian and American Christians.

A fifth area of influence might well be the inculcation of Christian ethics into non-Christian or secular areas of national life. Here again, many Christians reject the very idea from fear of syncretism and absorption or from insistence on narrow sectarian credit. Yet Jesus did not concern himself with labels or with credit. Nearly fifty years ago an India missionary wrote:

More and more in India the ideals and principles of Christ are becoming the working basis of organizations for social and economic betterment, which do not avowedly accept his leadership. . . . One mission of the Church is to apply the Gospel to social means and to shape public opinion in harmony with Christ's ideals.[13]

Historically this has been true, as earlier chapters have shown. The Brahmo Samaj, the Servants of India Society, the Gandhian movement, and *Sarvodaya,* all have acknowledged the importance of Christian ideals. It is one of the glories—and the shame—of Christianity that some Christians today point to the Ramakrishna Mission as having inherited from the Church the moral and social leadership which Christian missions first brought to India. Yet Devanandan rightly voiced his regret that followers of Jesus appear unable to apply their vision and their influence collectively. In Andhra 30 per cent of the population are *Harijans* and 75 per cent of those are Christian. In Kerala 30 per cent of the total state population is Christian. Yet because they are disunited—denominationally, socially, theologically, politically—they forfeit the witness they ought to make in the name of Christ.

In still another direction, Christians are making a contribution through their partnership in *Sarvodaya* and other movements of community service. In certain areas the focal center bears the name as well as the spirit of Christ. Listen to the testimony of an anonymous American missionary, who has devoted his life to building such spiritual bridges.

The Ashrams welcome members of all nations, castes, classes and creeds. They are common ground for hundreds of us. Christukula has been my spiritual home. . . . Dr. T. R. Anantharaman, Scientist of Bangalore, agreed with me that India was ready for the gift of the Eternal Christ as never before. Tragically, this is not sensed by Christian Missions; the Indian Church is not ready to give this precious gift. Perhaps India must seek the Living Christ, as did Rama Krishna, without benefit of church or mission!

Very few Westerners have so completely identified themselves, in dress and mode of life and thought, as this one. Because he has deviated from the "straight and narrow" path of orthodoxy (theological, social, administrative), he has been given "leave of absence" (on self-support) by his mission board. Lest no one condemn one church agency, it can be surmised that the other major denominations would all do likewise with anyone unwilling to conform to established practices and policies. "Can the West realize that it witnesses to a carpenter-saint, who gave up even his home that he might serve the needy?" Scattered over the face of the country there are many more Indian Christians who have chosen to take their stand with *Sarvodaya* or related experiments. It may be that through them, also, the ethics and the "spirituality" of the Man of Galilee may be injected into the lifeblood of humble, rural India.

One final role which the Christian Church can play should not be minimized, as it often is. In an unprecedented address before the Student Christian Association, V.K.R.V. Rao, former Vice-Chancellor of Delhi University, declared: "The greatest contribution of Christianity is the creation of an atmosphere in which the teachings of Jesus Christ are spread through the very air of India," rather than by counting the number of converts. He went on to outline a dual role for Indian Christians today. The first is internal, toward Christian members:

. . . to locate and promote the Christian spirit . . . not merely knowledge, but the absorption of the New Testament into life . . . to make Christianity the warp and woof of life (as no one has done perfectly but Christ) . . . permeating of the whole being with something of the teachings of Jesus Christ . . .

The second is external, since there cannot be one religion, Rao maintains, in the midst of so many diverse traditions, cultures and psychologies: to help fertilize and water the seeds (of social and ethical progress?) planted by Nehru, for in the next forty years of "spiritual conflict . . . we will need wisdom, charity, compassion, understanding, goodwill, fellowship." These can be infused into Indian society, he said, by Christians who are concerned with "action and deed, not argumentation and theology." [14]

Because of the many converging streams of Christian influence (missions, British literature, the Oxford-Cambridge education of men like Gandhi and Radhakrishnan and Nehru and a host of others) this "permeation" of Indian culture has probably gone further than in any other non-Christian country.

The Hindus have not, after all, been converted to Christianity, one-by-one as our great-grandfathers thought they would be. But the state, which in Europe is usually some way behind religion in its ethics, is in India now ahead of religion. That is because the state has been more willing to absorb Christian ethics. Even Hinduism has now come to pay reluctant lip-service to an ethic it did not possess of itself; few Brahmins would now speak out loud in favour of burning widows. So that perhaps after all there has been conversion of a kind. [15]

Thus, as Devanandan put it, Christianity's influence today seems to be largely as a catalyst rather than direct, sometimes even as an irritant to nag Hindu society into social reform. But it can have a deeper role than that. Vice-Chancellor Rao spoke of the next forty years of "spiritual conflict." Devanandan defined that situation as a metaphysical struggle in which India is searching for a theistic base to undergird democracy and social change. Even within nominally Christian ranks, he cited opposing poles of "untheological liberalism" (represented by Christian advocates of Sarvodaya) versus the neo-orthodoxy of Union Theological Seminary (!). He might even more validly have included the "fundamentalism" of many Bible-Christians, who are devoted to individual salvation and service but see no responsibility for the Church in social and political upheavals. "Do you really believe that Christianity is awake to these challenges and opportunities?" I asked Devanandan.

"No," he retorted, "I said, 'The Redeemer is already at work,' in spite of Christianity."

This chapter is written with a genuine measure of reluctance, in the knowledge that readers all along the religious spectrum will misunderstand or even take offense. Hindu friends will be disappointed to infer the same old Christian attitude of superiority and self-righteousness. Conservative Christians will detect major concessions to liberalism and syncretism. Both dangers must be acknowledged and faced. For scattered observations of the Church in India lead to moments of high admiration and deep discouragement, optimism and frustration. As a Christian, one can believe that the life-giving Gospel of Jesus Christ offers the clearest and surest way to participation in God's Love, and yet I neither expect nor demand the conversion, baptism and enrollment of four hundred million Indians. But India's conversion may take place in other ways. Presiding at a Good Friday Service in the garden of the New Delhi Y.W.C.A. Rajkumari Amrit Kaur remarked: "If a revival is needed anywhere, it is in the hearts of Indian Christians." If the Church in India is to contribute wisdom, compassion, and fellowship during the next forty years, it will need a broader understanding of the culture in which it lives, a broader concept of ethical responsibility, and a broader insight into the manifold workings of the Holy Spirit. It will also need a deeper dedication beyond itself—to the God it would worship and to His children whatever their color or caste or creed.

Chapter XV

Radhakrishnan's "Revised" Hinduism

The kindly professor, who was soon to become his nation's President, leaned back in his easy chair and crossed his legs, swathed in a voluminous *dhoti*. "Man as he is," the quiet voice explained, "is incomplete, unfinished, in transition. He has to grow into something larger, especially humanity and goodness. . . . Religion is the discipline which helps us to bridge the gulf between what we are and what we should be. . . . We can change our own nature." [1] For an hour and a half this world-famous philosopher patiently expounded the classical tenets of Indian thought, interpreting passages from his own copious writings, charting the beacon-lights of a more universal Hinduism yet to come. "The expressions of the Indian philosophical outlook have been inadequate," he admitted, "and they are always growing toward greater and greater adequacy. There is no such thing as standing still."

The brilliant mind of Sarvepalli Radhakrishnan has never stood still in nearly seventy-five years of intellectual pilgrimage, beginning in an orthodox Hindu home near Madras. From his early days Christian interpretation and misinterpretation of Hindu thought and practice have "provoked an incipient challenge," [2] to which Radhakrishnan has responded with eloquence, dignity and conviction. He has taught philosophy at Presidency College in Madras, at Mysore University, at Calcutta, and at Oxford. He has been Vice-Chancellor (President) of Andhra and Benares Universities, Ambassador to Moscow, a delegate to UNESCO, Vice-President and then second President of the Republic of India. Since he has written on Leibnitz and Tagore, Bergson and Bertrand Russell, and many phases of Indian thought, no summary of Radhakrishnan's philosophy could do him justice. These few pages can simply suggest his contributions to an understanding and a formulation of India's social ethics.

More than any other section of the book, this chapter demands a frank statement of thesis, in order that the evidence on both sides may be clearly cited. The thesis: that Radhakrishnan, as the outstanding spokesman for contemporary Indian philosophy, is drastically reinterpreting and reconstructing traditional Hinduism in the subconscious light of his own Western education, gradually creating a new *Weltanschauung* more consistent with democracy and a welfare state. It is a worthy task, fit for a modern "approximation to Plato's ideal of the philosopher king." [3] Men of goodwill, not too bound by personal or cultural dogmatisms, should welcome progress toward a world view. "The feeling of fellowship with the whole of humanity is implanted in our nature. We are members of a world community." [4]

The difficulty lies in Radhakrishnan's reluctance—or inability—to acknowledge the syncretism of his thought, the eclecticism of his total philosophy. He can be charged, as we shall see, with glorifying ancient Hinduism and condemning the ugliest elements of Christian history: persecution, discrimination, sectarianism. (Each of these sins of Christendom, be it noted, are violations of community, of the social and spiritual monism which marks most Eastern religions.) But Christians have been even more guilty of professing an ideal Gospel, ignoring its betrayal in practice, and decrying the vulgar, superstitious practices of Hinduism.

Certain Christian writers have maintained, with some validity, that the evils of the West have occurred because of human sin *in spite of* Christian teachings, whereas many of India's social evils have claimed religious sanction. But many Indians point to nineteen centuries in which Christendom accepted slavery as a social institution with hardly a word of moral protest. Nor is it yet proved that licensed prostitution or easy divorce is more ethical than polygamy, materialism more conducive to brotherhood than spiritualism, war more pleasing to God than nonviolence.

One reason for misunderstanding between Orient and Occident can be found in a perplexing paradox. The West, pragmatic and realistic, claims to base its ethics on a divine imperative. Yet with all its activism, Christendom has tolerated a wide range of practical conduct, but has demanded conformity and punished heresy in doctrinal, theological realms. Hinduism, stressing spirituality to the point of metaphysical idealism, has been extremely tolerant in belief, while enforcing a social pattern more rigid than any creedal orthodoxy. Like many people on both sides of the globe Radhakrishnan occasionally uses the term "religion" loosely. Sometimes, in the spirit of Gandhi and Vinoba, the President condemns "organized religion," the plural forms of which produce division and discord. At other times, he appeals for a universal spiritual quest which links man to man—and to ultimate truth.

Religion is the discipline which touches the conscience and helps us to struggle with evil and sordidness, saves us from greed, lust and hatred, releases moral power, and imparts courage in the enterprise of saving the world. . . . In its essence, religion is a summons to spiritual adventure. It is not theology, but practice and discipline. . . . The essence of religion is not in the dogmas and creeds, in the rites and ceremonies which repel many of us, but in the deepest wisdom of the ages.[5]

Unlike many Western admirers of Eastern religions, Radhakrishnan is not concerned with devising a new world faith, a syncretistic blending of doctrines which men from many cultures can adopt. This may well be the ultimate outcome of his reformulations. But he himself still speaks within a traditional Hindu framework. He accepts images not as objects of worship but as symbols for the weak and ignorant, idolatry as "a means to the development of the religious spirit, to the recognition of the Supreme who has his temple in all beings." [6] He would also point to similar symbols in the Cross, the Madonna, the statues of saints. Echoing the words of Gandhi, Radhakrishnan declares that "respect for the cow means respect for animals [especially the] foster-mother of the human race." Unlike Gandhi, he adds: ". . . but there is nothing religious about it . . . If cow protection is enjoined as a religious duty, it only shows that the tradition of centuries has not been snapped." [7] (Or that he himself represents a radical emancipation from many Hindu practices.)

More significant, for an ethical study, is the President's defense of caste. One can understand, if not wholly accept, an idealized view of historical origins. Radhakrishnan suggests several: racial purity, "virtue and valour," economic functions, social opportunities, "natural aptitude and vocation." Readily admitting that all these later congealed into the one factor of birth, upheld by false pride and discrimination, he asserts that "the caste spirit [of exclusiveness, jealousy, greed, and fear] must go." [8] Deploring the degradation and exploitation of untouchability, he insists that neither the *Bhagavad-Gita* nor the *Code of Manu* mentioned any outcaste group beyond the pale of society.

When all these points have been conceded, there remain certain fallacies in any attempted justification of caste. Once a person admits, even among other causes, that "caste was the Hindu answer to the challenge of society in which different races had to live together without merging into one," it is difficult to blame "the substitution of the principle of birth" for later "social crystallization and caste separatism." [9] The color consciousness implied in the term *varna* did not prevent an intermingling of Aryan and Dravidian races, although Brahminism remains strongest today in South India, where the racial encounter was prolonged. Somehow this color bar shifted to vocational groupings, but the denial of any moral issue from the start remains somewhat unconvincing. In fact, Radhakrishnan himself recognizes that segregation based on inherited status cannot be reconciled with democracy or enlightened humanism.

The theory of rebirth by which man's inborn nature and course of life are determined by his own past lives gives additional support to the view that man is born to the social function which is natural to him. It is not realized that the fact of ancestry, parentage, and physical birth may not always indicate the true nature of the individual. . . . Any system where an abstract power, caste, or Church decides a person's profession and place is an unnatural one.[10]

   This brief passage seems to abandon most of the traditional defenses. Its first sentence gives support to the law of *karma,* for Radhakrishnan often argues, as did Gandhi, that generally speaking a minister's son makes a better minister, or a coal miner's son a better adjusted miner. But the next two sentences demolish this rationalization by admitting that hereditary status is *not* a valid criterion for judging an individual, and that a socially imposed status is unnatural and unfair. Radhakrishnan knows full well that the caste system, whatever its origin, had no place for an Abraham Lincoln or an Ambedkar. Once segregation based on birth or social custom is disavowed, and freedom is granted for the individual to transcend caste, there is no caste. Social and personal differences remain of course, but they justify no arbitrary discrimination, by law or custom. Back in 1926 Radhakrishnan tried to defend the view of natural inequality as a basis for caste.

It is not true that all men are born equal in every way, and everyone is equally fit to govern the country or till the ground. The functional diversities of workers cannot be suppressed. . . . While we should remove the oppressive restrictions . . . and open to them opportunities of higher life, we should not be under the illusion that we can abolish the distinctions of the genius and the fool, the able organizer and the submissive worker.[11]

What this learned philosopher does not explain is how caste contributes in *any* way to the discovery and utilization of these diversities of gifts. The assumption that the accident of birth separates the genius and the fool, the organizer and the laborer, into distinct castes, appears both scientifically and morally absurd. Radhakrishnan's statement that "caste divisions are [note the present tense!] based on individual temperament, which is not immutable,[12] becomes a travesty on all that caste has ever meant in India.
   There remains one further approach, which does not justify

caste but pleads for its acceptance—and purification. That is the voice of order at the expense of freedom, of social justice at the cost of individual injustice. It is a familiar plea in American race relations.

We are not so certain to-day as we were a century ago that the individualistic conception of society is the last word in social theory. . . . There is much to be said . . . for the system of caste which adheres to the organic view of society and substitutes for the criterion of economic success and expediency a rule of life which is superior to the individual's interest and desires. Service of one's fellows is a religious obligation. To repudiate it is impiety. Democracy is not the standardizing of everyone so as to obliterate all peculiarity.[13]

Here, subtly and unexpectedly, creeps in the religious sanction, the veritable "opiate of the people." Here people are asked to accept voluntarily what cruel custom has long imposed. When the author adds a plea for gradualism, for a realistic acceptance of "laws and conditions" until "room and time are found for each to take his natural level," the argument takes on a conservative tone which most Indian leaders, including Radhakrishnan himself, would repudiate today. In fact, he remarked to this writer without equivocation:

All these divisions into caste and untouchability, etc., have violated that fundamental concept . . . that every man is a spark of the divine. They have betrayed and distorted and corrupted the image of the Divine in the human individual. This institution of caste requires to be scrapped, and equality of the individual established in social fact and not merely in philosophical theory.

In other words, what Radhakrishnan seems to have done in his later years is to discard all justifications of caste, traditional or psychological, philosophical or sociological. In their place he stresses the Universal Soul, and persons as individual sparks of it. For him this just as truly represents Hinduism, despite his own declaration that "religion . . . is more behaviour than belief," [14] despite the fact that the practice of caste has been more typically definitive of Hinduism than any creed.

This emphasis on "the image of the Divine in the human individual" strikes another paradoxical note which adds to the confusion between East and West, between traditional Hinduism and its new interpretations. Is religion primarily solitary or primarily social? Radhakrishnan has given his answer clearly and repeatedly: "Religion is based on the discovery of the essential worth of and dignity of the individual and his relation to a higher world of reality." [15] In the Jowett Lectures delivered in London in 1930 he contrasted Oriental and Occidental perspectives:

Religion in the East is the cultivation of the Interior Life . . . the attainment of spiritual freedom . . . essentially the private achievement of the individual won by hard effort in solitude and isolation. . . . In the West, religion is a social phenomenon, a matter of the ecclesia, of the community. . . . Religion in the West is a support for social stability and a shield against the innovator. . . . The Eastern religions are directed to the salvation of the individual soul rather than to the maintenance of society. The Western convert religion into a sort of police system for the sake of social order.[16]

Now this contradicts a popular assumption. Christianity, especially Protestantism, has almost claimed a monopoly on individualism, on personal salvation. A rediscovery of the Social Gospel characterized the late nineteenth century, and a renewed emphasis on the doctrine of the Church marks mid-twentieth-century theology. On the other hand, Hinduism has been traditionally labeled the most group-centered of all great religions. In few other advanced cultures do religious sanctions so thoroughly dominate individual conduct and social relationships. As an Indian writer put it: "Religion formed the core of life—social, cultural and spiritual; it was the central point of reference in relation to almost all aspects of life." [17] Thus, modern man in the West—whether Communist or Christian or something in between—seeks to revitalize social ethics by a new awareness of interdependence, of collective responsibility. At the same time, Eastern thought seeks to expand the horizons of duty beyond family, tribe and caste, by renewed emphasis on the sanctity and freedom of every individual.

Let us look briefly at the contemporary philosopher's transmutation of certain basic Hindu doctrines. *Dharma* (moral law?) has

been central—but undefinable. In fact, many Indians would say
that *dharma* is incomprehensible to an Occidental. Radhakrishnan
explains that "moral ideals about social relationships are not absolute, but relative to the needs and conditions of different types of
society. Though *dharma* is absolute, it has no absolute and timeless content." [18] Some such universal standard lies behind all ethical
theory, whether it be called natural law, moral law, the law of love
—or the dialectic. For most contemporary ethics, even in a religious framework, the application admits some degree of relativism.
Legalistic morality finds new adherents, East or West.

What one presumes to challenge in the writings of Radhakrishnan is not the validity, the necessity, or the wisdom of such an
interpretation. Every friend of India would agree that "we should
introduce changes today, and make the content of Hindu *dharma*
relevant to modern conditions." But even Western historians may
question whether, in fact, "social flexibility has been the chief
character of Hindu dharma." [19] Like the ancient Hebrews, the
Vedic writers (as well as the later *Upanishads* and *Code of Manu*)
gave to the "eternal law" social and moral content which proved
exceedingly inflexible. Of course Radhakrishnan admits that institutions developed "as formidable obstacles" to social progress and
ethical self-realization. But he describes these as entirely man-
made, presumably unrelated to the absolute *dharma,* at the time
insisting that the principles of *dharma* can be and must be incorporated into new patterns. In less guarded moments he has even
declared that Indian civilization has *always* stood for equal rights
for all and a classless society! [20]

The doctrine of *karma,* being more specific, has been even
more troublesome. Radhakrishnan defines it as "the rule of law not
only in outward nature, but also in the world of mind and morals." [21]
But he goes on to qualify it with two assertions which other
scholars find less evident in traditional Hinduism. In the first place,
the modern philosopher stresses the *present* creation of *karma* instead of the past, immediate responsibility for our own fulfillment
rather than determinism from a previous incarnation. "We are
every moment making our characters and shaping our destinies," [22]
for this life instead of a life beyond. In fact, Radhakrishnan's chief

modification here is to separate *karma* from *samsara,* to say little or nothing about transmigration and the rebirth to come.

The second revision of traditional Hinduism is to modify the law of *karma* by divine mercy.

There is room for repentance and consequent forgiveness on this scheme. . . . Forgiveness is not a mitigation of God's justice but only an expression of it. We can insist with unflinching rigour on the inexorability of the moral law and yet believe in the forgiveness of sins.[23]

The most objective reader could not fail to see more Christianity than orthodox Hinduism in such a statement. For long periods of Indian history *karma* has been accepted as absolutely determinative, with every word and act of commission or omission marked in the record book for the next rebirth. Furthermore, the essential monism of Hindu philosophy, which Radhakrishnan generally shares, leaves little room or meaning for a personal God who forgives repentant sinners.

The interminable discussions of freedom and determinism which characterize all philosophical speculation find as convincing an "answer" in this "new" Hinduism as in any other system. Radhakrishnan uses the familiar analogy that *karma* represents the cards dealt to us; we can decide our bid, choose what suit to lead, play freely, win or lose, according to our own talents—and instincts. He admits, further, that "unfortunately, the theory of *karma* became confused with fatality in India when man himself grew feeble and was disinclined to do his best. It was made into an excuse for inertia and timidity and was turned into a message of despair and not of hope." [24] The fact that what he describes as an unfortunate corruption represents the characteristic Hinduism of many centuries seems to support the contention that the President preaches a revised standard version.

Another basic dogma of Hinduism is *maya,* illusion. If all existence, all sensation, as well as all external environment, is deceptive and unreal, then moral effort to change society has little value or meaning. Here, again, Radhakrishnan takes several avenues of escape from this dilemma. First, he reminds his readers that the concept of *maya* is not basic to most Hindu systems of thought, but

was introduced and popularized by Sankara in the eighth century
A.D.[25] Then he hastens to add that *advaita* (monism) presents the
only rational approach to the relation between the empirical world
and the Absolute. A doctrine of Creation raises problems of meth-
odology and purpose. A "Manifestation" of the Infinite offers an inadequate picture of the Divine. "Transformation" suggests either
pantheism or division; is all or part of God transformed into a
physical state?

At the same time, Radhakrishnan says, Sankara's assertion of
ultimate monism should not be interpreted as subjectivism, a denial
of sense experience, a rejection of finitude, above all as illusionism.
Rather, *maya* signifies the divine mystery, the creative force, the
imperfect form of the perfectly Real. With metaphysical subtlety it
labels all incompleteness as unreal. "When the Hindu thinkers ask
us to free ourselves from *maya*, they are asking us to shake off our
bondage to the unreal values which are dominating us. They do not
ask us to treat life as an illusion or be indifferent to the world's welfare." [26] Yet millions of *sadhus,* ascetic holy men of this and countless generations, have obviously understood *maya* as a basis for renunciation and withdrawal. These mendicants, indifferent to the
world, Radhakrishnan dismisses as "not the true representatives of
the genius of India." [27]

The doctrine of *moksha,* salvation or liberation, comes in for
similar treatment. Despite centuries of concentration on escape, on
the search for *Nirvana,* on release from the cycle of rebirth, this
learned philosopher insists that "the Hindu ideal affirms that man
can attain his immortal destiny here and now," [28] that *"moksha* or
liberation is to be achieved here and now, on earth, through human
relations." [29] If what he means is that ethical behavior helps to advance the soul toward the ultimate goal of reunion with Brahma,
the moral incentive is obvious, and the doctrine can be reconciled
with *karma* and *samsara.* But if he implies any kind of "social salvation," or the complete attainment or achievement which his language asserts, he is going far beyond traditional Hinduism. Such an
emphasis suggests also a "this-worldly" goal far more humanistic
than Christianity, for which "the Kingdom of Heaven is within
you" *but also* awaiting Divine fulfillment.

What, then, is the basic "theology" of Sarvepalli Radhakrishnan? Like most Hinduism, it partakes of conflicting schools of thought, Eastern and Western, without any profound awareness of contradiction. He seems to accept the positive aspects of Sankara's *advaita vedanta:* a timeless and universal monism. As a scholar he recognizes the importance of knowledge, yet stresses the ultimate primacy of intuition, uniting subject and object. As a mystic, he speaks of God as personal (in the sentence about forgiveness, for example) because he believes that ordinary man cannot comprehend more abstract concepts.[30] These very compromises of language make one wonder whether Radhakrishnan is writing for an Eastern or Western audience, whether he can succeed in reconciling Hindu metaphysics with social ethics.

Thanks to these reformulations of traditional Hindu thought, Radhakrishnan sees an important role for religion in transforming social life. In fact, he acknowledged in a speech to an international gathering in New Delhi, that "ancient doctrines do not help us to solve modern problems." [31] Along with the need for meditation and solitariness, he insists that "religion is not an opiate for the disorders of the spirit. It is a dynamic for social advance. . . . Life is one, and in it there is no distinction of sacred and secular." [32] Here Radhakrishnan follows a familiar Gandhian line, an alternation between spiritual withdrawal and human service, both equally encompassed in Absolute Truth. In earlier writings, however, he has admitted that Hinduism failed to inspire such selfless conduct. "The superiority of Western religion lies in the fact that the individual seeks his salvation in service to others. . . . Religion is not only life-transcending, but also life-transforming. True worship is in the service of suffering humanity." [33]

This tribute to Christianity opens the way for other references which indicate, however briefly and superficially, Radhakrishnan's own subconscious orientation. From his training at Madras Christian College, his years of study and teaching in Oxford, his breadth of world vision, he could not help but absorb some feeling for Christianity. Speaking of the nineteenth-century reformers, he attributes their success to "the awakening of the social conscience, brought about by the spread of Western ideas," then hastens to add that "it is in accordance with the spirit of Vedic tradition and practice." [34] Repeatedly he discusses love in terms that sound like a blend of Reinhold Niebuhr and Mohandas Gandhi:

The opposite of love is hate, not force. There are occasions when love will use force. Love is not mere sentimentality. It can use force to restrain the evil and protect the good. . . . Non-violence is not a physical condition, but a mental attitude of love. . . . In an imperfect world, where all men are not saints, force has to be used to keep the world going. . . . The teaching of the Cross is that we cannot redeem the world of an evil like war, unless we are prepared to endure the suffering which it involves. . . . Is it for us to consider the consequences of adherence to the spirit of love? God will see to the victory of good over evil. It is our duty to apply everywhere and at all times the law of love.[35]

Declaring that God must be both transcendent and immanent, that religion must be both spiritual and ethical, he unites the two in a sublime phrase: "If there are no crucifixions, there will be no resurrections." [36] To a group of American Christians, Radhakrishnan told of a radio appearance with the Mormon Choir, which sang, "Were you there when they crucified the Lord?" (Note that he substituted "the" for "my.") His own brief meditation, he recalled, pointed out that the question does not refer to physical presence at a particular spot two thousand years ago, but to the challenge of where you are and what you are doing when Jesus' principles are crucified today.

It may be that Radhakrishnan's vehement attack on many aspects of Christianity (as contrasted with sincere appreciation for Jesus' life and teachings) stem from a subconscious awareness of his own indebtedness. The most bitter objections, among many Indians interviewed, focus on the dogmatic intolerance of Christianity (or Judaism or Islam). Deep but sincere resentment must have activated Radhakrishnan's statement (even back in 1939) that "it would by no means be a triumph divine or human if atheistic Communism of Russia were to be overcome by the dogmatic religions. Opposition to both these extremes is perhaps the greatest tribute that a mind of any spirituality can render to God." [37] One can hope that the gentle philosopher spoke only in religious

terms, and that he has had more recent occasion (including am-
bassadorship to Moscow) to reappraise the "dogmas" of atheistic
Communism. One might also hope that Christianity has learned
something of tolerance and wisdom in its approach to religions and
cultures of the East.

Many of the most serious criticisms of Hinduism, as a foundation for social ethics, came from Albert Schweitzer in *Indian
Thought and Its Development*. Many of the most vigorous rebuttals
have come from Radhakrishnan in *Eastern Religions and Western
Thought*. For this reason it may be appropriate to summarize the
points of this chapter by reference to the latter book. It should be
noted, not by way of refutation but in humble confession, that
Radhakrishnan's retorts are often couched in terms of Christianity's
weaknesses. If we accept the elements of truth contained therein, we
may not only "prove" that Radhakrishnan's Hinduism has been
profoundly influenced by the West, not only acknowledge Christianity's need for similar reinterpretation, but discover unexpected
areas of understanding and common experience.

Schweitzer's main thesis declares that Hinduism, despite its
many spiritual virtues, lacks a significant ethical dynamic because
its essential theme is "world-and-life negation." Defining *moksha*
as release from sense experience, and *maya* as the illusion of the
physical world, he finds no basis for affirming life, and hence no
basis for positive morality. Add to these doctrines a fatalistic view
of *karma* and a socially and religiously stratified society, and one
can find little incentive for democracy, action or social ethics. As
we have seen, Radhakrishnan denies many of these interpretations.
But he also rejects Schweitzer's conclusions on the ground that the
missionary draws too sharp a dichotomy between mystical and
practical religion and then assigns them too arbitrarily to East and
West.

Radhakrishnan insists that spiritual and ethical elements are
complementary facets of all insight into truth. The alleged other-
worldliness of Hinduism, he says, is no different from the Christian
affirmation of a higher and better reality transcending human existence. "Religion springs from the conviction that there is another
world beyond the visible and the temporal with which man has
dealings, and ethics require us to act in this world with the com-

pelling vision of another." [38] The idea that spiritual perfection
requires withdrawal from social responsibility is as unfair to Jesus
as to the *Gita,* Radhakrishnan maintains. He cites Schweitzer's own
admission, in *The Quest for the Historical Jesus,* that "the teaching of this historical Jesus was purely and exclusively world-
renouncing." Once again, the reader suspects that Schweitzer
searches for ethics in practice, to the neglect of certain original
teachings of Christianity—while Radhakrishnan describes Hinduism in terms of philosophical and metaphysical doctrines, to the
neglect of social and moral practices.

In attempting to define *maya,* the Hindu scholar warns "against
the temptation to regard what is not completely real as utterly illusory. . . . Human experience is neither ultimately real nor completely illusory." [39] He goes on to explain that the empirical reality
of the world is negated only when perfect intuition or knowledge is
attained in *moksha.* The world is not null and void in terms of immediate, practical, moral obligation. Nor is *moksha* an extinction
of the ego, any more than Christ renounced his selfhood when he
sacrificed personal desire in Gethsemane. The Christian would in-
stantly reply, "Christ fulfilled his selfhood rather than renouncing
it!" This is apparently Radhakrishnan's view of Hinduism.

Furthermore, the Westerner judges ethics in terms of action
and consequences. The Easterner judges ethics in terms of spirit
and intention. "The question is not, What shall I *do* to be saved?"
Radhakrishnan asserts, "but In what *spirit* shall I do? Detachment
of spirit and not renunciation of the world is what is demanded
from us. . . . When one realizes that all beings are but the self,
one acts not selfishly but for all beings." [40] To the charges that ultimate truth is supraethical and that Hinduism considers inner peace
more important than outward activity, Radhakrishnan acquiesces,
although he does not believe that such lines can be sharply drawn.
"Like all Eastern religions Christianity also preaches a gospel of
renunciation, of passivity, of withdrawal from the traffic of external
things. The Cross signifies that progress is achieved not by those who
fight for it, but by those who suffer for it." [41]

In arriving at such a synthesis, Radhakrishnan may be misreading the unique and absolute claims of Christianity. But he also
reveals to open-minded Christian readers some of their own mis-

understandings of the Gospel. In accenting the differences between theory and practice, Western critics may be unjustly condemning Hinduism. At the same time, they may succeed in showing where new emphases have been incorporated, new interpretations devised. As Radhakrishnan wisely says: "We delude ourselves into thinking that defects of our society are peripheral while those of others are central to their religions." [42]

The President's voluminous writings are impressive, not only for the brilliance of his philosophic mind, but for the gentleness of his religious spirit. How rare and fortuitous to have a statesman who can move serenely between political and academic realms, pleading for national integrity and character, warning that "in our practice we have distorted, corrupted, and betrayed the divine image in man." [43] It is because of his deep awareness of the need for social change that Radhakrishnan labors so diligently to give it moral and spiritual foundations. However valiantly he may defend the past, he acknowledges the host of contemporary problems which "require to be considered in a liberal spirit." With equal courage he calls for "insubordination to outworn customs . . . to disturb the complacency of the majority, who acquiesce in obsolete forms of thought and feeling. The new emphasis on the dignity and freedom of man demands a reshaping of the social order." [44]

Radhakrishnan does not presume to say where that "new emphasis" originates. He would certainly point out that it is relatively recent in Western society as well as in the East. What matters is that some effort is being made to formulate and propagate a Hinduism which can keep pace with scientific, political and social changes in the modern world. Or, as he himself defines his aim: "What is wrong with Hindu religion? How can we make it somewhat more relevant to the intellectual climate and social environment of our time?" [45] One fearful alternative is ideological (as well as economic) revolution, discarding the moral and spiritual traditions of the past, as China seems to be doing. The other, equally frightening, might well be religious (as well as political) reaction, in which the dead hand of the past, the inertia of mass superstition, drags India back from the twentieth century.

Unfortunately Radhakrishnan's influence appears limited to a small circle of intellectuals, in India and abroad. Tragic though it

may seem, most politicians and many social reformers see no need
for a new religious viewpoint, a spiritual renaissance. Perhaps more
than any other nation in the modern world, India possesses the
heritage to appreciate the role of spiritual values and to find place
for them in her program of progress. "Every religion is passing
through a period of self-criticism. They have to transform themselves or they will fade away. Here also a kind of change is taking
place, but the framework will remain." To the scholarly, philosophical strengthening and restructuring of that framework of Hinduism,
Radhakrishnan has made the greatest contribution since Ramanuja.

Conclusion

"So What?"

Prime Minister Nehru arrived half an hour late from a committee meeting (a rather unprecedented delay for his clock-work schedule) and ushered me from the enormous reception room into a secluded study. When I referred to my China experience as background for my interest in India, a visible wave of sadness flitted across his face, but he made no comment. Perched somewhat restlessly on a straight chair above my deep sofa seat, he indicated by a courteous but unmistakable gesture that the interview should begin. In a sense, I stammered, still genuinely awed to be in such a presence, you have voiced my basic questions when you ask early in *The Discovery of India:* "What of today? Are there any springs still functioning from which we can refresh and strengthen ourselves?"

The Prime Minister responded: "So what?" I gulped incredulously, wondering if the interview were at an end. This seemed hardly an auspicious opening for my prized interview with a world statesman, yet I trembled even more at the thought of retreating down that long hall, across the spacious reception room, around the corner to my rented bicycle, out the curving driveway to the imposing gates. Then I looked up and saw the faint, whimsical smile that flickered in the tired eyes. At least I could prove my sincerity, the love for India that had brought me to this country and to this august moment. So I summarized three primary questions, to let the Prime Minister select his preferred route: *What are these springs that you seem to think are necessary for India? What are the specific ethical bases on which modern India is building? What are the sources of your own profound ethical and social concerns?*

"That is difficult to answer," Nehru replied. "An ethical question is always difficult." Despite his opening retort, Panditji was never one to evade a difficult question.

I suppose India has quite strong ethical roots. Only they have often been rather covered up by all kinds of other things: superstitions, social practices, and all that, resulting in a kind of stagnating condition. . . . There are definite sources of strength in it, and I should like India—if she can—to disentangle those elements which have that depth and vitality, and get rid of those social forms and practices and superstitions. Looking at it from the social-economic point of view, we became quite static, and are changing very slowly.

Much of it is not entirely the fault of the people. Other conditions helped in keeping that [static situation], and we are beginning to come out of it. The question is not whether but in what shape they will come out. That is, to put it in another way, how to modernize our social set-up and yet keep the ethical roots which have distinguished India so much in the past.

How can this be done? I interposed. "It is difficult," the Prime Minister said again, "because the first apparent effect is a shattering one"—the effect of industrialization and all that produces new conditions and social change. "At the same time," he went on, "they are such deep roots that I hardly think they will be pulled out. I suppose after a number of rather earthquake shocks we will try to settle down."

As this sober, gentle, little man spoke of the revolutionary turmoil in his country and the world, I began to suspect that his abrupt query had been aimed at himself as much as at me. For Nehru too was wondering *So what?* Nehru too would have liked to know whether there were "any springs still functioning" from which India could refresh and strengthen herself. Nehru too was seeking to bridge the vast chasm between ancient, rural, Hindu society and modern, industrial, democratic socialism. These chapters have represented a reporter's notebook, not a prophet's crystal ball. These final pages aim to bring together some scattered observations and to suggest their significance for India and for her friends around the globe. If certain views appear to be stated in dogmatic terms, or to rest on insufficient evidence, a need for brevity is a partial excuse.

The psychological, moral and religious ingredients for democracy and social welfare cannot be derived from traditional Hinduism. To be sure, certain altruistic traits are common to humanity in every culture, race and age. Hospitality, succor in time of emergency, friendliness, these are too universal to be denied in any national character, or in any vast assortment of sacred writings. But democracy presupposes some concept of equality, in practice as well as theory, some freedom to alter the social structure and to protect minorities. Social welfare assumes a basic concern for people as people, the reality and importance of human needs, the initiative to repeal injustices. Such attitudes are denied by the philosophical tenets of caste, *karma, maya,* and *moksha.* Even Gandhi asserted, "We cannot dismiss the suffering of our fellow-creatures as unreal and thus provide a moral alibi for ourselves." [1] No effort to stress Buddhist compassion or Hindu monism can cancel out the obvious ethical lag recognized by most objective students. "In Buddhism love is affirmed as a principle of unity and harmony, but disavowed as a dynamic impulse. Buddhism is, therefore, unable to escape an enervating ambiguity in its statement of the love ideal." [2] One of India's leading political scientists stated the problem even more explicitly in these words:

We cannot put our religion to work for social processes because it is not organized. . . . [It is] the general view of Indian observers too that . . . each fellow himself is not bad, but there is no concern for neighbor, and everything is chaotic. Collectively, it is said, they [Indians] have no ethics.[3]

Whatever the ancient moral heritage of India, its renaissance must be credited to the West. Even if contemporary ethics can be traced to the *Vedas* and *Upanishads,* they have remained smothered and choked for so long that they would scarcely have burst forth without the sharp prodding of modern education. Says Hallam Tennyson:

Two hundred years of missionary effort in spreading Christ's ideal of human service and His call for right worldly activity have had their effect. Western virtue has been crossed with Indian vision. It is this that has given birth to the most exciting and important spiritual movement of our time.[4]

In actual social reform, Christian missionaries had far less influence than they should have had, far less than they might have had if they had displayed more charity, tolerance and insight. On the one hand, British commercialism and officialdom feared the possible consequences of social change; on the other hand, Christians spurned the proffered support of reformers, like Raja Rammohun Roy, who were not yet ready to accept theological and doctrinal formulations of the Christian faith.

Nevertheless, missionaries set an irresistible example of individual concern and sacrificial service. "It must be confessed," wrote D. S. Sarma in his *Renaissance of Hinduism,* "that the emphasis which our religious leaders, especially those belonging to the Samaj movement and the Ramakrishna Mission, have laid on social service is due to the object-lession provided by Christian missions." [5] But the real impact came from the liberal idealism of British thought in general. The conscience of East India Company officers may have been dull, the religion of early missionaries narrow, but Indian students could not escape the Christian ethics which permeated literature, philosophy and embryonic social reform in England.

Men like Locke, Milton, Burke and Mill moulded the mind of nineteenth century India. Even those who disclaimed their Christian heritage implanted elements of the Gospel in Asian soil, to sprout hopefully, to droop again under the merciless rays of colonialism, but never wholly to die.

Strangely enough, many Indian thinkers are still unwilling to acknowledge this catalytic function for Christianity. An Indian writer commented in a popular journal:

In the deeper region of religions, there are striking contrasts with karma and metempsychosis, on the one hand, and with freedom of the will and denial of transmigration of soul, on the other. In the sphere of philosophy, what is emphasized in the Occident is a disinterested quest for knowledge, while what is sought for in India is salvation, freedom from the cycle of birth and death. That is why, according to the philosophers trained in the traditional fashion, occidentalised thinkers like Aurobindo and Radhakrishnan have simply distorted and sophisticated Indian philosophy.[6]

As an Indian Christian explained to me, this denial of indebtedness is "not lack of historical veracity, it is lack of historical consciousness." Hindus like Radhakrishnan, he asserted, are sincerely unaware of what they have absorbed from the West. They do not care to ask of specific ideas: What? From where? How? When? Suffice it to say, it is here in Hinduism, a part of our culture. In other words, "Hinduism has the ability to integrate new elements by reinterpreting itself." [7] This summarizes precisely what seems to be happening, at a profound metaphysical level among Radhakrishnan's few disciples, on a practical, popular level among the masses who dare to question *karma* or to violate caste.

Malcolm Pitt, missionary, scholar, now professor at Hartford Seminary Foundation, is undoubtedly right when he warns:

I have become increasingly convinced that, though it is an interesting academic exercise to ferret out these sources, from the Indian point of view such a study is irrelevant. The Indian genius of synthesis has produced the present renaissance, and there is considerable resentment and bewilderment at any analytical approach to the totality. . . . We are scarcely understanding the Indian point of view unless approached— as you apparently intend to—from the point of view of constructive interaction rather than rational analysis alone.[8]

Still the process must go on, with or without conscious analysis. P. D. Devanandan, one of the keenest appraisers of the Indian social and religious scene, described his country as in the midst of a metaphysical crisis, seeking some theistic basis for inevitable social change. This accounts, he suggested, for the resurgence of interest in Ramanuja's theistically oriented philosophy, or for the multitudes who crowd the Ramakrishna Mission and the lectures of Krishnamurti. Similarly, what Roland Scott writes of the nineteenth-century reformers applies with equal cogency to India's leaders today: "They were conscious that, in trying to break religion loose from its association with undesirable social practice, they must provide a metaphysical basis for the new ideals and values." [9]

Granted that such a metamorphosis is taking place, what are its principal characteristics? One is the effort to develop a sense of wider responsibility. For thousands of years the Indian social pattern has emphasized duties: duties toward the joint family, duties toward the caste, duties toward the village, reluctant duties toward the wielder of political power. Such obligations are narrowly circumscribed. Furthermore, they give rise to an obverse stress on rights. Faith in *karma* and obedience to *dharma* tend to reduce initiative, as well as the decision-making so essential for democracy. No wonder the Constituent Assembly debated so heatedly the relative merits of Fundamental Rights and specific social duties. No wonder Nehru himself warned that august body that "there is no such thing as freedom without responsibility." [10] Unless and until the vast, unorganized, largely illiterate, tradition-bound citizenry of India can broaden its horizons of responsibility, democracy and social welfare will both remain external, ultimately ineffectual impositions.

Closely allied to a sense of responsibility is the need for personal initiative. A news reporter described a Nehru speech in these trenchant words: "What troubled him was this amazing capacity of the people to ask for help and their amazing incapacity to do something themselves." [11] Individualism, creativity, experimentation—these are essential ingredients of social change; these are also predominantly Western concepts. To be sure, India has known great periods of artistic creativity in the past. Despite those who

blame foreign invasions for recent sterility, it should be noted that
the few outstanding geniuses of the modern period have been
those, like Rabindranath Tagore, most thoroughly exposed to Western influence. But scientific and technological inventiveness has
always been scarce; few significant social transformations have
taken place since Asoka (250 B.C.).

Encouragement to individual achievement and fulfillment will come
with exposure to Western ambition and Western ideas of love; will these
mean the loss of loyalty, responsibility, and devotion which have been
the fruits of Indian institutions, including the joint family and regional
and caste loyalties as well as the religious sense of oneness of people
and the cosmos? [12]

With such concerns in mind many Westerners, as well as Indians, are questioning the wisdom of such a social revolution, such
transformation of values. At least two general answers can be given.
One is the evidence that Indian social traditions are not so noble and
glorious—and never were! Take, for example, village life with its
vaunted security, interdependence and simple happiness. Speaking
as a deeply hurt "Untouchable," B. R. Ambedkar challenged the
Constituent Assembly: "What is the village but a sink of localism,
a den of ignorance, narrow-mindedness and communalism?" [13] Even
Nehru in his autobiography quotes Mahatma Gandhi as "often" referring to the Indian village as a "dung heap." [14] Yet this was the
same Gandhiji who repeatedly told Indians as well as Occidentals:
"Go to villages; that is India; therein lies the soul of India."

The second answer is that modernization, with its concomitant
social upheavals, is inevitable. One may readily concede that India
will remain predominantly rural for generations to come, that
decentralization must be stressed wherever possible, that local self-
government should remain the cornerstone of democracy. Nevertheless, the naive assumptions of Vinobaji and Jayaprakash Narayan, that heavy industries, public services, large-scale development
programs can grow from the "grass-roots," strikes most educated
observers (Eastern or Western) as unrealistic and absurd. Even if
capital resources could somehow be made available, scientific re-
sourcefulness and initiative do not emerge at the local level—least
of all in India. Nor can a viable modern state be administered by

gram raj (village government), no matter how enticing the picture of bucolic simplicity may appear. A "progressive" delegate to the Constituent Assembly inquired: "Would our friends with Gandhian ideas tell us whether they are prepared to follow those ideas to their logical conclusions" (by abolishing armies, legislatures, judicial systems, and accepting maximum salaries of five hundred rupees per month)? [15]

One conclusion, therefore, endorses the government's basic program of democratic state socialism. "Socialism" because a poverty-stricken country cannot afford the waste which capital development entails under private competition, and a caste-ridden, communally divided society has not yet produced the will and motivation for universal concern. "State" because an embryonic democracy lacks the political and ethical experience for pluralistic interaction. Those rabid individualists who fail to see the necessity for centralized planning need only look at the authoritarian alternatives recently adopted in Korea, Pakistan and other underdeveloped areas, and be thankful that India clings at least to the form of parliamentary democracy.

India needs strong central government, subject of course to popular controls, in order to prevent further fragmentation. Some experts would say that Nehru's greatest mistake in domestic policy was consenting to linguistic realignment of states. This principle has led to the belated division of Bombay and to violent demands from the Punjab and certain minority tribes. Despite self-righteous claims of tolerance, religious passions in India run high, especially when the sizable Muslim minority resists uniform civil laws on marriage, property, inheritance, and so on. Equally deep and equally serious are regional loyalties and prejudices. Speaking of the fearful possibility that "India will break up completely" (linguistically, religiously, emotionally, politically), Frank Anthony, the Anglo-Indian spokesman, remarked sadly: "There will be no emotional bond, none whatever. . . . Nobody thinks of himself as an Indian. . . . That is one of the dangers we face." [16] Indeed, it is one of the very greatest dangers India faces, and the need for genuine, heart-felt unity, patriotism, national consciousness, represents one of the greatest moral and political challenges for Government leaders. Yet an outspoken Indian public servant has written:

"The elementary fact that stares even the casual observer in the face is that Hindu theory does not provide for the conception of community." [17]

This need for national unity may be one factor which tempted the Government to embark on the seizure of three Portuguese enclaves in December 1961. True, these tiny bits of land surrounded by Indian territory had rankled long as the last vestige of colonialism in Southern Asia. True, the Salazar regime had shown itself, in Angola and wherever else it rules, one of the most ruthless and intransigent of dictatorships, utterly unwilling to join the modern world in the inevitable "freedom march." True, personal and political exploitation and repression marked the administration of Goa, which also served as a focal point of smuggling into India, as Macao does for Communist China.

Within India itself, Nehru was under attack from Communists for tolerating imperialism in Goa, as he was condemned by anti-Communists for failing until 1962 to resist Chinese aggression along the Tibetan border. Yet despite all the extenuating circumstances, there is no doubt that India's use of force (Menon belligerently denied the terms "aggression" or "invasion") cost India heavily in Western esteem. Those who admired the nation's earlier proof that passive resistance can achieve its goals had to be reminded afresh that Gandhi conceded the use of force when *neither* side was spiritually prepared for nonviolence. But Nehru's own moral pronouncements were henceforth to be seriously impaired in their effectiveness.

From an ethical standpoint (quite apart from political gains or losses) the world's outcry against the Goa move may be good for India. It may remind the country of Gandhi's basic message, that morality cannot be separated from policy, if either is to be effective. The effort of some secular leaders to remove religion from social reform, in order to avoid the rigid conservatism of orthodox groups, has sometimes entailed the opposite result of removing social reform from religious concern, thus compartmentalizing spiritual from practical issues. Such a chasm often exists in diplomacy as well. Prime Minister Nehru knew this. At least Alexander Campbell quoted him as saying: "There is hardly a country that has such high ideals as India, and there is hardly a country where the gap between ideals and performance is so great." [18] But whether his associates knew it, or whether he himself applied it to foreign relations, the very attempt to justify and "moralize" the "police action" in Goa forced many Indians to re-examine the relevance of their ethical and spiritual foundations, especially the relationship of means to ends. (Nor should officials in other lands who bear responsibility for Suez or Guatemala or Cuba "cast the first stone.")

The reaction over Goa may also induce India to take a second look at her own dual standard of ethics applied to the Cold War. A young Indian diplomat told a group of Americans in Delhi that United States policy should be based on altruistic concern for mankind (in such matters as foreign aid), whereas India's emerging statehood required that it be guided by enlightened self-interest. A similar attitude prevailed when the West protested Nehru's instantaneous censure of Franco-British action at Suez, followed by his hesitant equivocation over Soviet suppression in Hungary, or his failure to condemn vehemently and forthrightly Russia's resumption of nuclear testing. Nehru and many other Indians have sometimes explained candidly, but unconvincingly, that they expect a higher moral standard from the West and therefore are more deeply hurt by the faults of democracy than of Communism. With stinging force this boomerang now applies to the land of Buddha and Gandhi.

To be sure, there have been voices warning that India's spirituality was *maya* (unreal, illusion). After his journey around the world in futile quest of a faith, Arthur Koestler declared somewhat cynically:

To look at Asia for mystic enlightenment and spiritual guidance has become as much an anachronism as to think of America as the wild West. . . . [The East] prefers intuition to reason, symbols to concepts, self-realization through the annihilation of the ego to self-realization through the unfolding of individuality. . . . The messianic arrogance of the Christian crusader is matched by the Yogi's arrogant attitude of detachment towards human suffering.[19]

Speaking for Anglo-Indians, Frank Anthony asserted: "Religion is nothing at all. We don't bother about that. Indian Christians are completely divided along denominational lines." In other words, such voices are saying, religion has become irrelevant to modern nation-building. Whatever the importance of spiritual values in the past, they have lost their effectiveness for tomorrow.

Not all of India has yet discarded its religious heritage. Perhaps, as a British missionary wrote some decades ago, "A country like India cannot be permanently secularized." [20] because secularism does not plumb the ultimate questions which man—especially Indian man—continues to ask. A College Radio Discussion Contest, broadcast in New Delhi on February 14, 1960, took as its topic: "Should the traditional way of life be changed for a modern industrial society?" One speaker revealed the tension which splits the country today by saying, "Spiritual values will have to be preserved, although the fatalistic attitude which is characteristic of India should be removed as soon as possible." Here were echoes of Judge Ranade, warning against "a general indifference to secular well-being almost bordering upon fatalism." Yet here was a young "modern" pleading for the preservation of India's spiritual values.

Many people are repeating this plea. Few are doing much about it. Not many are even asking How? A young, perceptive Labor Attaché in the United States Embassy probed deeply into Indian philosophy as well as into problems of everyday life. In frequent conversations and in an unpublished manuscript he summarized his conclusion thus:

The leaders of India, who are more or less agnostic, and the masses of India, who are still bound by the institutions of caste and the joint family, will be more and more tempted to employ totalitarian short-cuts in an effort to keep up the race for national domination in Asia. If this be the case, then the leaders and people of India, if they are serious in their verbal commitments to democracy, must attempt to re-examine the Hindu faith to see if it can provide an adequate ideological foundation for democracy itself.[21]

This calls not for a defensive apologetic, such as Radhakrishnan offers, but for a frank recognition of the weaknesses of traditional Hinduism and of necessary "borrowings" from the thought and culture of the West. One might suggest as a starting point, the emphasis on action to be found in the *Bhagavad-Gita*. But the action required for democracy and social change will have to be responsible action, concerned action, not merely motivated by duty and wrapped in detachment.

At the same time, the West must not match India's social rigidity and "intolerant toleration" with political arrogance or religious dogmatism. Missionaries and Indian Christians should be less concerned with winning converts—important though such redeemed individuals are—than with permeating Indian life and culture with Christian ethics and Christian love. By sacrificial service and by active involvement in the social and political problems of their country, they will be able to demonstrate the transforming power of their Gospel. At the same time, they will be manifesting not only concerned and sympathetic devotion in the spirit of Christ, but respect for the nation and its culture (Hindu, Muslim, Sikh, Parsi, Buddhist, Jain, Christian) as a part of God's creation and God's purpose. They will be showing the relevance of Christianity to all of human life. As Burgess concludes, "In brief, India must find her own soul, her own faith, and her own distinctive form of democratic ideology if she is to save herself."

Is this possible for India? Is it possible for the West? There is the way of religion. Christian pietists and Hindu fatalists will react to the quotation just above by retorting, "Of course, India cannot save herself: only God can do it." In the dedication to his book, Ambedkar, Hindu outcaste and Buddhist convert, says: "[Our] ancient society . . . was a society of man plus God while modern society is a society of men only. . . . As an Oriental I belong to a society which is still ancient and in which God is a much more important member than man is." [22] If there is one theme intended to characterize this book, it is the conviction that God is indispensably at work—in Hindu India and Christian America. Parallel to that is the equally firm conviction that a person's or a nation's concept of God and of His moral demands does make a difference. Hence, to speak of India's "saving herself" implies a rejection not of divine grace, but of the fatalism in any religion which nullifies human effort.

There is the way of science. For many people, both East and West, science and religion still wage unholy war. Devout believers in God too often speak as if science threatens Him instead of confirming His power. Materialists, on the other hand, have made of science a jealous and omniscient god who will some day prove his omnipotence. One of the greatest Asian philosophers of the twentieth century, Hu Shih of China, seeks to dispel this dichotomy. Acknowledging that Orientals have exaggerated their "spirituality" and misconceived its rivals, he declares:

We should learn to understand and appreciate that science and technology are not materialistic but are highly idealistic and spiritual values. . . . For modern science is the cumulative achievement of that which is the most spiritual and indeed most divine in man, namely, the creative intelligence of man.[23]

Thus, one of the most significant insights of Vinoba Bhave brings together "science and spirituality." In other words, India's progress and India's ethics need not split asunder between opposing poles of science and religion.

There is the way of politics. This heading includes the vast network of partisan, economic, international relationships which threaten to atomize India and the world. No Westerner dare offer political advice, even if he possessed infallible wisdom. One might, however, echo the hope expressed by Frank Moraes that a realignment, especially of the Congress, might provide more democratic freedom and give greater stature to the able leaders of Opposition, both Right and Left. Obviously India cannot "save herself" economically. The country is full of experts and advisors and survey teams examining every aspect of development. Astute observers like Walter Lippmann and Barbara Ward have urged outside aid to India as high as a billion dollars a year until that country achieves a "break-through" into self-perpetuating growth. Not only humanitarianism, but the ultimate self-interest of the West demands some such support, undeterred by differences of political perspective or military alliances.

None of these instruments will be effective in saving India if she loses her inner moral integrity. This, not the possible collapse of the United Nations, was the greatest threat of the Goan crisis. If cynicism and corruption spread at the Center or in local administration, economic aid would become "Operation Rathole." Observers generally agree that Communism represents no serious threat to India so long as a stable government maintains unity and

even a bare modicum of material and social progress. But if Lal
Bahadur Shastri, or any other successor to Nehru, is unable to hold
the scattered loyalties of the country together, if religious and political reactionaries attempt to turn back the clock, India might well
fall into regional, linguistic, communal and partisan fragments
ready to be swept up by a long arm across the Himalayas.

There is the way of education. The cult of John Dewey still
has countless followers in Asia, those who believe that the proper
guidance of the intellect will solve all other problems. Hinduism's
optimistic view of the nature of man, its confidence that a divine
spark shines in every man and that evil is an illusion, undergirds
this faith in rational progress. Secularists who are dubious about
any transcendent values are confirmed in their prejudice against
religion by its institutional forms. In fact, the most common difficulty in discussing religion in India proved to be uncertainty as to
whether the speaker thought of it as a divisive, antisocial, outmoded system or as a vague ethical spirituality.

Late in 1959, the Government appointed a Committee on
Religious and Moral Instruction to make investigations and recom-
mendations as to the role of educational institutions in religious
training. When the Committee made its report five months later,
prominent educators spoke scornfully of its failure to consult those
with experience and convictions, implying that the document represented an "armchair"—or a bureaucratic office—survey. More
seriously, like so many official studies, the Prakasa Report on Religious and Moral Instruction seemed destined to gather dust in
files and libraries, devoid of implementation.

Nevertheless, certain principles and observations could be significant guideposts. Here are a few excerpts from the Report:

The old bonds that kept men together are fast loosening and the various new ideologies that are coming to us, and which we are outwardly
accepting without inwardly digesting their meanings, are increasingly
worsening the situation. The only cure, it seems to us, is the deliberate
inculcation of moral and spiritual values from the earliest days of our
lives. If we lose these, we shall be a nation without a soul; and our attempts to imitate the outer forms of other lands, without understanding their inner meanings . . . would only result in chaos and confusion.

Specific suggestions include a comparative study of the lives and teachings of great religious leaders; the inculcation of social service, good manners, and true patriotism; a strengthening of religious values in the home; a period of silent meditation opening each school day; promotion of "the virtues of reverence and courtesy which are badly needed in our society"; preparation of literary materials designed to instill appreciation of the common cultural heritage from many faiths; state assistance to religious institutions in lieu of specific religious instruction in state schools; a concerted effort to uplift moral standards in business and politics. These represent enormous tasks for India—and for the West.

It is claimed that when John Ruskin was informed with great excitement that the first cable had been opened from England to India, he replied calmly and wisely: "But what do you have to say to India?" The past century has brought tremendous changes to the world. The West has said many things to the Orient, not all of them kind and helpful. But minds as alert and hearts as sensitive as those of India could not remain aloof from the modern world, however justified their fears of materialistic value standards. With the inevitable science and industry, with the technological and political machinery, India has begun to assimilate the fundamental principles of democracy and social welfare.

At the same time, the West is learning that Asia has something to say, something vital and essential. There is a strength as well as frailty in Hindu adaptation, for that is what has enabled India to survive and adjust through four thousand years or more. So, again, an ancient civilization is undergoing tumultuous change: in the social patterns of its rural villages, in the gracious intellects of its philosopher-statesmen. Objective, analytical scholars in the West may argue as to whether Hinduism will remain Hinduism without "sacred cows" and caste, or whether vague concepts of *karma* without worship or sect will even constitute a religion. Let us hope that India will retain her colorful festivals, as a source of cultural unity and an increasingly profitable tourist attraction. For Indians will continue to regard themselves as Hindus, reconciling science and spirituality, absorbing unobtrusively a modicum of Christian ethics. And whatever direction the country's foreign policy may take in the future, India has earned a place in history as the supreme example of a people who won its freedom by patient, passive perseverance, under the leadership of a little man who believed that means must be as moral as aims.

In December 1959, President Eisenhower told the joint houses of the Indian Parliament that "the welfare of America is bound up with the welfare of India." Then he added: "The most heartening and hopeful phenomenon in the world today is that the people have experienced a great awakening. They recognize that only under a rule of moral law can all of us realize our deepest and noblest aspirations." India and the United States may follow very different paths—religiously, politically, economically, culturally. Among many things which they share in common, however, one shines forth conspicuously in the nineteen-sixties: both nations are looked to by the rest of the world as the conscience of mankind, and both are bitterly criticized when they fail to perform that role. Each, therefore, must help the other to understand, to enhance, and to fulfill its moral and spiritual heritage and destiny.

Not all British members of the Indian Civil Service left their offices with sympathy and goodwill. Yet ten years after Independence, Sir Percival Griffiths paid this tribute to the former colonial empire:

It is the most successful example of a Parliamentary democracy in the East; secondly, it is the scene of the greatest experiment in socialism ever conducted in a freedom-loving country; while, thirdly, it is the only great country wholly outside either of the international blocs. . . . A reasonable impatience is the keynote of modern India.[24]

In a warmly honest message from the University of Madras, Professor Bhaskaran expressed the nation's dilemma in these terms:

Really India is not a very complex land (though here many would disagree—CL), only it has got on for thousands of years without government, without a self-conscious and sophisticated élite, in fact without any notion of deliberate planning or program. Quite organic and natural. Now some of us propose to change all this and I approve of the urge. We are all trying to help each other to get to know what we want and to set about getting it. That is where the apparent confusion and cross purposes become very visible. But we shall settle down.[25]

In orientation lectures for Americans newly arrived in India, U.S. Embassy officials acknowledged the enormous difficulties which confront the country and confessed their recurrent moods of hopelessness and frustration. Yet with equal unanimity, with equal candor, and with equal realism, they affirmed their faith that somehow India will muddle through. This writer shares that confidence. As one of those diplomats said, the deluge may still come, years after Nehru's death, when the comparative weakness of his successors has been thoroughly exposed and when partisan, communal frictions have had time to fester. But India possesses remarkable human and spiritual resources for growth. A culture which can produce in one century Rammohun Roy, Rabindranath Tagore, Mohandas Gandhi and Jawaharlal Nehru need not boast only of its ancient past. As Gardner Murphy says in his UNESCO study: "I believe that a fair acquaintance with the men and women who govern India's affairs, whether at a political, economic, literary, artistic, educational, or cultural level, will convince the observer that India is capable of solving her own problems." [26] And as Nehru told the Constituent Assembly out of his own burgeoning rediscovery of his native land: "Whether we are men and women of destiny or not, India is a country of destiny." [27]

Selected Bibliography

Like this book, the following bibliography makes no pretense of being definitive or comprehensive. It is made up, rather, of those works which have come directly to the author's attention, which proved readily accessible in libraries, or which relate especially to the leaders interviewed. I am particularly indebted to the libraries of the Delhi Orientation Center, Delhi University, the United States Information Service, Sapru House, Serampore College, Leonard Theological College, and Duke University.

Aiyar, Alladi Krishnaswami, *The Constitution and Fundamental Rights,* Srinivasa Sastri Institute of Politics, Madras, 1955, 80 pp.

Aiyer, P. S. Sivaswami, *Evolution of Hindu Moral Ideals,* Calcutta University, 1935, 242 pp.

All-India Women's Conference, Twenty-Eighth Session (Kanpur), A.I.W.C. Central Office, New Delhi, 1959, 135 pp.

Alter, James P. and Jai Singh, Herbert, *The Church in Delhi,* National Christian Council of India, 1962, xii + 166 pp.

Ambedkar, B. R., *What Congress and Gandhi Have Done to the Untouchables,* Thacker, Bombay, 1945, 399 pp.

Andrews, C. F., and Mukerji, Girija, *The Rise and Growth of the Congress in India,* George Allen and Unwin, London, 1938, 304 pp.

Asirvatham, Eddy, *Christianity in the Indian Crucible,* Y.M.C.A. Publishing House, Calcutta, 1955, 244 pp.

Azad, Abul Kalam, *India Wins Freedom,* Orient Longmans, Calcutta, 1959, 252 pp.

Bhagavad-Gita (Annie Besant, trans.) Natesan, Madras, 1907, 264 pp.

Binani, G. D., and Rao, T. V. Rama (eds.), *India at a Glance,* Orient Longmans, Calcutta, rev. 1954, 1756 pp.

Blunt, Edward (ed.), *Social Service in India,* H. M. Stationery Office, London, 1938, 447 pp.

Bowles, Chester, *Ambassador's Report,* Harper, New York, 1954, 415 pp.

Bowles, Chester, *Ideas, People and Peace,* Bodley Head, London, 1958, 189 pp.

Brecher, Michael, *Nehru: A Political Biography,* Oxford University Press, 1959, 682 pp.

Brown, D. Mackenzie, *The White Umbrella,* University of California Press, Berkeley, 1958, 204 pp.

Campbell, Alexander, *The Heart of India,* Alfred A. Knopf, New York, 1958, 333 pp.

Carey, S. Pearce, *William Carey,* Carey Press, London, 1923 (rev. 1934), 439 pp.

Carstairs, G. Morris, *The Twice-Born,* Hogarth Press, London, 1957, 343 pp.

Chakravarti, S. C. (ed.), *The Father of Modern India,* Rammohun Roy Centenary Committee, Calcutta, 1935, 190 + 572 + xxxviii pp.

Chandran, J. R., and Thomas, M. M., *Political Outlook in India Today,* Committee for Literature on Social Concerns, Bangalore, 1956, 176 pp.

Chandran, J. R., and Thomas, M. M., *Religious Freedom,* Committee for Literature on Social Concerns, Bangalore, 1956, 128 pp.

Chandrasekhar, Sripati, *Hungry People and Empty Lands,* University of Baroda, 1952, 306 pp.

Chandrasekhar, Sripati, *India's Population, Fact and Policy,* John Day, New York, 1946, 117 pp.

Chandrasekhar, Sripati, *Population and Planned Parenthood,* George Allen and Unwin, London, 1955, 108 pp.

Chirol, Valentine, *India,* E. Benn, London, 1926, 352 pp.

Committee on Religious and Moral Instruction, *Report,* Ministry of Education, Government of India Press, New Delhi, 1960, 21 pp.

The Constituent Assembly Debates, Vols. I-XII + Index, Government of India, New Delhi, 1946-1949.

The Constitution of India, Government of India Press, Delhi, 1958.

Cousins, Norman, *Talks with Nehru,* John Day, New York, 1951, 64 pp.

Desai, A. R., *Social Background of Indian Nationalism,* Popular Book Department, Bombay, 1948 (rev. 1954), 407 pp. (also published by Oxford University Press, 1948).

Deshmukh, C. D., *In the Portals of Indian Universities,* University Grants Commission, New Delhi, 1959, 336 pp.

Devanandan, P. D., *The Gospel and the Hindu Intellectual,* Christian Institute for the Study of Religion and Society, Bangalore, 1959, 28 pp.

Devanandan, P. D., *Living Hinduism,* Christian Institute for the Study of Religion and Society, Bangalore, 1959, 28 pp.

Devanandan, P. D., *Resurgent Hinduism,* Christian Institute for the Study of Religion and Society, Bangalore, 1959, 24 pp.

Devanandan, P. D., and Thomas, M. M. (eds.), *The Changing Pattern of Family in India,* Christian Institute for the Study of Religion and Society, Bangalore, 1960, 166 pp.

Devanandan, P. D., and Thomas, M. M. (eds.), *Christian Participation in Nation-Building,* National Christian Council of India, Bangalore, 1960, 325 pp.

Devanandan, P. D., and Thomas, M. M. (eds.), *Communism and the Social Revolution in India,* Y.M.C.A. Publishing House, Calcutta, 1953, 88 pp.

Devanandan, P. D., and Thomas, M. M. (eds.), *Community Development in India's Industrial Urban Areas,* Committee for Literature on Social Concerns, Bangalore, 1958, 151 pp.

Devanandan, P. D., and Thomas, M. M. (eds.), *Cultural Foundations of Indian Democracy,* Y.M.C.A. Publishing House, Calcutta, 1955, 110 pp.

Devanandan, P. D., and Thomas, M. M. (eds.), *Human Person, Society and State,* Committee for Literature on Social Concerns, Bangalore, 1957, 140 pp.

Devanandan, P. D., and Thomas, M. M. (eds.), *India's Quest for Democracy,* Y.M.C.A. Publishing House, Calcutta, 1955, 64 pp.

Devanesen, Chandran, *The Cross Is Lifted,* Friendship Press, New York, 1954, 68 pp.

Dhawan, Gopinath, *The Political Philosophy of Mahatma Gandhi,* Navajivan Publishing House, Ahmedabad, 1946, 407 pp.

Dutta, Bhupendranath, *Swami Vivekananda, The Socialist,* Khulna Press, Bengal, 1929.

Ebenstein, William, *Great Political Thinkers,* Holt, Rinehart and Winston, New York, 1951, 903 pp.

Empty Shoes, A Study of the Church of South India, National Council of the Protestant Episcopal Church, New York, 1956, 153 pp.

Farquhar, J. N., *The Crown of Hinduism,* Oxford University Press, 1913, 469 pp.

Farquhar, J. N., *Modern Religious Movements in India,* Macmillan, New York, 1924, 471 pp.

Finegan, Jack, *India Today!,* Bethany Press, St. Louis, 1955, 208 pp.

Fischer, Louis, *The Life of Mahatma Gandhi,* Jonathan Cape, London, 1951, 593 pp.

Fleming, Daniel J., *The Social Mission of the Church in India,* Association Press, Calcutta, 1913.

Gandhi, M. K., *Communism and Communists,* Navajivan Publishing House, Ahmedabad, 1959, 24 pp.

Gandhi, M. K., *My Socialism,* Navajivan Publishing House, Ahmedabad, 1959, 56 pp.

Gandhi, Mohandas K., *The Story of My Experiments with Truth,* Public Affairs Press, Washington, 1948 (and other editions since 1927, *Autobiography*).

Gandhi, M. K., *What Jesus Means to Me,* Navajivan Publishing House, Ahmedabad, 1959, 49 pp.

Gokhale, B. G., *The Making of the Indian Nation,* Asia Publishing House, Bombay, 1958, 355 pp.

Gora (G. Ramachandra Rao), *An Atheist with Gandhi,* Navajivan Publishing House, Ahmedabad, 1951 (rep. 1958), 60 pp.

Griffiths, Percival, *The British Impact on India,* MacDonald, London, 1952, 500 pp.

Griffiths, Percival, *Modern India,* E. Benn, London, 1957, 255 pp.

Hopkins, E. Washburn, *Ethics of India,* Yale University Press, New Haven, 1924, 265 pp.

Hoyland, John S., *Gopal Krishna Gokhale,* Y.M.C.A. Publishing House, Calcutta, 1933, 200 pp.

Husain, S. Abid, *The National Culture of India,* Jaico Publishing House, Bombay, 1955.

Husain, S. Abid, *The Way of Gandhi and Nehru,* Asia Publishing House, Bombay, 1959, 184 pp.

Hutton, J. H., *Caste in India,* Oxford University Press, 1946 (rep. 1960), 320 pp.

Immanuel, Rajappan D., *The Influence of Hinduism on Indian Christians,* Leonard Theological College, Jabalpur, 1950, 251 pp.

India, 1959, Ministry of Information and Broadcasting, Government of India, Delhi, 1959, 562 pp.

Indra, *The Status of Women in Ancient India,* Minerva Bookshop, Lahore, 1940, 324 pp.

Ingham, Kenneth, *Reformers in India,* 1793-1833, Cambridge University Press, 1956, 150 pp.

Jennings, Ivor, *Some Characteristics of the Indian Constitution,* Oxford University Press (Madras), 1953, 86 pp.

Jones, E. Stanley, *Along the Indian Road,* Abingdon, New York, 1939, 248 pp.

Jones, E. Stanley, *Christ at the Round Table,* Abingdon, New York, 1928, 328 pp.

Jones, E. Stanley, *The Christ of the Indian Road,* Abingdon, New York, 1925, 213 pp.

Jones, E. Stanley, *Mahatma Gandhi,* Abingdon, New York, 1948, 160 pp.

Joshi, G. N., *The Constitution of India,* Macmillan, London, 1954, 466 pp.

Kabir, Humayun, *Science, Democracy and Islam,* George Allen and Unwin, London, 1955, 126 pp.

Karanjia, R. K., *The Mind of Mr. Nehru,* Allen and Unwin, London, 1961, 112 pp.

Kellock, James, *Mahadev Govind Ranade,* Association Press, Calcutta, 1926, 204 pp.

Koestler, Arthur, *The Lotus and the Robot,* Macmillan, New York, 1961. (also published by Hutchinson, London, 1960).

Lin Yutang, *The Wisdom of China and India,* Random House, New York, 1942, 1104 pp.

Majumdar, J. K. (ed.), *Raja Rammohun Roy and Progressive Movements in India,* 1775-1845, Art Press, Calcutta, 1941, 552 pp.

Manikam, Rajah B. (ed.), *Christianity and the Asian Revolution,* Diocesan Press, Madras, 1954, 293 pp.

Marshman, John Clark, *The Life and Times of Carey, Marshman and Ward,* Longman, Brown, Green, London, 1859.

Masani, M. R., *The Communist Party of India,* Macmillan, New York, 1954, 302 pp.

Mayhew, Arthur, *Christianity and the Government of India,* Faber and Gwyer, London, 1929, 260 pp.

Mayhew, Arthur, *The Education of India,* Faber and Gwyer, London, 1926, 306 pp.

Mehta, Asoka, *Democratic Socialism,* Bharatiya Vidya Bhavan, Bombay, 1959, 192 pp.

Mehta, Asoka, *Studies in Asian Socialism,* Bharatiya Vidya Bhavan, Bombay, 1959, 241 pp.

Methodist Episcopal Church, *Conference Minutes* (Indian Mission or Central Conference), 1864-1916.

Ministry of Community Development and Cooperation, *Democratic Decentralisation,* Government of India, New Delhi, 1959, 10 pp.

Ministry of Community Development and Cooperation, *Our Programme At Work,* Government of India, New Delhi, 1959, 19 pp.

Ministry of Community Development and Cooperation, *Revised Programme of Community Development,* Government of India, New Delhi, 1959, 88 pp.

Moore, Charles A. (ed.), *Philosophy—East and West,* Princeton University Press, 1944, 334 pp.

Moraes, Frank, *Jawaharlal Nehru,* Jaico Publishing House, Bombay, 1959, 514 pp. (also published by Macmillan, New York)

Moraes, Frank, *India Today,* Macmillan, New York, 1960, 248 pp.

Mukerjee, Radhakamal, *The Dynamics of Morals,* Macmillan, London, 1950, 530 pp.

Müller, F. Max, *Rammohan to Ramakrishna,* Susil Gupta, Calcutta, 1952, 165 pp. (orig. pub. 1884, 1898, 1899)

Munshi, K. M., *Our Greatest Need and Other Addresses,* Bharatiya Vidya Bhavan, Bombay, 1953, 266 pp.

Munshi, K. M., *Our Sovereign Democratic Republic,* University of Madras, 1955, 11 + 12 pp.

Munshi, K. M., *Sparks from the Anvil,* Bharatiya Vidya Bhavan, Bombay, 1956, 146 pp.

Murphy, Gardner, *In the Minds of Men,* Basic Books, New York, 1953, 306 pp.

Narain, Dhirendra, *Hindu Character,* University of Bombay, 1957, 238 pp.

Narayan, Jayaprakash, *A Plea for Reconstruction of Indian Polity,* Akhil Bharat Sarva Seva Sangh, New Delhi, 1959.

Natarajan, S., *A Century of Social Reform in India,* Asia Publishing House, Bombay, 1959, 208 pp.

Nehru, Jawaharlal, *The Discovery of India,* John Day, New York, 1946, 595 pp. (also published by Signet Press, Calcutta, 1945, 615 pp., rep. 1956)

Nehru, Jawaharlal, *Independence and After,* John Day, New York, 1950.

Nehru, Jawaharlal, *Jawaharlal Nehru, an Autobiography,* John Lane, London, 1936 (rep. 1947), 623 pp. (also published as *Toward Freedom,* John Day, New York, 1941, 445 pp.).

Nehru, Jawaharlal, *Nehru on Gandhi,* John Day, New York, 1941.

Nehru, Krishna, *With No Regrets,* John Day, New York, 1945, 160 pp.

Northrop, F. S. C., *The Meeting of East and West,* Macmillan, New York, 1947, 531 pp.

Noss, John B., *Man's Religions,* Macmillan, New York, rev. 1956, 784 pp.

O'Malley, L. S. S., *Modern India and the West,* Oxford University Press, 1941, 834 pp.

Panikkar, K. M., *Hindu Society at Cross Roads,* Asia Publishing House, Bombay, 1955, 103 pp. (a very slightly revised version of *Hinduism and the Modern World*)

Panikkar, K. M., *Hinduism and the Modern World,* Kitabistan, Allahabad, 1938, 115 pp.

Park, Richard L., and Tinker, Irene (eds.), *Leadership and Political Institutions in India,* Princeton University Press, 1959, 486 pp.

Paton, William, *Social Ideals in India,* United Council for Missionary Education, London, 1919, 104 pp.

Perry, Edmund, *The Gospel in Dispute,* Doubleday, Garden City, New York, 1958, 230 pp.

Prabhu, J. M. Lobo, *New Thinking,* India Book House, Bombay, 1959, 161 pp.

Prasad, Narmadeshwar, *The Myth of the Caste System,* Samjna Prakashan, Patna, 1957, 319 pp.

Pylee, M. V., *Constitutional Government in India,* Asia Publishing House, Bombay, 1960, 745 pp.

Radhakrishnan, S., and Muirhead, J. H., *Contemporary Indian Philosophy,* George Allen and Unwin, London, 1936 (rev. 1952).

Radhakrishnan, S., *East and West in Religion,* George Allen and Unwin, London, 1933 (rep. 1949), 146 pp.

Radhakrishnan, S., *Eastern Religions and Western Thought,* Clarendon Press, Oxford, 1939, 394 pp.

Radhakrishnan, S., *The Hindu View of Life,* George Allen and Unwin, London, 1927, 133 pp.

Radhakrishnan, S., *Religion and Society,* George Allen and Unwin, London, 1947, 242 pp.

Radhakrishnan, S., and Moore, Charles A., *A Source Book in Indian Philosophy,* Princeton University Press, 1957.

Raichur, Sunder Raj Sathianathan, *Religion in Public Education in India,* Council of Christian Education, Methodist Church in Southern Asia, Mysore, n.d., 166 pp.

Rajagopalachari, C., *Hinduism: Doctrine and Way of Life,* Bharatiya Vidya Bhavan, Bombay, 1959, 132 pp.

Ramabhai, Suresh, *Vinoba and His Mission,* Akhil Bharat Sarva Seva Sangh, Sevagram, 1954, 246 pp.

Ramachandran, V. G., *Fundamental Rights and Constitutional Remedies,* Eastern Book Company, Lucknow, 1959, 572 pp.

Ranganathananda, *Eternal Values for a Changing Society,* Advaita Ashrama, Calcutta, 1958, 244 pp.

Ranganathananda, *The Ramakrishna Mission,* Sri Ramakrishna Math, Madras, 1940 (rev. 1956), 50 pp.

Ranganathananda, *Religion in India Today,* Promoting Enduring Peace, West Haven, Conn., n.d., 20 pp.

Rao, C. V. H. (ed.), *Social Welfare in India,* Planning Commission, Government of India, New Delhi, 1955, 850 pp.

Ray, Benoy Gopal, *Gandhian Ethics,* Navajivan Publishing House, Ahmedabad, 1950 (rep. 1958), 59 pp.

Redding, Jay Saunders, *An American in India,* Bobbs-Merrill, Indianapolis, 1954, 277 pp.

Rolland, Romain, *The Life of Vivekananda and the Universal Gospel,* Advaita Ashrama, Almora, 1953, 384 pp.

Roosevelt, Eleanor, *India and the Awakening East,* Harper, New York, 1953, 237 pp.

Roy, M. N., *Politics, Power and Parties,* Renaissance, Calcutta, 1960, 216 pp.

Samuel, V. C., *The Ramakrishna Movement,* Christian Institute for the Study of Religion and Society, Bangalore, 1959, 35 pp.

Sarma, D. S., *The Renaissance of Hinduism,* Benares Hindu University, 1944, 686 pp.

Sastri, L. S., *The Constitution of India,* Law Book Company, Allahabad, 1950, 383 pp.

Sastri, V. S. Srinivasa, *The Rights and Duties of the Indian Citizen,* Calcutta University Press, 1927 (rev. 1948), 116 pp.

Schuster, George, and Wint, Guy, *India and Democracy,* Macmillan, London, 1941, 444 pp.

Schweitzer, Albert, *Indian Thought and Its Development,* Hodder and Stoughton, London, 1936, 272 pp.

Scott, Roland W., *Social Ethics in Modern Hinduism,* Y.M.C.A. Publishing House, Calcutta, 1953, 243 pp.

The Secular State of India, Y.M.C.A. Publishing House, Calcutta, n.d., 10 pp.

Sen, Sachim, *The Political Thought of Tagore,* General Printers and Publishers, Calcutta, 1947, 360 pp.

Shukla, V. N., *The Constitution of India,* Eastern Book Company, Lucknow, 1950, 468 pp.

Singh, Anup, *Nehru, The Rising Star of India,* George Allen and Unwin, London, 1940.

Smith, George, *The Life of William Carey,* J. M. Dent, London, 1909, 326 pp.

Social Legislation, Its Role in Social Welfare, Planning Commission, Government of India, New Delhi, 1956, 418 pp.

Soper, Edmund Davison, *The Religions of Mankind,* Abingdon, New York, rev. 1951, 253 pp.

Spear, Percival, *India, Pakistan and the West,* Oxford University Press, 1958.

Tagore, Rabindranath, *Nationalism,* Macmillan, New York, 1917, 159 pp.

Tagore, Rabindranath, *The Religion of Man,* Macmillan, New York, 1931, 244 pp.

Tagore, Rabindranath, *A Tagore Testament,* Philosophical Library, New York, 1954, 117 pp.

Tahmankar, D. V., *Lokamanya Tilak,* John Murray, London, 1956, 340 pp.

Tennyson, Hallam, *Saint on the March,* Victor Gollancz, London, 1955, 223 pp. (published in the United States as *India's Walking Saint,* Doubleday, Garden City, New York, 1955, 224 pp.)

They Belong to the Ages, United States Information Service, Delhi, n.d.

Thomas, P., *Christians and Christianity in India and Pakistan,* George Allen and Unwin, London, 1954, 210 pp.

Thompson, Edward, *Rabindranath Tagore, Poet and Dramatist,* Oxford University Press, 1926 (rev. 1948), 330 pp.

Thompson, Edward, *Suttee,* George Allen and Unwin, London, 1928, 165 pp.

Toynbee, Arnold, *Christianity Among the Religions of the World,* Scribner's, New York, 1957, 116 pp.

Vyas, K. C., *The Social Renaissance in India,* Vora, Bombay, 1957, 206 pp.

Walker, F. Deaville, *William Carey, Missionary Pioneer and Statesman,* Student Christian Movement, London, 1926, 320 pp.

Wallbank, T. Walter, *India in the New Era,* Scott, Foresman, Chicago, 1951, 204 pp.

Ward, Barbara, *India and the West,* Norton, New York, 1961, 256 pp.

Webb, Clement C. J., *The Contribution of Christianity to Ethics,* University of Calcutta, 1932, 121 pp.

Weber, Max, *The Religion of India,* Free Press, Glencoe, Ill., 1958, 392 pp.

Wilson, Dorothy Clarke, *Fly with Me to India,* Abingdon, New York, 1954, 127 pp.

Wiser, William H., and Charlotte Vail, *Behind Mud Walls,* Agricultural Missions, New York, 1930 (rep. 1951), 180 pp.

With the Kings in India, Gandhi National Memorial Fund, New Delhi, 1959, 24 pp.

Wolseley, Roland E., *Face to Face with India,* Friendship Press, New York, 1954, 176 pp.

Woodruff, Philip, *The Men Who Ruled India* (2 vols.), Jonathan Cape, London, 1953.

Yasin, Mohammed, *A Social History of Islamic India,* Upper India Publishing House, Lucknow, 1958, 234 pp.

Notes

Introduction

[1] Jawaharlal Nehru, *The Discovery of India,* John Day, New York, 1946.

[2] M. K. Gandhi, *The Story of My Experiments with Truth,* Public Affairs Press, Washington, 1948, p. 5.

[3] Quoted, Louis Fischer, *The Life of Mahatma Gandhi,* Jonathan Cape, London, 1951, p. 23.

[4] Nehru, *op. cit.,* p. 14.

[5] George Schuster and Guy Wint, *India and Democracy,* Macmillan, London, 1941, pp. 81-82, 86-87.

[6] Cf. *Goals for Americans,* Prentice-Hall, New York, 1960.

[7] *The Christian Century,* February 3, 1960.

[8] *Time* (Pacific Edition), February 22, 1960.

[9] D. Mackenzie Brown, *The White Umbrella,* University of California, Berkeley, 1958, p. 84.

Chapter I

[1] *The Bhagavad-Gita,* XII, 13 and 17, translated by Annie Besant, Natesan & Co., Madras, 1908, pp. 182-183. (Subsequent quotations in this chapter from the *Gita* are from this translation.)

[2] Sarvepalli Radhakrishnan and Charles A. Moore (Eds.), *A Source Book in Indian Philosophy,* Princeton University Press, 1957, p. 27; cf. E. Washburn Hopkins, *Ethics of India,* Yale University Press, New Haven, 1924, p. 44.

[3] Albert Schweitzer, *Indian Thought and Its Development,* Hodder and Stoughton, London, 1936, p. 43, cf. p. 36.

[4] *Ibid.,* p. 45.

[5] P. S. Sivaswamy Aiyer, *Evolution of Hindu Moral Ideals,* Calcutta University, 1935, p. 92.

[6] Schweitzer, *op. cit.,* p. 178.

7 *Ibid.,* p. 188.
8 Hopkins, *op. cit.,* p. 225.

also lecture at Delhi University Orientation Center, August 10, 1959.

27Quoted, Soper, *op. cit.,* p. 130.

Chapter II

1 Edmund D. Soper, *The Religions of Mankind,* Abingdon, New York, rev. ed., 1951, p. 120.

2 Quoted, John B. Noss, *Man's Religions,* Macmillan, New York, rev. ed., 1956, p. 151, cf. p. 153.

3 *Ibid.,* p. 154.

4 Schweitzer, *op. cit.,* pp. 82-83.

5 *Ibid.,* pp. 80, 81, 83.

6 Nehru, *op. cit.,* p. 119.

7 B. G. Gokhale, *The Making of the Indian Nation,* Asia Publishing House, Bombay, 1958, p. 247.

8 *Ibid.,* p. 24.

9 Schuster and Wint, *op. cit.,* p. 22.

10 Nehru, *op. cit.,* p. 166.

11 Hopkins, *op. cit.,* p. 142.

12 Edmund Perry, *The Gospel in Dispute,* Doubleday, Garden City, 1958, p. 195.

13 F. Max Müller, *Rammohan to Ramakrishna,* Gusil Gupta, Calcutta, 1952, pp. 12-13.

14 Hopkins, *op. cit.,* p. 137.

15 *Ibid.,* pp. 165-166.

16 Nehru, *op. cit.,* p. 166.

17 *Social Welfare in India,* Planning Commission, Government of India, New Delhi, 1955, p. xi (italics added).

18 Soper, *op. cit.,* p. 131.

19 *Ibid.,* p. 134.

20 Mohammed Yasin, *A Social History of Islamic India (1605-1748),* Upper India Publishing House, Lucknow, 1958, p. 14.

21 Frank Moraes, *India Today,* Macmillan, New York, 1960, pp. 38-39.

22 Yasin, *op. cit.,* pp. 44-45.

23 *Ibid.,* p. 180.

24 Quoted, T. Walter Wallbank, *India in the New Era,* Scott, Foresman, Chicago, 1951, p. 84.

25 Quoted, C. F. Andrews and Girija Mukerji, *The Rise and Growth of the Congress in India,* George Allen and Unwin, London, 1938, p. 52.

26 M. M. Begg, personal interview, Delhi College, Delhi, January 29, 1960;

Chapter III

1 Quoted, Fischer, *op. cit.,* p. 184.

2 Quoted, Arthur Mayhew, *Christianity and the Government of India,* Faber and Gwyer, London, 1929, p. 39.

3 Quoted, Schuster and Wint, *op. cit.,* pp. 76-77.

4 Mayhew, *op. cit.,* p. 24.

5 Quoted, *ibid.,* p. 26.

6 Philip Woodruff, *The Men Who Ruled India,* Vol. I, "The Founders," Jonathan Cape, London, 1953, p. 145.

7 *Ibid.,* p. 220.

8 Mayhew, *op. cit.,* p. 92.

9 Kenneth Ingham, *Reformers in India 1793-1833,* Cambridge University Press, 1956, p. 10.

10 Quoted, Woodruff, *op. cit.,* p. 257.

11 Quoted, Jatindra Kumar Majumdar (Ed.), *Raja Rammohun Roy and Progressive Movements in India (1775-1845),* Art Press, Calcutta, 1941, pp. 97-98.

12 Edward Thompson, *Suttee,* George Allen and Unwin, London, 1928, p. 52.

13 Quoted, Satis Chandra Chakravarti (Ed.), *The Father of Modern India,* Rammohun Roy Centenary Committee, Calcutta, 1935, Part II, p. 19.

14 Quoted, Majumdar, *op. cit.,* pp. 121-128.

15 Quoted, *ibid.,* pp. 139-148.

16 F. Deaville Walker, *William Carey, Missionary Pioneer and Statesman,* Student Christian Movement, London, 1926, p. 310.

17 Quoted, Majumdar, *op. cit.,* p. 153.

18 Quoted, *Social Welfare of India, op. cit.,* p. 588.

19 Quoted, Woodruff, *op. cit.,* p. 327.

20 Nehru, *op. cit.,* p. 316.

21 Alexander Campbell, *The Heart of India,* Alfred A. Knopf, New York, 1958, p. 30.

22 Quoted, Schuster and Wint, *op. cit.,* p. 77.

23 Quoted, Moraes, *op. cit.,* p. 53.

24 Nehru, *op. cit.*, p. 412, cf. pp. 317-318.

25 Wallbank, *op. cit.*, p. 77.

26 William Ebenstein, *Great Political Thinkers*, Holt, Rinehart and Winston, New York, 1951, p. 450.

27 Quoted, Andrews and Mukerji, *op. cit.*, p. 88.

28 A. Ranganathan, "The Impact of British Liberalism on Indian Thought," *The Hyphen*, July, 1958, p. 17.

29 Quoted, Andrews and Mukerji, *op. cit.*, p. 80.

30 Wallbank, *op. cit.*, p. 60.

31 Katherine Mayo, *Mother India*, Harcourt, Brace, New York, 1927; a cruelly devastating "exposure" of the worst social conditions frequently refuted and still bitterly resented by many Indians.

32 Alexander Campbell, *The Heart of India*, Knopf, New York, 1958, p. 30.

33 Sachin Sen, *The Political Thought of Tagore*, General Printers and Publishers, Calcutta, 1947, p. 210.

34 *Social Welfare in India, op. cit.*, p. 6.

35 Moraes, *op. cit.*, p. 57.

Chapter IV

1 Schuster and Wint, *op. cit.*, p. 64.

2 Mayhew, *op. cit.*, p. 14.

3 Ingham, *op. cit.*, p. 96.

4 Quoted, Majumdar, *op. cit.*, p. xxiii.

5 Quoted, *ibid.*, pp. 23-29.

6 Quoted, *ibid.*, p. 70.

7 Andrews and Mukerji, *op. cit.*, p. 56.

8 P. Thomas, *Christians and Christianity in India and Pakistan*, Allen and Unwin, London, 1954, pp. 69-70; cf. Rajappan D. Immanuel, *The Influence of Hinduism on Indian Christians*, Leonard Theological College, Jabalpur, 1950, Chap. II.

9 John C. Marshman, *The Life and Times of Carey, Marshman and Ward*, Longman, Brown, Green, London, 1859, Vol. I, p. 158.

10 Quoted, S. Pearce Carey, *William Carey*, Carey Press, London, 1923, p. 192, cf. pp. 177-178, 195.

11 Ingham, *op. cit.*, p. 16.

12 Quoted, Woodruff, *op. cit.*, p. 125.

13 Quoted, Mayhew, *op. cit.*, pp. 214-215 and 122.

14 Marshman, *op. cit.*, Vol. I, p. 157.

15 Thomas, *op. cit.*, p. 182.

16 Cited, Ingham, *op. cit.*, pp. 37 ff.

17 *Ibid.*, p. 37.

18 Quoted, Mayhew, *op. cit.*, p. 145.

19 George Smith, *The Life of William Carey*, J. M. Dent, London, 1909, p. 205.

20 Ingham, *op. cit.*, p. 33.

21 Mayhew, *op. cit.*, pp. 105-110.

22 Quoted, *ibid.*, p. 218.

23 Minutes of the First Session, Indian Mission Annual Conference, Methodist Episcopal Church (in library of Leonard Theological College, Jabalpur).

24 Mayhew, *op. cit.*, p. 178.

25 *Ibid.*, p. 184.

26 *Ibid.*, pp. 175-176.

27 Kenneth Scott Latourette, *The Great Century* (*A History of the Expansion of Christianity*, Vol. VI), Harper and Row, New York, 1944, p. 204.

28 *Ibid.*, pp. 200-201; cf. Schuster and Wint, *op. cit.*, pp. 104-105.

29 J. N. Farquhar, *Modern Religious Movements in India*, Macmillan, New York, 1919, p. 1.

Chapter V

1 Saurendra Nath Tagore, lecture, Delhi University, November 10, 1959.

2 Chakravarti, *op. cit.*, Part II, p. 46.

3 Majumdar, *op. cit.*, p. xix; cf. Andrews and Mukerji, *op. cit.*, p. 25.

4 Quoted, Schweitzer, *op. cit.*, p. 211.

5 Chakravarti, *op. cit.*, Part II, p. 59.

6 Andrews and Mukerji, *op. cit.*, p. 16.

7 Quoted, Chakravarti, *op. cit.*, Part II, p. 61.

8 Saurendra Nath Tagore, lecture, *op. cit.*

9 Quoted, *ibid.*, p. 87.

10 Farquhar, *op. cit.*, p. 19.

11 Nehru, *op. cit.*, p. 315.

12 Quoted, Chakravarti, *op. cit.*, p. 47.

[13] Müller, *op. cit.*, p. 17.
[14] Quoted, Farquhar, *op. cit.*, p. 32.
[15] Majumdar, *op. cit.*, pp. xxvii-xxviii; cf. Andrews and Mukerji, *op. cit.*, p. 26.
[16] Quoted, Vyas, K. C., *The Social Renaissance in India,* Vora, Bombay, 1957, p. 18.
[17] Quoted, Müller, *op. cit.*, p. 20.
[18] Quoted, Schweitzer, *op. cit.*, p. 212.
[19] *Ibid.*
[20] Quoted, Vyas, *op. cit.*, p. 50.
[21] Quoted, *ibid.*, p. 63.
[22] Farquhar, *op. cit.*, p. 42.
[23] Vyas, *op. cit.*, p. 129.
[24] Quoted, Müller, *op. cit.*, p. 58.
[25] Quoted, Farquhar, *op. cit.*, p. 68.
[26] Rabindranath Tagore, *Nationalism,* Macmillan, New York, 1917, pp. 118-119, 123.
[27] *Ibid.*, p. 123.
[28] *Ibid.*, pp. 137-138.
[29] Schweitzer, *op. cit.*, p. 244.
[30] Quoted, "Speaking Generally," *The Statesman,* July 28, 1959, p. 6.
[31] Louis Fischer, *op. cit.*, pp. 146-147.
[32] James Kellock, *Mahadev Govind Ranade, Patriot and Social Servant,* Association Press, Calcutta, 1926, p. 12; cf. Brown, *op. cit.*, pp. 81-82.
[33] Quoted, *ibid.*, p. 88.
[34] *Ibid.*, p. 166.
[35] M. G. Ranade, "Note on Professor Selby's Published Notes of Lectures on Butler's Analogy and Sermons," quoted, *ibid.*, p. 150.
[36] Quoted, *ibid.*, p. 145.
[37] *Indian Social Reform,* Vol. II, p. 91, quoted, *ibid.*, p. 93.
[38] Quoted, *ibid.*, pp. 12-13.
[39] Valentine Chirol, *India,* Ernest Benn, London, 1926, p. 108.
[40] *Social Welfare in India, op. cit.*, p. 793, italics added.
[41] Quoted, John S. Hoyland, *Gopal Krishna Gokhale, His Life and Speeches,* Y.M.C.A. Publishing House, Calcutta, 1933, pp. 144n-145n.
[42] *Social Welfare in India, op. cit.*, p. 11.
[43] Hoyland, *op. cit.*, p. 130.
[44] *Social Welfare in India, op. cit.*, p. 10.

Chapter VI

[1] Vyas, *op. cit.*, p. 74.
[2] *Social Work in India, op. cit.*, p. 9.
[3] Nehru, *op. cit.*, p. 337.
[4] Farquhar, *op. cit.*, p. 121.
[5] Quoted, Farquhar, *op. cit.*, p. 120, cf. p. 115.
[6] *Ibid.*, p. 111.
[7] *Social Welfare in India, op. cit.*, p. 10.
[8] Quoted, Vyas, *op. cit.*, p. 124.
[9] Quoted, K. M. Munshi, *Sparks from the Anvil,* Bharatiya Vidya Bhavan, Bombay, 1956, p. 69.
[10] Quoted, *ibid.*
[11] *Ibid.*, p. 66.
[12] Fischer, *op. cit.*, pp. 152-156.
[13] Quoted, Munshi, *op. cit.*, p. 68.
[14] Quoted, D. V. Tahmankar, *Lokamanya Tilak,* John Murray, London, 1956, p. 50.
[15] Quoted, *ibid.*, p. 320.
[16] Suresh Ramabhai, *Vinoba and His Mission,* Akhil Bharat Sarva Seva Sangh, Sevagram, 1954, p. 190.
[17] S. Natarajan, *A Century of Social Reform in India,* Asia Publishing House, Bombay, 1959, p. 85.
[18] Munshi, *op. cit.*, radio speech at Aurobindo's death in 1950.
[19] Roland Scott, *Social Ethics in Modern Hinduism,* Y.M.C.A. Publishing House, Calcutta, 1953, p. 77.
[20] Quoted, *ibid.*, p. 36.
[21] Quoted Brown, *op. cit.*, p. 124; cf. Andrews and Mukerji, who call Aurobindo the "greatest of all in intellectual eminence," *op. cit.*, p. 185.
[22] Quoted, Richard L. Park and Irene Tinker (Eds.), *Leadership and Political Institutions in India,* Princeton University Press, 1959, p. 288.
[23] Quoted, Max Müller, *op. cit.*, p. 162.
[24] Nehru, *op. cit.*, pp. 337-338.
[25] Quoted, Schweitzer, *op. cit.*, p. 217.
[26] Müller, *op. cit.*, p. 137.
[27] Scott, *op. cit.*, p. 48.
[28] Both of the judgments above from Vyas, *op. cit.*, pp. 97-98; cf. Farquhar, *op. cit.*, p. 199.
[29] Quoted, Vyas, *op. cit.*, p. 102.
[30] Quoted, Nehru, *op. cit.*, p. 339.

81 Quoted, Scott, *op. cit.*, p. 54.

82 Quoted, Romain Rolland, *The Life of Vivekananda and the Universal Gospel*, Advaita Ashrama, Almora, 1953, p. 169.

33 Quoted, *ibid.*, pp. 151-152.

34 Quoted, Brown, *op. cit.*, pp. 89-104; cf. Bupendranath Dutta, *Swami Vivekananda, the Socialist*, Khulna Publishing Company, Bengal, 1929.

35 Quoted, Vyas, *op. cit.*, p. 109.

36 Quoted, Rolland, *op. cit.*, pp. 166-167, 10.

37 Schweitzer, *op. cit.*, p. 221.

38 *Ibid.*, p. 219.

Chapter VII

1 Schuster and Wint, *op. cit.*, p. 91.

2 Quoted, Andrews and Mukerji, *op. cit.*, p. 165.

3 Quoted, *ibid.*, p. 160.

4 Quoted, B. R. Ambedkar, *What Congress and Gandhi Have Done to the Untouchables*, Thacker and Co., Bombay, 1945, pp. 7-8.

5 Quoted, *ibid.*, pp. 8-9.

6 Quoted, *ibid.*, pp. 9-10.

7 Cf. *ibid.*, pp. 17 ff.

8 Quoted, Vyas, *op. cit.*, p. 144.

9 Quoted, *ibid.*, p. 149.

10 Cf. *ibid.*, pp. 152-154.

11 Quoted, *ibid.*, p. 167.

12 Quoted, Hoyland, *op. cit.*, p. 137.

13 Quoted, *ibid.*, p. 146.

14 M. K. Gandhi, *Young India*, October 20, 1920, and December 29, 1920.

15 *Social Welfare in India*, *op. cit.*, p. 12.

16 S. Abid Husain, *The Way of Gandhi and Nehru*, Asia Publishing House, Bombay, 1959, p. xvii.

17 Quoted, Hallam Tennyson, *Saint on the March*, Victor Gollancz, London, 1955, p. 34.

18 Fischer, *op. cit.*, p. 525.

19 Frank Anthony, personal interview, New Delhi, April 21, 1960.

20 Cf. Moraes, *op. cit.*, Chapter X.

Chapter VIII

1 M. K. Gandhi, selected quotations from "They Belong to the Ages" (Lincoln and Gandhi), United States Information Service, New Delhi, undated.

2 Fischer, *op. cit.*, p. 288.

3 *Young India*, quoted, Brown, *op. cit.*, p. 146.

4 M. M. Begg, personal interview, Delhi, January 29, 1960.

5 Quoted, Fischer, *op. cit.*, p. 402.

6 Schuster and Wint, *op. cit.*, p. 104.

7 Fischer, *op. cit.*, p. 28.

8 Gandhi, *op. cit.*, p. 18.

9 Fischer, *op. cit.*, p. 56.

10 Gopinath Dhawan, *The Political Philosophy of Mahatma Gandhi*, Navijivan Publishing House, Ahmedabad, 1946, p. 25.

11 Schweitzer, *op. cit.*, p. 230.

12 Quoted, Fischer, *op. cit.*, p. 117.

13 Gandhi, *op. cit.*, pp. 113-114.

14 Fischer, *op. cit.*, p. 362.

15 Gandhi, *Young India*, October 6, 1921.

16 *Ibid.*

17 *Ibid.*, Vol. II, p. 1078.

18 Quoted, Fischer, *op. cit.*, p. 488.

19 Quoted, *ibid.*, p. 328.

20 Quoted, *ibid.*, p. 320.

21 The nearest passage to be found in G. Ramachandra Rao (Gora), (*An Atheist with Gandhi*, Navajivan Publishing House, Ahmedabad, 1958) quotes the Mahatma as saying: "So long as you feel akin with mankind you accept God in practice" (p. 31, cf. pp. 14, 30, 48).

22 Gandhi, *Harijan*, November 18, 1939 (italics added).

23 Pyarelal Nayar, personal interview, New Delhi, March 19, 1960.

24 Quoted, Fischer, *op. cit.*, p. 329.

25 Quoted, Dhawan, *op. cit.*, p. 25.

26 Gandhi, *Harijan*, March 23, 1940.

27 Gandhi, *The Story of My Experiments With Truth*, *op. cit.*, pp. 96 et seq.

28 Quoted, Fischer, *op. cit.*, p. 465.

29 Quoted, *ibid.*, p. 330.

30 Gandhi, *Harijan*, August 29, 1936.

31 Dhawan, *op. cit.*, p. 58; cf. personal interview, Lucknow, March 1, 1960.

32 Gandhi, *Young India*, 1920, p. 164.

33 Schweitzer, *op. cit.*, pp. 230-232.

34 Quoted, Ambedkar, *op. cit.,* p. 288; cf. Vyas, *op. cit.,* pp. 176-179; Rao, *op. cit.,* p. 57.

35 Quoted, Husain, *op. cit.,* p. 40.

36 Nehru, *Toward Freedom,* John Day Company, New York, 1941, p. 318.

37 Quoted, Ambedkar, *op. cit.,* p. 107.

38 Gandhi, *Young India,* October 6, 1921.

39 Gandhi, *Young India,* November 4, 1932.

40 Quoted, Ambedkar, *op. cit.,* p. 85; cf. Fischer, *op. cit.,* p. 334.

41 Quoted, Ambedkar, *op. cit.,* p. 78.

42 Gandhi, *Young India,* May 25, 1921.

43 *Ibid.,* October 20, 1920.

44 Quoted, Fischer, *op. cit.,* pp. 165-166.

45 Quoted, *ibid.,* p. 145; cf. Schweitzer, *op. cit.,* p. 234 ff.

46 Cf. Fischer, *op. cit.,* p. 527; J. B. Kripalani, *Vigil,* Vol. X, No. 49, February 2, 1960, p. 772, and personal interview, New Delhi, November 27, 1959.

47 Gandhi, *Young India,* August 11, 1920.

48 Quoted, Fischer, *op. cit.,* p. 374.

49 John Gunther, *Inside Asia* (Harper & Row, New York, 1939), pp. 392-393.

50 Gandhi, *Young India,* p. 804.

51 Quoted, Fischer, *op. cit.,* p. 262.

52 Cf. Schweitzer, *op. cit.,* pp. 227 ff.

53 Cf. Rao, *op. cit.,* p. 40.

54 Quoted, Brown, *op. cit.,* p. 143.

55 Cf. Schweitzer, *op. cit.,* pp. 237-238, cf. pp. 227 ff.

56 Gandhi, *Young India,* November 20, 1924.

57 Cf. Tennyson, *op. cit.,* p. 180.

58 K. M. Panikkar, personal interview, New Delhi, March 24, 1960.

59 Quoted, Fischer, *op. cit.,* p. 446.

60 Quoted, *ibid.,* p. 331.

61 A. R. Desai, *Social Background of Indian Nationalism,* Popular Book Depot, Bombay, 1954, p. 328.

62 Schuster and Wint, *op. cit.,* pp. 119-120.

63 Gandhi, *Young India,* January 8, 1925.

64 Rajkumari Amrit Kaur, personal interview, New Delhi, November 7, 1959.

65 Fischer, *op. cit.,* p. 408.

66 Husain, *op. cit.,* p. 36; cf. Gandhi, *Harijan,* February 11, 1939.

67 Quoted, Fischer, *op. cit.,* p. 120.

68 Quoted, *ibid.,* p. 408.

Chapter IX

1 *The Constitution of India,* modified to April 1, 1958, Government of India Press, Delhi, 1958. Excerpts from the Constitution will be identified only by Article, not page, because of the variety of editions available.

2 Constituent Assembly, *The Constituent Assembly Debates,* Government of India, New Delhi, 1946-1949, Volume I, p. 59.

3 *Ibid.,* p. 60.

4 *Ibid.,* Volume XI, pp. 612-613. Volume XI, pp. 612-613.

5 *Ibid.,* Volume VII, p. 341.

6 *Ibid.,* p. 938.

7 *Ibid.,* p. 40.

8 *Ibid.,* Volume XI, pp. 975-979.

9 V. G. Ramachandran, *Fundamental Rights and Constitutional Remedies,* Volume I, Eastern Book Company, Lucknow, 1959, p. 269.

10 Constituent Assembly, *op. cit.,* Volume VII, pp. 606-607.

11 *Ibid.,* p. 612.

12 Ramachandran, *op. cit.,* p. 269.

13 Constituent Assembly, *op. cit.,* Volume VII, p. 666.

14 *Social Legislation, op. cit.,* pp. 220-222.

15 Constituent Assembly, *op. cit.,* Volume XI, pp. 610-611.

16 *Ibid.,* Volume III, p. 384.

17 *Ibid.,* Volume VII, p. 726.

18 *Ibid.,* p. 761.

19 *Ibid.,* pp. 771-772.

20 *Ibid.,* p. 809.

21 *Ibid.,* Volume VII, pp. 876, 882, 890-891, 938, *et passim.*

22 *Ibid.,* p. 41; cf. V. N. Shukla, *The Constitution of India,* Eastern Book Company, Lucknow, 1950, p. lxi.

23 Quoted, Percival Griffiths, *Modern India,* Ernest Benn, London, 1957, p. 126.

[24] K. M. Munshi, *Our Sovereign Democratic Republic*, University of Madras, 1955, Lecture II, pp. 10-11.

[25] Constituent Assembly, *op. cit.*, Volume I, p. 62.

[26] *Ibid.*, Volume VII, pp. 544-545.

[27] *Ibid.*, pp. 547-548.

[28] Cf. *Time*, February 17, 1961, pp. 26-27.

[29] Constituent Assembly, *op. cit.*, Volume VII, pp. 575-576.

[30] *Ibid.*, pp. 568-581.

[31] *Ibid.*, pp. 670-671.

[32] *Ibid.*, Volume XI, p. 942.

[33] *Ibid.*, Volume VII, p. 601.

[34] *Ibid.*, p. 38.

[35] *Ibid.*, Volume XI, pp. 993-994.

Chapter X

[1] *Empty Shoes: A Study of the Church of South India*, National Council of the Protestant Episcopal Church, New York, 1956, p. 5.

[2] Nehru, *The Discovery of India, op. cit.*, p. 680.

[3] *Ibid.*, p. 64.

[4] Jawaharlal Nehru, personal interview, New Delhi, February 25, 1960.

[5] "Nehru Explains India's 'Split Personality,' " *New York Times* Magazine, March 11, 1956, p. 13.

[6] M. Mujeeb, personal interview, Jamia Millia Islamia, New Delhi, December 13, 1959.

[7] Cf. Fischer, *op. cit.*, pp. 461-462.

[8] Nehru, personal interview, February 25, 1960; cf. *Christian Century*, July 8, 1964, pp. 883-885.

[9] Husain, *op. cit.*, p. 152.

[10] Nehru, *Toward Freedom, op. cit.*, p. 242.

[11] *Ibid.*, p. 377.

[12] *Ibid.*, pp. 71-72.

[13] Cf. Winburn T. Thomas, "To Prime Minister Jawaharlal Nehru," *Christian Century*, December 23, 1959, p. 1499.

[14] Nehru, *The Discovery of India, op. cit.*, p. 16; cf. *Christian Century*, July 8, 1964, p. 885.

[15] *Ibid.*, p. 15.

[16] *Ibid.*, p. 16.

[17] Nehru, *The Discovery of India, op. cit.*, pp. 63-64.

[18] *Ibid.*, p. 477.

[19] *Ibid.*, p. 80.

[20] *Ibid.*, p. 136.

[21] *Ibid.*, 85-86; cf. Scott, *op. cit.*, p. 10.

[22] *Ibid.*, p. 243.

[23] Quoted, Husain, *op. cit.*, p. 143.

[24] Nehru, *Toward Freedom, op. cit.*, p. 230.

[25] *Jawaharlal Nehru, An Autobiography*, John Lane, the Bodley Head, London, 1947, pp. 551-552 (a chapter omitted from the American edition, *Toward Freedom;* one wonders whether because of its pacifism or socialism).

[26] Anup Singh, personal interview, New Delhi, February 15, 1960.

[27] Hans Morgenthau, *New York Times* Magazine, August 27, 1961, pp. 25, 76-77.

[28] Nehru, *The Discovery of India, op. cit.*, p. 251.

[29] Quoted, *Deccan Herald*, January 16, 1960, p. 8.

[30] Nehru, *The Discovery of India, op. cit.*, p. 113.

[31] *Ibid.*, p. 523.

[32] Anup Singh, personal interview, February 15, 1960.

[33] Mujeeb, personal interview, December 13, 1959.

[34] Munshi, personal interview, April 12, 1960.

[35] Nehru, *Toward Freedom, op. cit.*, p. 353.

[36] Cf. Krishna Nehru, *With No Regrets*, Asia Press, John Day, New York, 1945, p. 138.

[37] Nehru, *Toward Freedom, op. cit.*, p. 242.

[38] Dhirendra Narain, *Hindu Character*, University of Bombay, 1957, p. 116.

[39] Krishna Nehru, *op. cit.*, p. 139.

Chapter XI

[1] C. Rajagopalachari, personal interview, Madras, January 8, 1960.

[2] Moraes, *op. cit.*, p. 225; cf. pp. 229-230.

[3] Quoted, *The Statesman*, New

Delhi, August 2, 1959, pp. 1 and 9.
  [4] Quoted, *The Statesman,* New Delhi, August 3, 1959, p. 7.
  [5] Mahesh, Chandra, *The Statesman,* New Delhi, August 5, 1959.
  [6] Rajagopalachari, personal interview, Madras, January 8, 1960.
  [7] *Ibid.*
  [8] Quoted, *The Statesman,* January 25, 1960.
  [9] *The Statesman,* April 9, 1960.
  [10] K. M. Munshi, *Sparks from the Anvil, op. cit.,* p. 29.
  [11] K. M. Munshi, personal interview, New Delhi, April 12, 1960.
  [12] M. R. Masani, personal interview, New Delhi, March 30, 1960.
  [13] *Ibid.*
  [14] Moraes, *op. cit.,* p. 97.
  [15] J. B. Kripalani, personal interview, November 27, 1963.
  [16] Asoka Mehta, personal interview, December 2, 1959.
  [17] M. N. Roy, *Politics, Power, and Parties,* Renaissance Publishers, Calcutta, 1960; cf. review in *Hindu Weekly Review,* September 19, 1960, p. 5.
  [18] Jay Saunders Redding, *An American in India,* Bobbs-Merrill, Indianapolis, 1954, p. 255.
  [19] Quoted, M. R. Masani, *The Communist Party of India,* Macmillan, 1954, p. 21.
  [20] Quoted, *ibid.,* pp. 42-43.
  [21] Quoted, *ibid.,* p. 43.
  [22] Quoted, Moraes, *op. cit.,* p. 123.
  [23] Masani, *op. cit.,* pp. 231-234.
  [24] Hiren Mukerjee, *Gandhiji: A Study,* National Book Agency, Calcutta, 1958.
  [25] Hiren Mukerjee, personal interview, New Delhi, April 4, 1960.
  [26] Quoted, Tennyson, *op. cit.,* p. 209.
  [27] Nehru, *New York Times,* August 23, 1958.
  [28] Nehru, *New York Times* Magazine, March 11, 1956, p. 13.
  [29] Frank Anthony, personal interview, April 21, 1960.

Chapter XII

  [1] Rajendra Prasad, personal interview, Rashtrapati Bhavan, New Delhi, April 16, 1960.

  [2] Nehru, *Autobiography, op. cit.,* p. 489 (omitted from the American edition, *Toward Freedom*).
  [3] K. M. Munshi, *Our Greatest Need,* Bharatiya Vidya Bhavan, Bombay, 1953, p. 202.
  [4] G. Ramachandran, personal interview, New Delhi, February, 1960.
  [5] Pyarelal Nayar, personal interview, March 19, 1960.
  [6] Quoted, Tennyson, *op. cit.,* p. 45.
  [7] Quoted, *ibid.,* p. 68.
  [8] Quoted, *ibid.,* p. 69; cf. Ramabhai, *op. cit.,* p. 165.
  [9] Donald Groom, personal report, Quaker Centre, Delhi, January 21, 1960; this approximates the percentage estimated by Tennyson, *op. cit.,* April 1954.
  [10] Quoted, Donald Groom, personal interview, Bulandshahr, April 20, 1960.
  [11] Cf. *Time,* June 13, 1960, pp. 29-30; July 30, 1961, p. 69.
  [12] Quoted, Tennyson, *op. cit.,* pp. 110-111.
  [13] Vinoba Bhave, personal interview, Bulandshahr, April 20, 1960.
  [14] Tennyson, *op. cit.,* p. 171, cf. p. 195.
  [15] Radhakrishnan, Foreword to Ramabhai, *op. cit.,* p. vi.
  [16] Campbell, *op. cit.,* p. 229.
  [17] Tennyson, *op. cit.,* p. 213.
  [18] Jayaprakash Narayan, lecture, Sapru House, New Delhi, December 28, 1959.
  [19] Fischer, *op. cit.,* p. 414.
  [20] Masani, *op. cit.,* p. 54.
  [21] Campbell, *op. cit.,* p. 177.
  [22] Quoted, Tennyson, *op. cit.,* p. 140, cf. p. 139.
  [23] J. P. Narayan (Narain), *A Plea for Reconstruction of Indian Polity,* Akhil Bharat Sarva Seva Sangh, Central Electric Press, Delhi, 1959.
  [24] Quoted, *The Statesman,* New Delhi, October 27, 1959, pp. 1f.
  [25] J. P. Narayan, group discussion, Delhi, January 21, 1960.
  [26] Open forum, New Delhi, March 27, 1960.
  [27] *The Statesman,* New Delhi, February 11, 1960.
  [28] *The Statesman,* New Delhi, October 31, 1959.

Chapter XIII

[1] B. S. Murthy and group interview, Ministry of Community Development, New Delhi, November 26, 1959.

[2] Cf. *The Statesman,* New Delhi, January 22, 1960.

[3] Ralph Richard Keithann, printed letter, October 1, 1961.

[4] Quoted, *The Statesman,* New Delhi, November 8, 1959.

[5] Quoted, Narain, *op. cit.,* pp. 156-157.

[6] Radhakrishnan, *Religion and Society, op. cit.,* p. 184 (italics added).

[7] Indira Gandhi, personal interview, New Delhi, April 12, 1960.

[8] Mrs. Lakshmi Menon, personal interview, New Delhi, April 11, 1960.

[9] Rajkumari Amrit Kaur, personal interview, November 7, 1959.

[10] Ranganathananda, "Ethics of Social Work," Y.W.C.A., New Delhi, February 19, 1960.

[11] Ranganathananda, personal interview, New Delhi, April 18, 1960; cf. Ranganathananda, *Eternal Values for a Changing Society,* Advaita Ashrama, Calcutta, 1958.

[12] Quoted, *Time,* Pacific Edition, January 11, 1960, p. 19.

[13] Quoted, Radhakrishnan, *Religion and Society, op. cit.,* p. 189.

[14] Rajkumari Amrit Kaur, address on "The Commonwealth of Children," Duke University, October 6, 1961.

[15] Gardner Murphy, *In the Minds of Men,* UNESCO, Basic Books, New York, 1953, pp. 244-245.

Chapter XIV

[1] Quoted, Mayhew, *op. cit.,* p. 189.

[2] Quoted, *ibid.,* p. 93.

[3] William Paton, *Social Ideals in India,* United Council for Missionary Education, London, 1919, p. 57.

[4] *Ibid.,* p. 53.

[5] William Richey Hogg, "India and Indian Christianity—Some Observations," Perkins School of Theology *Journal,* Fall, 1955, p. 17 (corrected).

[6] J. M. Lobo Prabhu, *New Think-*

ing, India Book House, Bombay, 1959, p. 146.

[7] P. D. Devanandan and M. M. Thomas, *India's Quest for Democracy,* Y.M.C.A. Publishing House, Calcutta, 1955, pp. 58-59.

[8] Cf. J. W. Pickett, *Christian Mass Movements in India,* Abingdon, New York, 1933; and Donald McGavran, *Bridges of God,* Friendship Press, New York, 1955.

[9] *Times of India,* March, 1955, quoted, Hogg, *op. cit.,* p. 17.

[10] Rajah D. Manikam, *Christianity and the Asian Revolution,* Joint East Asia Secretariat, Madras, 1954, p. 87.

[11] Rajappan D. Immanuel, *op. cit.,* p. 84.

[12] Quoted, *The Missionary Herald,* American Board of Commissioners for Foreign Missions, Volume II, No. 4, November, 1960, p. 1; cf. Chandran Devanesan, personal interview, Tambaram, January 9, 1960.

[13] Daniel J. Fleming, *The Social Mission of the Church in India,* Association Press, Calcutta, 1913, pp. 16 and 21.

[14] V.K.R.V. Rao, lecture, Student Christian Movement, Delhi University, August 23, 1959; cf. personal interview, February 2, 1960.

[15] Woodruff, *op. cit.,* p. 265.

Chapter XV

[1] S. Radhakrishnan, personal interview, New Delhi, February 26, 1960.

[2] G. D. Binani and T. V. Rama Rao, (eds.), *India at a Glance,* Orient Longmans, Calcutta, rev. 1954, p. 13.

[3] *Ibid.*

[4] S. Radhakrishnan, *Eastern Religions and Western Thought,* Clarendon Press, Oxford, 1939, p. 40.

[5] *Religion and Society, op. cit.,* pp. 42-43.

[6] *Ibid.,* pp. 121-123.

[7] *Ibid.,* pp. 128-129.

[8] *Ibid.,* p. 133; cf. pp. 340-376, and *The Hindu View of Life,* George Allen and Unwin, London, 1927, pp. 92-123.

[9] *Eastern Religions and Western Thought, op. cit.* p. 373.

10 *Ibid.*, p. 374.

11 *The Hindu View of Life, op. cit.,*
p. 114.

12 *Religion and Society, op. cit.,* p.
129.

13 *The Hindu View of Life, op. cit.,*
pp. 115-116.

14 *Eastern Religions and Western
Thought, op. cit.,* p. 60.

15 *Religion and Society, op. cit.,* p.
42.

16 *East and West in Religion,* George
Allen & Unwin, London, 1933-1949, pp.
54-56.

17 Gokhale, *op. cit.,* p. 211.

18 *Religion and Society, op. cit.,* p.
114.

19 *Ibid.*, p. 115.

20 Speech at Jullunder, reported in
The Statesman, November 8, 1959.

21 *The Hindu View of Life, op. cit.,*
p. 72.

22 *Ibid.*

23 *Ibid.*, pp. 73-74.

24 *Ibid.*, p. 76.

25 Cf. *The Hindu View of Life, op.
cit.,* pp. 61 ff.

26 *Eastern Religions and Western
Thought, op. cit.,* p. 47.

27 *Ibid.*, p. 109.

28 *Ibid.*, p. 54.

29 *Religion and Society, op. cit.,* p.
104.

30 Cf. Gokhale, *op. cit.,* pp. 256-
257.

31 *The Statesman,* November 22,
1959.

32 *Religion and Society, op. cit.,* pp.
76 and 105.

33 *East and West in Religion, op. cit.,*
p. 69.

34 *Religion and Society, op. cit.,* p.
180.

35 *Ibid.*, pp. 202-210.

36 *Eastern Religions and Western
Thought, op. cit.,* p. 301.

37 *Eastern Religions and Western
Thought, op. cit.,* p. 290.

38 *Ibid.*, p. 82.

39 *Ibid.*, p. 86.

40 *Ibid.*, pp. 101-102.

41 *Ibid.*, p. 108.

42 *Ibid.*, p. 323.

43 Quoted, *The Statesman,* February
26, 1960.

44 *Religion and Society, op. cit.,* pp.
115-119; cf. "Hinduism and the West"
in L.S.S. O'Malley, ed., *Modern India
and the West,* Oxford University Press,
London, 1941, pp. 338-353.

45 S. Radhakrishnan and J. H. Muirhead, eds., *Contemporary Indian Philosophy,* George Allen and Unwin, London, 1936 (rev. 1952), p. 258.

Conclusion

1 *Harijan,* July 21, 1946.

2 Reinhold Niebuhr, *An Interpretation of Christian Ethics,* Harper and
Brothers, New York, 1935, p. 84,

3 R. Bhaskaran, personal interview,
University of Madras, January 11, 1960.

4 Tennyson, *op. cit.,* pp. 189-190.

5 D. S. Sarma, *The Renaissance of
Hinduism,* Benares Hindu University,
1944, p. 639.

6 A.M. Ghose, "Should the History
of India be Rewritten?" *Illustrated
Weekly of India,* Vol. LXXX, No. 26,
June 28, 1959.

7 John G. Arapura, personal conversation, Serampore, March 3-5, 1960.

8 Malcolm Pitt, personal letter, April
16, 1958.

9 Scott, *op. cit.,* p. 45.

10 *Constituent Assembly Debates,
op. cit.,* Volume VII, p. 319.

11 *Indian Express,* November 21,
1957; quoted, Narain, *op. cit.,* p. 183.

12 Murphy, *op. cit.,* p. 57.

13 *Constituent Assembly Debates,
op. cit.,* Volume VII, p. 39, cf. pp. 522-
526.

14 Nehru, *Toward Freedom, op. cit.,*
p. 348.

15 *Constituent Assembly Debates,
op. cit.,* Volume VII, p. 385.

16 Frank Anthony, personal interview, New Delhi, April 21, 1960.

17 K. M. Panikkar, *Hinduism and
the Modern World,* Kitabistan, Allahabad, 1938, p. 92 *et passim.*

18 Quoted, Campbell, *op. cit.,* p. 24.

19 Arthur Koestler, *The Lotus and
the Robot,* Macmillan, New York, 1961,
pp. 276, 281, 282.

20 Paton, *op. cit.,* p. 42.

21 David Burgess, "Can Hinduism

and Hindu Culture Provide an Ideological Foundation for Democracy in India?" unpublished manuscript, 1959, pp. 18-19.

[22] Ambedkar, *op. cit.,* Dedication.

[23] Hu Shih, "Science is Spiritual Achievement," *The Asian Student,* November 18, 1961, p. 5.

[24] Griffiths, *op. cit.,* pp. 239 and 242.

[25] R. Bhaskaran, personal postcard, February 3, 1960.

[26] Murphy, *op. cit.,* p. 235.

[27] *Constituent Assembly Debates, op. cit.,* Vol. VII, p. 322.

Index

313